THE CLASSICS
OF **WESTERN
SPIRITUALITY**

THE CLASSICS OF WESTERN SPIRITUALITY
A Library of the Great Spiritual Masters

President and Publisher
Mark-David Janus, CSP

EDITORIAL BOARD

SCHLEIERMACHER
Christmas Dialogue,
The Second Speech, *and Other Selections*

Edited, Translated,
and with an Introduction
by Julia A. Lamm

Paulist Press
New York / Mahwah, NJ

Library of Congress Cataloging-in-Publication Data

Schleiermacher, Friedrich, 1768–1834.
    [Works. Selections. English]
    Schleiermacher : Christmas dialogue, the Second speech, and other selections / edited, translated, and with an introduction by Julia A. Lamm.
        pages cm. — (Classics of Western spirituality)
    Includes bibliographical references and index. ISBN 978-0-8091-0607-3 (alk. paper) — ISBN 978-0-8091-4878-3 (alk. paper) — ISBN 978-1-58768-366-4
    1. Schleiermacher, Friedrich, 1768–1834. 2. Spirituality—Christianity. I. Lamm, Julia A., 1961- writer of added commentary. II. Title.
    B3092.E5L36 2014
    230'.044—dc23

2014011515

Published by Paulist Press
997 Macarthur Boulevard
Mahwah, New Jersey 07430

www.paulistpress.com

Printed and bound in the
United States of America

For Brian, Dawn, and Heather

CONTENTS

CONTENTS

About the Contributor

JULIA A. LAMM is Associate Professor of Theology at Georgetown University in Washington, DC, where she has taught courses on the history of Christian thought, the doctrine of God, philosophical theology, and Christian mysticism since 1989. She received her B.A. in history and philosophy from the College of St. Catherine, and her M.A. in religious studies and Ph.D. in Christian theology from the University of Chicago. She is author of *The Living God: Schleiermacher's Theological Appropriation of Spinoza* (Pennsylvania State University Press, 1996) and numerous scholarly articles on the theology and philosophy of Friedrich Schleiermacher. She was awarded an Alexander von Humboldt Fellowship from Germany to research and write *Schleiermacher's Plato*, currently in progress. She is editor of the *Wiley-Blackwell Companion to Christian Mysticism* (2013).

PREFACE

A volume on Schleiermacher's spirituality could be quite thick indeed, or even a multivolume work. The present volume, relatively slender as it is, is designed to be enjoyable to read and easy to hold. The texts included in it have been chosen because they illustrate Schleiermacher's spirituality *and* because they are interesting texts about the spiritual life, texts that people having no particular interest in Schleiermacher might nevertheless enjoy reading. At the same time, specialists will hopefully appreciate the new translations of editions not previously translated, as teachers will perhaps welcome the collection of this particular array of texts in one volume. This volume, then, is meant to be a portal to Schleiermacher and to a particular way of thinking about Schleiermacher. As someone who has spent the last quarter century reading and writing about Schleiermacher's philosophy and doctrinal theology, I have found this approach to him, *via* his spirituality, challenging and illuminating. I hope readers will find the same.

When a project spans as long as seven years, as this one has, one's indebtedness and gratitude can only accrue. I want first to acknowledge the contribution and scholarship of Dawn DeVries. This volume began as a collaborative endeavor between the two of us, and a most enjoyable and rewarding one at that. Together we conceived the original design of the volume, conducted research in Berlin, and translated the first two drafts of the *Christmas Dialogue*. A series of family health emergencies did not permit her to continue in the project, but my debt and gratitude remain. Her expert knowledge of Schleiermacher and the Reformed theological tradition, and in particular her knowledge of Schleiermacher's sermons and his theory of preaching, have informed my own understanding of Schleiermacher for the past thirty years. She identified several sermons as appropriate for a volume on spirituality, two of which I have chosen to translate here. This book is dedicated to her; to B. A. Gerrish, whose meticulous and elegant scholarship has inspired two generations of Schleiermacher scholars; and to their extraordinary daughter, Heather Gerrish.

In the German Department here at Georgetown University, I am fortunate to have wonderful colleagues who have been generous with their time and knowledge. I am profoundly grateful to Astrid M. Weigert, who specializes in genre and gender in German Romanticism, especially the works of Dorothea Schlegel. Her expertise has proven invaluable. She graciously read our early translation of *Die Weihnachtsfeier: Ein Gespräch* (*The Christmas Celebration: A Dialogue*) and offered feedback and insight. She was equally generous in her moral support. Also in the German Department, I owe a special note of thanks to Friederike Eigler, who patiently responded to long queries about the syntax and meaning of some particularly difficult sentences; as she noted, Schleiermacher sometimes seems to have his own German. Finally, Mary Helen Dupree and G. Ronald Murphy, SJ, kindly helped on a couple of occasions with finding just the right translation for special terms.

One of the great benefits of working at a university is that one has, so close at hand, treasures of expert knowledge in different fields. For researching a polymath such as Schleiermacher, it takes a university. I want to thank my dear colleagues: Richard D. Bates in the Chemistry Department, for his description of the formation of crystals; William Blattner in the Philosophy Department, for his refined knowledge of Kantian terminology and modern philosophy; Alisa Carse in the Philosophy Department, for her help in the aesthetics of translating and for her ongoing support; Anthony R. DelDonna in the Department of Performing Arts, for so patiently answering questions about music in Germany in 1805, and for doing so with depth of detail. In my own Department of Theology, John W. O'Malley, SJ, has the misfortune of being my office neighbor and so is the person I bother the most, and I am indebted to him for his input on turns of phrase, his good cheer, and his encouragement; he often reminds me that translation is the ultimate interpretation. I am also grateful to Leo D. Lefebure; Daniel Madigan, SJ; James P. Walsh, SJ; and D. M. Yeager for their advice on particular matters. Carole Sargent in the Office of Scholarly Publications advised in the preparation of the original proposal and all along the way; she has been most generous and is a great asset to this university. Richard Brown, Director of Georgetown University Press, has also been most generous with his time and expert advice.

Farther afield, Richard Crouter graciously read early drafts of the introduction and gave candid feedback, and the ensuing exchange of ideas was most stimulating. Brent Sockness helped me sort through particular issues, especially in regard to Schleiermacher's ethics. Ruth Albrecht of Hamburg University was generous in answering my many questions about Pietism and pointing me to the best resources. Peter Albert graciously read the introduction with a sharp editorial eye.

In the last year of the project, I had the uncanny good luck of being assigned a research assistant versed in Romantic German. Taraneh Wilkinson has been an immense help in going over the translations of the *Christmas Dialogue* and the second *Speech* for readability, and in providing me with a literal translation of the sermons so that I could then shape them according to Schleiermacher's particular style and vocabulary. I look forward to seeing her own work on Schleiermacher in the future. In previous years, other talented research assistants also aided me in tracking down secondary sources and sorting through Schleiermacher's correspondence; my sincere thanks to Maureen Walsh, Jerusha Lamptey, and Rahel Fischbach. And at the very end, Matthew Taylor was of great help with page proofs.

Bernard McGinn, the general editor of this series, and Nancy de Flon, the academic editor at Paulist Press, have both been most patient and encouraging, even when deadlines were missed. I am deeply grateful to both of them for all they have done.

I thank Georgetown University for providing me with a summer grant to conduct research in Germany. I also thank the Alexander von Humboldt Stiftung for its ongoing support. I am grateful, too, to staff members at the Staatsbibliothek in Berlin and at the Library and Archives of the Berlin-Brandenburgische Akademie der Wissenschaften.

My most profound thanks and deepest debt go to my family— my husband, Alan C. Mitchell, and our beautiful son, Aidan, now almost twelve years old. They are the two great loves of my life, and they have been endlessly patient and loving. I have been occupied in some way or another with this volume for more than half of Aidan's life, and he is glad to see it completed even more than I am.

Julia A. Lamm
Washington, DC
May 31, 2013

ABBREVIATIONS

ASL   *Aus Schleiermachers Leben. In Briefen.* 4 vols. Berlin: Reimer, 1860; reprint, Berlin & New York: Walter de Gruyter, 1974.

BO   F. D. E. Schleiermacher, *Brief Outline on the Study of Theology.* Translated by Terrence N. Tice. Atlanta: John Knox Press, 1966.

CF   F. D. E Schleiermacher, *The Christian Faith.* English translation of *Glaubenslehre* (1830/31). Translated and edited by H. R. Mackintosh and J. S. Stewart. Edinburgh: T. & T. Clark, 1928. Since 1976, published in the United States by Fortress Press, Philadelphia.

Gl.   F. D. E. Schleiermacher, *Der christliche Glaube nach den Grundsätzen der evangelischen Kirche im Zusammenhange dargestellt* (Berlin, 1830/31), 2 vols. (*Glaubenslehre*). In KGA 1:13/1–2. Edited by Rolf Schäfer. Berlin and New York: Walter de Gruyter, 2003.

KGA   *Friedrich Daniel Ernst Schleiermacher Kritische Gesamtausgabe.* Edited by Hans-Joachim Birkner, Gerhard Ebeling, Hermann Fischer, Günter Meckenstock, Kurt-Victor Selge, et al. Berlin and New York: Walter de Gruyter, 1983–.

OR1   F. D. E. Schleiermacher, *On Religion: Speeches to Its Cultured Despisers,* 1st edition (1799). Translated and edited by Richard Crouter. Cambridge, UK: Cambridge University Press, 1988.

OR3   F. D. E. Schleiermacher, *On Religion: Speeches to Its Cultured Despisers,* 3rd edition (1821). Translated by John Oman. New York: Harper, 1958.

SW   *Friedrich Schleiermachers Sämmtliche Werke.* Berlin: G. Reimer, 1834–64.

1

SCHLEIERMACHER'S SPIRITUALITY

An Introduction

Friedrich Schleiermacher (1768–1834) was a virtuoso of spirituality. To some this claim will be obvious; to others, dubious. Either way, it needs to be explained. *Spirituality* was not Schleiermacher's term, nor was it (or a cognate in German) even a real option for him in Prussia in the early nineteenth century, since the English word was derived from the French *spiritualité*, and its revival and application in the early twentieth century occurred in decidedly Catholic contexts.[1] As a Reformed preacher and theologian, Schleiermacher's preferred term was *piety* (*Frömmigkeit*). The Protestant Reformer John Calvin (1509–64), at the beginning of his *Institutes on the Christian Religion*, had defined *piety* (*pietas*) as "that reverence joined with love of God which the knowledge of his benefits induces."[2] Similarly, Schleiermacher's more formal definitions of *piety* are found in the opening chapters of his own dogmatic magnum opus, *The Christian Faith*.[3] Piety, he wrote, "considered purely for itself, [is] neither a knowing nor a doing but is a determination of feeling or of the immediate self-consciousness" (§3); and "the self-identical essence of piety is this: that we are conscious of ourselves as absolutely dependent or, which is the same thing, as being in relation to God" (§4).[4]

Arguably, when it comes to Schleiermacher's notion of piety, scholars have taken two basic approaches: on the one hand, there has been a strong focus on his *theory* of piety and religion, a focus that has figured large in the history of the modern study of religion, due to the contentious nature of these debates; on the other hand, there has been a tendency to focus on Schleiermacher's personality and

1

personal piety, in part because the biographical details are so telling and interesting. Both approaches risk becoming too one-sided. The former approach, in its important task of seeking precision and coherence, can lose sight of how, according to Schleiermacher, *feeling* (to choose just one key term) actually functions in the life of an individual and community. The latter approach, in its equally important task of trying to know the person, can lend itself to hagiographic-like treatments. In either case, theory and practice become disconnected from each other.

This introduction to Schleiermacher and his spirituality does not begin with an examination of his own definitions of *piety*. Were we to begin with these later, formal definitions, we would begin with his more abstract and scientific theoretical formulations without having a real sense of the richly textured content of how he understood it or how he himself lived and practiced a specifically Christian piety. As Schleiermacher himself made clear, there is no religion in the abstract. Religion, hence piety, is always particularized, always culturally and historically embedded. What is more, the study of spirituality as an academic field has grown significantly in recent years, and its rubrics and methods can enable us to approach Schleiermacher anew by helping us to appreciate how capacious his understanding of piety was and, at the same time, by requiring us to expand our view of his spirituality, since current definitions of spirituality tend to be more comprehensive than older ones. Let me briefly indicate four ways in which recent scholarship on spirituality can help inform our understanding of Schleiermacher's practice as well as his theory of the Christian life, in ways that are appreciative yet critical, and in ways that help correct certain common misperceptions.

First, in the current academic study of Christian spirituality, scholars generally tend to offer two related kinds of definitions of the term *spirituality*: a more general or "anthropological"[5] definition that identifies spirituality as an ongoing realization of a profoundly human propensity or ideal; and, connected to that, a more specific definition of *Christian spirituality*. So, to give but one example, Sandra Schneiders defines *spirituality* in general as "the actualization of the basic human capacity for transcendence and...as the experience of conscious involvement in the project of life-integration through self-transcendence toward the horizon of ultimate value one perceives."[6] She then goes on to fill in what "self-transcendence" and "horizon of ultimate value" mean in a specifically Christian context.[7] Schleiermacher, too, insisted on the need to articulate definitions that are both universal and particular, with the two mutually informing one another. Where such new definitions will be informative for us in considering Schleiermacher's spirituality is in the stress they place on practice, process, and the ongoing integrative activity of the spiritual life. Taken alone, Schleiermacher's own definitions of *piety* may seem to (or at least have been taken to) emphasize passivity, seclusion, and interiority. Yet his actual descriptions of pious people in general (in the *Speeches*, for example) and of the Christian life in particular (such as in the *Christmas Dialogue, The Christian Faith,* and his sermons) in fact do emphasize practices, processes, and the cultivation of certain attitudes and relations. This is in part what he meant by *Bildung*—one of the "keywords"[8] in Germany during his lifetime.

Second, as already suggested in the previous point, the current consensus of scholars in the field is that the scope of what falls under spirituality needs to be widened. In the words of Rowan Williams, our understanding of spirituality "must now touch every area of human experience, the public and social, the painful, negative, even pathological byways of the mind, the moral and relational world."[9] Again, Schleiermacher's definitions of *piety* alone do not suggest any "public and social" reach, when in fact his understanding, experience, and practice of piety were profoundly social and did take public and even political form. This may surprise many familiar with his famous phrase that religion is not a knowing or a doing, but a feeling. Yet this is precisely why it is necessary to use a broader rubric to help see how Schleiermacher's spirituality was related to just about every aspect of his life. In doing so, we can correct a common but apparently almost intractable misunderstanding of Schleiermacher's piety (a view shared alike by people who themselves espouse this view of spirituality and by critics who find it terribly problematic)— namely, that spirituality is essentially an interiorization on the part of individuals.[10] Schleiermacher does indeed stand in relation to recent developments in the study of spirituality—not, however, because of an overemphasis on interiority and withdrawal from the world but precisely because he held together the theoretical and the practical, the exterior and interior, the individual and the whole, and so forth.

Third, the current academic field of the study of Christian spirituality can help inform our understanding of Schleiermacher's practice and theory of piety because, increasingly, scholars emphasize the historical-contextual nature of spirituality. Bernard McGinn succinctly describes this approach as one that "emphasizes spirituality as an experience rooted in a particular community's history rather than as a dimension of human existence as such (not that it excludes this)."[11] Philip Sheldrake devotes an entire book to this approach:

> In specifically Christian terms, the notion of "spirituality" refers to the way our fundamental values, lifestyles, and spiritual practices reflect understandings of God, human identity, and the material world as the context for human transformation. All Christian spiritual traditions are ultimately rooted in, and are interpretations of, the Hebrew and Christian scriptures and particularly in the four Gospels. The connection to these foundational texts is not simple, however. Spiritual traditions and texts, in all times and places, are also attempts to reinterpret these foundational scriptural texts, and the values they portray, within specific historical and cultural circumstances.[12]

Again, we find here a key aspect of contemporary theory that is not at all foreign to Schleiermacher's thought, since he was perhaps the first Christian theologian to take seriously modern historical consciousness and to try to understand religious communities (their practices as well as their doctrinal propositions) in terms of their particular historical context. "Religious people are thoroughly historical," he insisted.[13]

Fourth, the academic study of spirituality is by no means strictly theological, nor need it be tied to a specific religious tradition. Broader humanist strands of scholarship are also instructive here. Influential in the past few decades, for instance, is the work of Pierre Hadot, a philosopher specializing in ancient philosophy who has been instrumental in retrieving the notion of "spiritual exercises" as a philosophical activity.[14] As we shall see, Schleiermacher's own work on Socrates and Plato was a precursor to such dialogical readings of ancient philosophy, and his writing style as well as his theory of religious language offer excellent examples of writing as a spiritual exercise (see the section below entitled "Schleiermacher's Writing as Spiritual Exercise").

In summary, the rubric of spirituality, as that has been shaped in the past quarter-century by the study of spirituality in a broader ecumenical and humanist setting, offers a chance to consider certain aspects of Schleiermacher's thought in a new light. At the same time, Schleiermacher's multifaceted spirituality—as that comes through in his writing, preaching, friendships, teaching, as well as his ecclesial and civic leadership and social engagement—has much to offer the field of spirituality, both as practice and as academic inquiry. It may also serve as a challenge to scholars in the fields of theology and philosophy. Can his theology and philosophy even be understood apart from his spirituality?

This introduction to Schleiermacher's spirituality is divided into three main sections, each of which takes a different starting point: (1) Schleiermacher's life and works, with a special view to his spirituality; (2) Schleiermacher's writing as spiritual exercise; and (3) main themes in Schleiermacher's spirituality. There is no one correct place to start. Readers should decide where to begin based on their own inclinations. It is an *introduction* in three senses. It introduces readers to Schleiermacher and, for those already familiar with him, to a new lens through which to read him. It also serves as an introduction to the selection of texts in this volume, insofar as each section includes discussion of the texts, especially of the two title pieces.[15] Finally, it is introductory in that it is an initial foray that hopes to generate further discussion on Schleiermacher and spirituality.

Schleiermacher's Life and Works, with a Special View to His Spirituality[16]

Childhood and Youth, 1768–1785

Born in Breslau on November 21, 1768, Friedrich Daniel Ernst Schleiermacher would become the fourth and third generation of

Reformed pastors on both the maternal and paternal sides of the family, respectively. His mother, Elisabeth Maria Katharina Stubenrauch (1736–83), was the daughter and granddaughter of court chaplains at the Reformed (Calvinist) Cathedral of Berlin (*Berliner Dom*)—or more properly, the *Supreme Parish Church*; her brother, Samuel Ernst Timotheus Stubenrauch (1738–1807), was a *Gymnasium* professor of church history at Halle and later a preacher at Drossen and Landsberg-an-der-Warthe. Friedrich's paternal grandfather, Daniel Schleyermacher (1697–ca. 1765), was a Reformed preacher in Elberfeld who had become involved with a radical Pietist movement headed by Anna von Büchel and Elias Eller, an association that led to serious accusations and to his having to flee to Holland in disgrace. Friedrich's father, Johann Gottlieb Adolph Schleyermacher (1727–94), was a Reformed chaplain in the Prussian army. In 1778, as a result of the war of the Bavarian Succession (1778–79), Gottlieb moved his family from Breslau to Pless while he camped with Prussian troops near Gnadenfrei. There he came into contact with the Pietist settlement, the *Herrnhuter Brüdergemeine*, known in English as the Moravian Church, which had originally been established in the early eighteenth century on land owned by Graf Nikolaus Ludwig von Zinzendorf (1700–1760), under his protection and with his largesse. Gottlieb, along with some of his troops, underwent a spiritual awakening, and his former reserve about Pietism was lifted somewhat. After the Treaty of Teschen the next year, the family moved to Anhalt, but by 1782 the parents had decided that their children's (Friedrich, his sister Friederike Charlotte, and brother Johann Carl) religious and educational formation should be entrusted to the *Brüdergemeine* (Congregation) at Herrnhut.

While waiting in Gnadenfrei for several weeks to hear final word about whether he and his siblings would be accepted (by means of a lottery system), the fourteen-year-old Schleiermacher had his own religious awakening. Years later he would describe this experience to a friend: "No other place has fostered the lively reminiscence of the entire course of my spirit as this place has—from the first awakening of the better things up to the point where I now stand. Here arose in me, for the first time, the consciousness of the relation of the human person to a higher world—admittedly in an inferior form."[17]

All three children were accepted into the Congregation.

Charlotte stayed with the community at Gnadenfrei, while Friedrich and Carl were sent to the Moravian school at Niesky. Schleiermacher would not see his parents again. His mother died that autumn, in 1783, and his father, with whom he would correspond over the next decade, died in 1794.

The fairly liberal curriculum and schedule at Niesky provided Schleiermacher with a strong education in languages, science, and math. In particular, he immersed himself in ancient Greek literature and philosophy. Religiously speaking, the emphasis was not so much on dogma as on the inner religious life supported by communal worship. The children were protected from what were deemed the evils of the world so that their inner lives might develop, grace might break through by the power of the Holy Spirit, they might focus their devotion to Jesus, and they might feel the joy of salvation and experience the immediate presence of God. The two years he spent at Niesky were on the whole happy years for Schleiermacher, ones he would remember with fondness. The teachers and students had close relationships, and he cultivated what would be lifetime friendships there—for instance, with Carl Gustav von Brinckmann and Johann Baptist von Albertini. The cultivation of friendship, which involved the open exchange of hearts and ideas, would always remain an essential part of Schleiermacher's spirituality. Still, this time was not without internal conflicts. Doubts or fears about certain Christian doctrines, such as eternal punishment, had plagued him since he was eleven. He did not sit easy with the Moravian emphasis on a "wounds-theology"[18] or with its views of the evil world or of human corruption, even though his sense of his own sinfulness weighed on him. He later wrote,

> Now commenced another struggle generated by the views held among the United Brethren relative to the doctrines of the natural corruption of man and of the supernatural means of grace, and the manner in which these doctrines were interwoven with every discourse and every lesson— a struggle which endured almost as long as I remained a member of the congregation. My own experience furnished me with abundant evidence in favour of the truth of the first of these two chief pillars of the ascetic-mystic system, and at length I came to look upon every good

action as suspicious, or as resulting merely from the force of circumstances. I was thus in that state of torture,...: my belief in the innate moral faculty of man had been taken from me, and as yet nothing had been substituted in its stead. For in vain I aspired after those supernatural experiences, of the necessity of which every glance at myself with reference to the doctrine of future retribution convinced me—of the reality of which, *externally to myself,* every lesson and every hymn, yes, every glance at the Brethren, so attractive while under their influence, persuaded me....Vain were the endeavours of my excellent mother to reconcile her own more correct views of the two doctrines with that which I was taught on this head in the congregation, and to tranquillize my heart.[19]

Formal Education and Spiritual Crisis, 1785–1790

Such concerns were only exacerbated when, in September 1785, he and ten classmates were sent to the seminary at Barby, where the Moravian Church educated its future teachers and preachers. There, within a very restrictive intellectual setting, Schleiermacher and his friends formed a philosophical club. They read as much of the forbidden literature and philosophy of the Enlightenment as they could get their hands on—such as Johann Wolfgang von Goethe's *The Sorrows of Young Werther* (1774), the poetry of Christoph Martin Wieland, Immanuel Kant's *Prolegomena to Any Future Metaphysics* (1783), and the leading philosophical and literary journals of the day. Their enthusiasm over these ideas put the members of the philosophical club at odds with the aims and methods of the curriculum at Barby and drew these free spirits into direct conflict with their superiors. Already within the first year, Schleiermacher had begun to complain to his father about the suspicions he and his classmates had due to the fact that their teachers did not allow them to read, nor did the teachers lecture on, other views or criticisms. Schleiermacher's English friend, Samuel Okely, left Barby at the end of 1786 (he died tragically in the following year).

Schleiermacher disclosed to his teachers the fact that he simply could not accept some of the basic dogmas of the church, and in

January 1787, he wrote the same to his father in a heartrending letter:

> I cannot believe that he who called himself only the Son of Man was the true, eternal God. I cannot believe that his death was a vicarious atonement, because he has never himself expressly said it, and because I cannot believe that it had been necessary, since God, who clearly created human beings not for perfection but only for the pursuit of perfection, could not possibly want to punish humans eternally because they have not become perfect.[20]

The son pleaded with his father to let him leave Barby and pursue nontheological studies at the University of Halle. "Given my mindset about the teaching and constitution of the Congregation," he wrote, "I would not be tranquil, peaceful or happy there."[21] The father relented, although not without warning him about the dangers of pride and the need for meekness. Friedrich Schleiermacher thus left the Moravian Church, a breach as painful as it was liberating.

He moved to Halle in April 1787, where he immediately matriculated at the university and was given lodging at the home of his beloved maternal uncle, Samuel Stubenrauch. The University of Halle had been an important center for (Lutheran) Pietism and was at this time a vibrant center for the German Enlightenment. Under the philosopher Johann August Eberhard, himself a student of the Enlightenment rationalist philosopher Christian Wolff, Schleiermacher studied such far-ranging topics as metaphysics, classics (especially Aristotle's *Nicomachean Ethics*), Kant's transcendental philosophy,[22] and English moral sense philosophy. When his aunt and uncle moved to Drossen in May 1789, where the latter had accepted a preaching position, Schleiermacher, still financially dependent, had little choice but to go with them. His time in Drossen was dry, lacking in social contact and with limited access to books. His disinterest in anything theological continued, with his intellectual energies continuing to be directed to matters of practical philosophy. By the end of the year, there, however, at the urging of his father and prompted by the need to earn a living, Schleiermacher forced himself to take the theology examination for the Reformed Church. He passed the examination in Berlin (1790), getting only "fair" in dogmatic theology, but his practical aim was achieved in that shortly thereafter he received a position as tutor in the home of nobility, Count and Countess von Dohna, in Schlobitten (East Prussia).

Early Career, 1790–1796

Schleiermacher's almost three years in Schlobitten (October 1790–May 1793) were significant for the development of his spirituality in two ways. The experience of living in the household of a large, loving family with distinguished women (the mother and the older daughters) inspired him and set in his mind a new ideal of family and sociability. Also, he met considerable success in his preaching; his sermons were well received, and he discovered a talent in himself that would inspire a genuine interest in religion and theology. Both of these points come through in a letter to his father in 1791:

> My heart is regularly nurtured here and needs not wilt under the weeds of erudition, and my religious sentiments do not die under theological musings. Here I enjoy the domestic life for which the human person is destined, and that life warms my feelings....[In my acquaintances] I learn patience and a suppleness that comes from the heart and is grounded in gratitude for social happiness. I am coming to know myself and others. I have models to emulate, and I feel that I am becoming a better person. Certainly thank God with me for his gracious foreordination, and wish me blessings to use it wisely.[23]

Differences in worldviews between the tutor and his employers (differences that were exposed, in part, through their respective responses to the French Revolution) led eventually to Schleiermacher's leaving Schlobitten in 1793. After a short stint in Friedrich Gedike's pedagogical seminars in Berlin,[24] Schleiermacher took the final set of his theological examinations and then accepted his first pastorate, in Landsberg an der Warthe (1794–96).

His scholarly writings from these early years, although mostly philosophical in nature, offer important insights into his spirituality. Indeed, from his earliest days, his spirituality had never been separate from his philosophical and literary pursuits. We find the young Schleiermacher immersed in questions of moral philosophy, for instance in "On the Highest Good" and "Notes on Kant: Critique of Practical Reason" (1789); "On Freedom" (1790–92); "On What Gives Value to Life" (1792/93). Here we find Schleiermacher sharing Kant's anti-eudemonism yet also rejecting Kant's notion of transcendental freedom. Rather than making the human agent an exception to natural causality, Schleiermacher placed the human squarely within the natural causal system. At the same time, however, he described causality in nonmechanistic terms and developed a moral determinism that allowed for novelty and freedom, albeit not absolute freedom, and that went hand in hand with a strong theory of "individuality."[25] This would remain central to his thought overall and would prove crucial for his spirituality: the human person is essentially related; human freedom is thus always finite and always stands in relation to dependency; or, to put it another way, spontaneity is always related to receptivity.

Schleiermacher pursued his reflections on practical philosophy when, in 1793–94, he became interested in one of the major debates of late eighteenth-century Germany, the Pantheist Controversy (*Pantheismusstreit*) between F. H. Jacobi (1743–1819) and Moses Mendelssohn (1729–86) over whether their mutual (deceased) friend Gotthold Ephraim Lessing (1729–81) was a "Spinozist."[26] Schleiermacher wrote two studies, "Spinozism" and "Brief Presentation of the Spinozistic System" (1793/94), one consisting mainly of notes on Jacobi's book and the other marking the beginning of more constructive positions, extending his thought from practical philosophy to larger metaphysical considerations of being (albeit in a post-Kantian framework). Significant here for the future development of his thought is that he grounds his practical philosophy in an ontology and a theory of individuation.[27]

Berlin and the Romantic Circle, 1796–1802

In 1796 Schleiermacher was assigned as the Reformed chaplain at the Charité Hospital, a hospital for the poor located just outside of

Berlin at that time.[28] This meant that, although his letters did not always convey this, he spent much of his days addressing the spiritual needs of sick (physically and mentally) patients and their families, who would have had very little hope for an improved life. His work there would leave an imprint on his theological work. As a recent biographer has pointed out, Schleiermacher's most important writing from this time, *On Religion: Speeches to Its Cultured Despisers* (1799), contains many "medical terms such as *asphyxia, sthenic death, euthanasia, dephlegmated spirit*."[29] Along with a Lutheran colleague, Schleiermacher was involved in the restructuring of the hospital, in particular the role of chaplains. There were also larger sociopolitical issues at stake here having to do with how the state understood and treated the poor, and Schleiermacher's activity on this score contributed to a tense relationship with the Director of the Poor.

In Berlin, several threads of personal connections came together for Schleiermacher. Old acquaintances from his mother's family were there, including Friedrich Samuel Gottfried Sack (1738–1817), the court chaplain and Schleiermacher's sponsor, as well as Johann Joachim Spalding (1714–1804), the famous Enlightenment philosopher and theologian.[30] His old friend from the Herrnhuter days and Halle, Brinckmann, was there, as were his former pupils from Drossen, Alexander von Dohna, who had obtained a position in the Royal Prussian Chamber of War and Domain, and his brother Wilhelm. The renewal of these latter friendships led quickly to his introduction to the literary and intellectual society of Berlin, most particularly into the circle of Markus and Henriette (de Lemos) Herz (1764–1847), whose home served as one of the most famous salons. To use one of Schleiermacher's own metaphors, it was there that those seeds of sociability and engaged discourse at Niesky and at Schlobitten blossomed and the man who would become the famous theologian, preacher, and philosopher came into view.

It is difficult to overstate the uniqueness of this particular constellation of brilliant talent that formed in Jena and Berlin just at this time and gave rise to what came to be called the "Romantic circle," or Early German Romanticism: the brothers August Wilhelm (1767–1845) and Friedrich (1772–1829) von Schlegel, Friedrich Wilhelm Joseph von Schelling (1775–1854), Johann Ludwig Tieck (1773–1853), Friedrich von Hardenberg aka "Novalis" (1772–1801),

Dorothea Mendelssohn Veit (1764–1839), and Schleiermacher him-self, among others.[31] Romanticism was a literary movement that, driven as it was by a new historical consciousness and imbued with the sense that the German language and culture could best capture the great classics, challenged classicism. Translation projects were at the heart of their activity, from Plato to Shakespeare. Their "philos-ophy of poetry" dissolved the typical categorization of literary forms and called for the establishment of an entirely new canon, one deter-mined not by epoch or genre but by the "element of poetry." In the Romantic canon, Plato, an ancient philosopher who attacked the poets, was a Romantic poet and artist; Shakespeare, a modern poet, was a Romantic philosopher; and Spinoza, a modern rationalistic philosopher, was a Romantic poet. Still, it was as much a philosoph-ical movement as it was literary, and indeed that was the point. Divisions between art, science, and life did not hold because they could not hold. As F. Schlegel famously defined *Romantic poetry*,

> Romantic poetry [*Poesie*] is a progressive, universal poetry. Its aim isn't merely to reunite all the separate species of poetry and put poetry in touch with philosophy and rhetoric. It tries to and should mix and fuse poetry and prose, inspiration and criticism, the poetry of art and the poetry of nature; and make poetry lively and sociable, and life and society poetical....It alone can become, like the epic, a mirror of the whole circumambient world, an image of the age.[32]

Contrary to some common assumptions about Romanticism, theirs was neither an utter rejection of the Enlightenment (*Aufklärung*) nor an appeal to emotionalism. Philosophically, they had cut their teeth on Kant's critical philosophy and thus can be considered "post-Kantians." And while emotions and sentiments were important to the Romantics, the Romantic genius was the one who would draw back from the immediacy of emotion and experience into a contemplative moment, reflect on those emotions and sentiments, and then give thoughtful expression to them, shaping them into a new work of art.

What the Romantics did reject was any notion of reason detached from life, an intellect separated from depth of emotion, a "self" abstracted from history, a transcendental freedom divorced from a real relationship to nature, and a philosophy devoid of poetry. All of this reflected their particular understanding of the "whole circumambient world." Their universe was not the mechanistic one found in so many of the philosophies of the Enlightenment. Profoundly influenced as they were by recent discoveries in chemistry and electricity,[33] their universe was a vital, charged, living organic universe supersaturated with the infinite. This worldview allowed the Romantics to account for novelty, progress, individuality, and genius. Central was the concept of *Bildung*, which can mean education, culture, formation, or development. As Frederick Beiser explains,

> The romantic ideal of *Bildung* was not only holistic but also individualistic. In other words, *Bildung* should consist in the development of not only our characteristic human power, which we all share as human beings, but also our distinctive individual powers, which are unique to each of us. The romantics stressed that each individual had to realize his human powers in his own unique and individual fashion. No two persons were ever alike; each had characteristics that distinguished him from everyone else; complete self-realization demanded actualizing these distinctive characteristics no less than our universal ones.[34]

This cultivation of individuality necessarily took place amidst sociability. Friendship, conversation, and *Symphilosophie* provided inspiration, context, and content to their project.

Friendship was always of vital importance to Schleiermacher, and by all accounts he was a genius at it, with an easy and engaged conversational style, an open and empathetic heart, and a generous attentiveness. The Romantic ideal of friendship was a complete sharing of oneself through conversation, correspondence, the arts, and other shared experiences. During these Berlin years, three of Schleiermacher's friendships in particular stand out as telling of his character and as instrumental in the development of his spirituality, in that he shared with these people his innermost thoughts and explored with them human possibility. First, his friendship with

Henriette Herz, which lasted his lifetime: here were two people—one Jewish and one Christian, one female and one male—who found a soulmate in each other and who sustained an intimate friendship that was not romantic.[35] Two short letters to Herz translated in this volume serve as examples of the importance of their friendship, and of friendship in general, to his spiritual life. Second, his friendship with Friedrich Schlegel: Schlegel moved in with Schleiermacher in 1797, and they remained roommates for almost two years in Berlin, collaborating on several projects. Schleiermacher defended Schlegel's novel *Lucinde* (1799), deemed scandalous by many because it was so sexually explicit, in his own *Confidential Letters on Lucinde* (1800), holding forth the idea of marriage as a spiritual union of love rather than as an external, civic form.[36] Finally, his love affair with Eleanore (Krüger) Grunow (1769–1837), the wife of a Lutheran pastor: their relationship lasted on and off for years, as he waited for her to make the decision to end her miserable marriage. In the end, she could not do so, a decision that Schleiermacher respected. The letter to Grunow translated in this volume was written on the occasion of her mother's impending death, and it lends insight not only to Schleiermacher's ideals of romantic love and friendship, but also to his understanding of death and eternity. Each one of these unconventional friendships raised the ire of Schleiermacher's superiors.

1. On Religion: Speeches to Its Cultured Despisers (1799)

On Schleiermacher's twenty-ninth birthday (November 21, 1797), several of his friends (the Dohna brothers, Henriette, Dorothea, and Friedrich Schlegel) showed up at his door, surprising him with a cake and birthday greetings. They challenged him to write a book, chiding him that there he was, almost thirty, without having really produced anything of his own. It took almost a year for the concept of the book to form (it would be on religion) and there was concern that it would not pass the censor. Finally, Schleiermacher's first major work was published anonymously in 1799, *On Religion: Speeches to Its Cultured Despisers*,[37] a work that, in addressing the greatest literary and philosophical talents of the age, in challenging the status quo of the Enlightenment and of bourgeois society, and in being nonetheless so intimate and expressive, is itself a consummate example of Early German Romanticism. The *Speeches on Religion*, as it is referred to, put Schleiermacher on the map, so to speak, and has become both a religious classic and a classic in the field of the study of religion.[38]

On Religion consists of five *Speeches*. The first is "Apology." From the start, it is clear that the *Speech* is a rhetorical tour de force, whether or not one agrees with its main points. Schleiermacher defends religion against the despisers' misconceptions of it, which have to do with "the different edifices of religion, from the meaningless fables of barbarous nations to the most refined deism, from the crude superstition of our people to the poorly stitched together garments of metaphysics and morals that are called rational Christianity."[39] He agrees that these are "without rhyme or reason"[40] and insists such things are not religion. In an oblique reference to his time at Herrnhut, Schleiermacher writes,

> Religion was the maternal womb in whose holy darkness my young life was nourished and prepared for the world still closed to it. In it my spirit breathed before it had discovered the world of external objects, experience, and scholarship. Religion helped me when I began to examine the ancestral faith and to purify my heart of the rubble of primitive times. It remained with me when God and immortality disappeared before my doubting eyes.[41]

In one swoop, Schleiermacher appeals to the despisers by emphasizing genius and tapping into their suspicion of forms, formulas, and demands for conformity. At the same time, he begins to redefine religion: it is not about doctrines or precepts. The task of his second *Speech* is to explain just what, then, it is.

The second *Speech*, "On the Essence of Religion," has probably proven to be the most famous, or infamous, of the five. Schleiermacher begins his second *Speech* by, as he was wont to do, shifting the terms of debate, from Cicero's question "What are the gods?" to "What is religion?" Not until the very end of the *Speech* does he even address the ideas of "God" and "immortality." Religion is not, Schleiermacher insists, a knowing (metaphysics) or a doing (ethics) but is instead *feeling*, "the necessary and indispensable third to those two."[42] "True religion," he writes, "is sensation and taste for the infinite."[43] The second *Speech* is peppered with such definitions that themselves have almost become "classics":

This seeking and finding in all that lives and moves, in all becoming and change, in all doing and suffering, and just having and knowing life itself in immediate feeling as this existence—this is religion;[44]

religion lingers with pleasure on every acting from God, on every activity through which the infinite reveals itself in the finite...;[45]

religion is the original and sworn enemy of all pedantry and all one-sidedness.[46]

In order to get at his meaning and his spirituality, it is important to attend to his method of proceeding. Because his addressees despise religion, the definitions ought not to be extracted from how he builds his argument, from how he arrives at such definitions almost by way of negation (by saying, that is, what religion is *not*), or from how, in the public space of a "speech," he draws his cultured audience along, pointing out their own contradictions and then turning them suddenly so as to behold what they most value, only to realize that that is religion. It is also important to attend to his descriptions of what pious people always do or never do, and of how the religious life is lived—its attitudes and demeanors. Thereby we can come to realize how Schleiermacher himself enacts those very attitudes and gestures in his rhetoric, and thus how he himself lived and embodied that spirituality.[47] Because this *Speech* is so critical in understanding Schleiermacher's spirituality—both as theory and as lived—a new translation of it, the first in English of the second edition (1806), is included in this volume.

The third *Speech*, "On Self-Formation for Religion," harkens back to Schleiermacher's youthful days at Niesky, arguing that religion cannot be taught ("We cannot teach them to intuit"[48]) but must instead be elicited, aroused, and cultivated. Religion, as he has already said in the second *Speech*, is not about imitation. "The universe creates its own observers and admirers, and we only wish to intuit how that happens as far as it allows itself to be intuited."[49] How this occurs is explained in the fourth *Speech*, "On the Social Element in Religion; or, On Church and Priesthood." Religion for Schleiermacher is necessarily social. If piety is social, it therefore belongs to a particular language and conceptual world, as well as to a particular set of practices, gestures, and customs that express and arouse the sense and the taste for the "infinite." Here is the beginning of his ecclesiology. It is remarkable, really, that Schleiermacher has been accused of being individualistic, since his understanding of the necessity of fellowship—of church—would always remain central to his thought.

The fifth and last *Speech* is "On the Religions." This *Speech* is critical for understanding his theory and philosophy of religion, inasmuch as Schleiermacher rejects the possibility of a natural religion, or Deism. Having introduced this point earlier, here he develops the idea explicitly: only "in the religions, you are to discover religion."[50] This is also critical for understanding his spirituality: the importance of multiplicity, plurality, and embeddedness. There is no "essence" without a concrete living reality. In this fifth *Speech*, Schleiermacher again returns to pantheism and personalism as two types of religion,[51] a point he had made at the end of the second *Speech*. And we also find here a rather unique clue into his understanding of a particularly Protestant expression of piety: in his definition of Christianity, he highlights the polemical nature, its

> intuition of the universal straining of everything finite against the unity of the whole and of the way in which the deity handles this striving, how it reconciles the enmity directed against it and sets bounds to the ever-greater distance by scattering over the whole individual points that are at once finite and infinite, at once human and divine.[52]

Thus, where he begins his *Speeches* with apologetics, he ends with polemics. Schleiermacher's rhetorical flourish gets somewhat ahead of him here, insofar as he would later also shift how religious polemics are executed, moving them from the territory of hostile warfare to a shop where bad ideas and worn-out paradigms could be carved away. In this last *Speech*, we also find Schleiermacher's first major christological claim outside the genre of a sermon. He explains that what he admires in Christ is not so much the "purity of the ethical teaching" or the "uniqueness of his character" but "the splendid clarity with which the great idea he had come to exhibit was formed in his soul, the idea that everything finite requires higher mediation in order to be connected with the divine."[53]

So then, in the *Speeches* and especially in the second *Speech*, what does Schleiermacher say about religion in general and pious people in particular, and what does that tell us about his spirituality? Let me touch on five relevant points.

First, in distinguishing religion as feeling from "a kind of think-ing" and "a manner of acting,"[54] Schleiermacher underscores religion or piety as fundamentally, though not exclusively, a receptive state. For him, both "knowing" and "acting" are kinds of activity in which we try to impose something onto the universe, but in doing so with-out any "feeling," we fail to "hear" the universe and attune ourselves to it, and consequently we risk losing contact with reality and sink into a "one-sided narrow-mindedness of...empty consciousness."[55] This Schleiermacher sees as arrogance that stands in contrast to the humility of the pious person, whose openness to the universe is a kind of courage.

Second, while piety is passive and inactive in the sense that it receives without trying to impose or control, it is not totally inactive. "Feeling" is an active kind of receptivity or susceptibility (*Empfänglichkeit*) according to which the pious take up what they receive, appropriating it in a distinctive way that becomes formative for their character. In his words, "The entire religious life consists in two elements: we surrender to the universe, letting ourselves be excited by the side of the universe turned towards the self; and then inwardly we reproduce this contact (which, as what it is and in its determinateness, is a particular feeling) assimilating it into the inner unity of our own life and existence."[56] For Schleiermacher, the pious life necessarily involves a "living" oscillating movement between self and other, individual and whole, interior and exterior, near and far.[57] In short, the spiritual life is what can be called an integrative process of expanding, refining, and attuning.

Third, when Schleiermacher speaks of the "universe," he does in part mean nature, but he does not mean nature as distinct from humanity or as separate from the fullness of divine activity. In the second *Speech* in particular, we see a deep respect for nature and the Romantic insistence that we are fully human only in relation to the universe and all it contains—or, more to the point, humans are a part of nature and are subject to the same eternal laws. Schleiermacher understands nature in organic and relational terms, so much so that he claims that we stand in relation even to the farthest star. At the same time, religion for him is not awe about the magnitude of the universe or about the intricate designs found in it; that is why he says that "exterior" nature is only the "forecourt of religion."[58] What he means by "universe" has more to do with the interconnectedness of all that is, due to the divine activity that is always and already present in and through the finite: "Your feeling is your piety insofar as it expresses, in the way described, the existence and life common to you and to the universe, and insofar as you hold the individual moments of this existence and life as an operating of God in you by means of the universe."[59] For Schleiermacher, natural causality and divine causality always coincide; they can never be separated, nor can they be collapsed.

Fourth, piety is only possible where there is love, communication, and intimacy. This is evident, of course, in Schleiermacher's correspondence, but it is also developed throughout the *Speeches*, especially in two examples he gives in the second *Speech*: his interpretation of Genesis 2,[60] and the analogy, clearly mystical in nature, he draws between religious feeling and sexual intercourse.[61] The spirituality developed in the *Speeches* is a kind of humanism that insists that we *value* humanity—that we value individuals, humanity as a whole, and humanity as an ideal toward which to strive. Schleiermacher rebukes the despisers for claiming to love humanity but for being contemptuous of individuals less cultured than they. Admitting to sometimes feeling such contempt himself, he advises that they then move from the individual to humanity itself and then back to the individual, in order to renew and rededicate themselves there.[62] What he calls "peregrinations through the entire realm of humanity" are critical for *Bildung*, for our own education, growth, and formation.[63]

And fifth, piety requires a surrender—a willingness to recognize one's own finitude and mortality by surrendering the deep desire for immortality and by surrendering some of our most cherished ideas, even and especially our ideas of God when they become divorced from an openness to divine activity.[64] It is not our concepts that make us religious.

The *Speeches on Religion* aroused the apprehensions of the censor, who was none other than his superior and longtime family friend, Sack. Schleiermacher had availed himself of the common practice of publishing his work anonymously, so when Sack called him into his office to discuss the work he was reviewing (in order to decide whether it should be granted the imprimatur), their relationship took on what one scholar has described as "an awkward, if not bizarre, aspect."[65] Sack had actually appreciated the defense of religion in the first *Speech*, but he considered the second *Speech* to be a defense of pantheism and, what was for him the same thing, atheism. Schleiermacher was never entirely able to shake off such charges over the following three decades, finding it necessary to add "Explanations" to the third edition (1821).

2. Letters on Jewish Emancipation

Shortly after the publication of the *Speeches*, Schleiermacher involved himself in a very public debate in Berlin about the civic status of Jews in Prussia. Because Jews were not allowed citizenship, it was suggested (somewhat satirically) that Jews be baptized as Protestant Christians in order to become full citizens with the rights that entailed. (Many Jews in Berlin had in fact converted to Christianity.) Schleiermacher published *Letters on the Occasion of the Political-Theological Task and the Open Letter of Jewish Householders*, in which he argued that Jews should be granted citizenship, without any requirement that they change their religion, because legal rights should not depend on religion.[66] Here we find three interrelated and fundamental commitments of Schleiermacher at play, the coming together of which speaks to his spirituality: he upholds political liberty and individual freedom; he rejects a notion of religion that is defined only in terms of exterior forms that have no relation to a person's authentic development; and he feels compelled to speak publicly about a matter of basic fairness and justice.

21

3. *Soliloquies* (1800)

Shortly after the publication of the *Speeches*, Schleiermacher wrote to the publisher J. C. P. Spener, presenting an idea for another work, this one in the form of a soliloquy—not in the tone of a teaching voice, he explained, but engaging the reflections of the average person.[67] He had jotted the main idea in his notes: "Self-intuition and intuition of the universe are reciprocal concepts; hence, every reflection is infinite."[68] In other words, it was to be a kind of companion piece to his *Speeches*: where that work had developed the idea of the intuition of the universe, this one would develop the other side, intuition of the self. Schleiermacher wrote the piece in a matter of three weeks, and it was published in January 1800 with the title *Soliloquies: A New Year's Gift*.[69] Similar to the *Speeches*, there are five *Soliloquies*: "Reflection," "Soundings," "Worldview," "Prospect," and "Youth and Age." Also similar to the *Speeches*, it was published anonymously. As the title and genre suggest, the *Soliloquies* is profoundly personal and autobiographical. It was intended, after all, as a gift of his own self, and therefore could very well have been included in this volume on Schleiermacher's spirituality, were more space available.

While a cursory glance might suggest that the *Soliloquies* is an exercise in subjective idealism, in fact it took a critical counterposition to Fichte's idealism. What was true for the *Speeches* remains true here: Schleiermacher intends a "higher realism." As we have already seen, he held that we discover our own selves and our freedom only in relation to others, only when we have discovered humanity. He writes in the first *Soliloquy*, "To behold humanity within oneself, and never to lose sight of the vision when once found, is the only certain means of never straying from its sacred precincts."[70] Schleiermacher outlines three stages of moral (in the broadest sense of the term) development: from the sensuous, to a "realization of humanity in its universal aspects" (when a person submits to duty), and then to "the still higher level of individuality."[71] He recounts,

> Thus there dawned upon me what is now my highest intuition. I saw clearly that each [person] is meant to represent humanity in [their] own way, combining its elements uniquely, so that it may reveal itself in every mode, and all

22

that can issue from its womb be made actual in the fullness of unending space and time.[72]

Although his notion of an ideal humanity can seem abstract, it is made real by the fact that it is discovered in intimacy and friendship:

This is the very thing of which I chiefly boast, that my love and friendship always have so high a source, that they have never been blended with any vulgar sentiment, have never been the offspring of habit or tender feeling, but ever an act of purest freedom orientated towards the individuality of other human beings.[73]

The self is only a self, only truly individual, in intimate relation to others and in recognizing their freedom.

This he lived, as is evident especially at this time in his relation to Eleanore. In addition, being in relation to others means one is also in relation to the world, as he goes on to explain in the third *Soliloquy*. And in "Prospect," he brings up marriage and how his freedom is necessarily limited by his future wife's freedom. He closes with "Youth and Age," touching on an attitude he sustained throughout his life, both in his theory and his practice: "I shall never consider myself old until I am perfect, and I shall never be perfect."[74]

4. The Plato Translation (1804–1828)

Schleiermacher began another major project during this earlier period in Berlin—a translation of the works of Plato.[75] Although some new translations of individual Platonic dialogues were being published in German, this was to be of the entire corpus. The project would occupy him intensely over the course of the next decade and indeed for his entire career; it also earned him admission to the Royal Prussian Academy of Sciences. Just about the time Schleiermacher finished writing his *Speeches*, Friedrich Schlegel had invited him to undertake this joint project of translating Plato's dialogues and setting them in chronological order. It was to be a great experiment in "symphilosophizing," a Romantic ideal. At the time, it was Schlegel who had name recognition; in fact, Schlegel had included only his own name in the public announcement of the project in 1800. In early 1801, Schleiermacher began his translation of the *Phaedrus*, which both men had considered to be the first of Plato's dialogues, although for different reasons. The collaboration fell through, and by August 1802, the project became Schleiermacher's alone. The first volume appeared in 1804, with subsequent volumes appearing in 1805, 1807, 1808, and 1828, and with a second edition (of the earlier translations) appearing in 1817. The general consensus was that Schleiermacher's translation had captured the spirit of Plato, but it was his interpretation as much as his translation that was to change the course of Plato studies.

In his introduction to *Plato's Works*, Schleiermacher insisted that the *content* of Plato's philosophy cannot be understood apart from its *dialogical form*, and yet most interpreters treated that form as incidental and as a nuisance; he rejected the esoteric reading of Plato, arguing against the notion of a secret, oral tradition and insisting that Plato's thought is presented clearly and exclusively in the written documents; he dismissed neo-Platonic traditions and their speculative interpretations of Plato; he argued that Plato is best understood as an artist and his dialogues therefore as a single work of art; and he used the tools of the new criticism so as to arrange the dialogues in proper order.[76]

Although piety per se is not at issue here, all of these interpretive decisions are, in fact, related to his spirituality. Most notably, the emphasis he places on dialogue (conversation and other forms of personal intercommunication) was carried over into just about every area of his life and his thought; it is perhaps most explicit in his *Christmas Dialogue* and in his ecclesiology. Furthermore, the fact that he rejects speculative, esoteric systems shows again his insistence that we not impose our wishes but deal with the reality before us; Plato's principles, he calmly stated, are to be read clearly enough in his writings. Finally, Schleiermacher's rejection of the neo-Platonic tradition must not go unnoted, since so much of Christian spirituality had presupposed just such a metaphysical scaffolding. His spirituality does not involve an ascent from the material to the spiritual but discovers the divine in and through the finite.

Stolp and Halle, 1802–1807

As we have seen, Schleiermacher's superior, Sack, was unhappy with the *Speeches on Religion*, but even before that, he had complained about Schleiermacher's associations (with Schlegel as roommate, with "Jews,"[77] and with Grunow) and so thought it best that his protégé leave Berlin and take a pastorate somewhere far away. This finally happened in the summer of 1802, when Schleiermacher was exiled to Stolp, in Prussian Pomerania near the Baltic Sea. Schleiermacher himself saw it as an opportunity to let Eleanore make a final decision about whether or not to leave her husband. During the short period of transition from Berlin to Stolp, Schleiermacher visited his sister Charlotte in Gnadenfrei. While there, he wrote to his friend and publisher, Reimer, about his happy memories of that place, declaring, "I can say that I have become a Moravian again after all, only of a higher order."[78]

Stolp itself was a lonely and often depressing time for him, but it was also a time of scholarly production and transition. Removed from the Romantic context and associations of Berlin, his style of writing transitioned from the deeply personal expression of the *Speeches* and the *Soliloquies* to a more "scientific" style. When not preaching or making pastoral rounds, Schleiermacher devoted himself to writing his *Basic Principles of a Critique of Previous Ethical Theories*,[79] which by his own admission is a tedious piece. Once that was finished, he turned immediately back to the Plato project, intensively preparing the first volume of *Plato's Works*, which included the groundbreaking general introduction along with introductions to and translations of the *Phaedrus*, *Lysis*, *Protagoras*, and *Laches*; he also began work on the second volume. Still, beleaguered by loneliness and north winds, Schleiermacher despaired that his life held no other future.

Finally, in 1804, with the intervention of King Friedrich Wilhelm III, Schleiermacher was appointed "Professor *extraordinarius* of Theology and Philosophy" at the University of Halle, the "extraordinary" referring to the fact that he was the first Reformed member of what had been a Lutheran faculty; in 1806 his position was changed to *ordinarius*, which meant he became a full-fledged member of the faculty. He encountered some difficulties in integrating with the faculty, but the tensions were not just due to denominational differences. Most of the faculty still represented the typical Enlightenment approach to religion, which was both rationalistic and supernaturalist, although orthodox Pietism was also present. Schleiermacher's former professor, Eberhard, regarded him as an atheist due to his *Speeches*. Still, Schleiermacher threw himself into his new life with eager energy. As professor for the first time and as university preacher (a position that he dearly wanted), Schleiermacher's career took off. Famous now for his work on Plato, Schleiermacher lectured on dogmatics, ethics, the New Testament, church history, encyclopedia and methodology, and hermeneutics.

In Halle, Schleiermacher once more enjoyed the company of good friends and stimulating minds. He became close with the Danish philosopher Heinrich (Henrik) Steffens (1773–1845), whose wife, Johanna, was the daughter of the composer Johann Friedrich Reichardt (1752–1814), in whose home Schleiermacher was often a guest. This more familial setting inspired Schleiermacher and, indeed, served as the backdrop for his *The Christmas Celebration: A Dialogue*, in his descriptions of both the home and the music. It also made Schleiermacher long all the more for a loving household of his own. Eleanore had finally decided to leave her husband in August 1805. Schleiermacher's hopes, however, were dashed in October, when, as he explained in a letter, Eleanore had been "suddenly assailed by her old doubts and scruples of conscience just before her announcement of the judgment of separation"[80] to her husband. Schleiermacher was devastated, his "grievous feeling"[81] lasting through November. Then, in early December, Schleiermacher cancelled his lecture on ethics to attend a concert at the town hall by the virtuoso Friedrich Ludwig Dülon (1769–1826), a blind flutist. So inspired was Schleiermacher that, upon leaving the concert, the idea of writing something on the joy of Christmas came to him suddenly.

5. The Christmas Celebration: A Dialogue (1806)

Three weeks later, on the morning of Christmas Eve, Schleiermacher submitted the manuscript of *The Christmas Celebration: A Dialogue*.[82] Although he himself admitted it was not a great literary feat and suffered from having been written too hastily, it has proven to be his most-printed work. The *Christmas Dialogue* takes place on Christmas Eve in the well-appointed home of a married couple, Ernestine and Eduard, and their daughter Sofie. Their home and marriage are clearly depicted by Schleiermacher as the ideal: it is a relationship defined by affection, freedom, and mutual respect; in their intelligence, generosity, and serenity, Ernestine and Eduard both exemplify what for him is the essence of Christian piety; little Sofie very clearly is a product of that love and represents the early bud of Christian piety; and such love, according to Schleiermacher, necessarily creates a hospitable place of community and joy. Several close friends (it is not clear if any are also relatives), all of whom are Protestant Christians and some of whom seem to have close ties to Pietism, gather to celebrate Christmas and exchange gifts. In addition to the hosts, there are three women, three men, and two boys.

Since it is a very gender-inflected text where marital relations are important (because, in part, Schleiermacher himself was so preoccupied at the time with his own marital prospects), the characters will be described in those terms: Agnes is the mother of the two boys and is pregnant, although no mention is made of her husband or her marital status; Leonhardt, who plays the skeptic, is an attorney and presumably single; Ernst and Friederike are a young engaged couple, the latter an accomplished musician; Karoline is a lively conversationalist about whom no information is given, but she seems to be quite familiar with Sofie's schooling and habits, so she might be a relative or governess; and finally the sage Josef, whose presence is anticipated, appears at the very end.

The scene reflects the growth of bourgeois society in Germany at the time: a parlor decked with flowers, lights, and very nice gifts; musical instruments and books; tea time and, later, drinking and toasting. The mood throughout is one of joy, but it is a joy shared with intimate friends who have obviously also shared times of real grief. One of the points Schleiermacher returns to throughout is that the joy and serenity experienced that night are not passing states. Having their grounding in the gift of Christ in the incarnation, they are enduring states that define Christian piety through times of weal and woe.

The form and structure of the *Christmas Dialogue* has been the topic of considerable debate. That debate has largely been shaped by the fact that for 150 years it was mostly male Protestant theologians who wrote about the piece, and their interest was almost exclusively on the men's three speeches on Christology toward the end. This myopic approach has been corrected in recent years.[83] Schleiermacher does not explicitly break the *Christmas Dialogue* down into sections, but clear literary transitions throughout the piece indicate five main sections or scenes:

1. An opening narrative that describes the scene and introduces the characters.
2. A conversation in which all the adults and the girl Sofie participate.
3. Three stories by women (Ernestine, Agnes, and Karoline) about Christmases past, each of them involving a woman and her infant child.
4. Three speeches by men (Leonhardt, Ernst, and Eduard) on the topic of the Christmas holiday, all of which address what relation Christmas actually has to Christ and his birth.
5. A very short scene at the end, when the sage Josef appears, chiding the men for giving boring speeches on an inexpressible subject and inviting the entire company to return to singing, conversing, and enjoying one another's company.

The *Christmas Dialogue* is important for understanding Schleiermacher's spirituality for several reasons. Inasmuch as it is about Christmas, it—more than the *Speeches* or the *Soliloquies*— focuses on an explicitly Christian piety. Like the *Speeches*, it makes an argument about the nature of piety at the same time that it displays, by means of examples and forms of speech, what piety looks like and how it is lived out. Yet whereas in the second *Speech*, for example, Schleiermacher describes piety in general, here in the *Christmas Dialogue*, he speaks exclusively of Christian piety: the experience of having been redeemed by Christ, the characteristics of a Christian community, authentic and inauthentic forms of Christian religiosity, properly Christian religious sentiments, and the meaning of Christian rituals such as baptism.

Moreover, the *Christmas Dialogue* develops the ideal of dialogue in a specifically Christian context. As has already been noted, part of Schleiermacher's groundbreaking work in Plato studies was his insistence that the *content* of Plato's work cannot be understood apart from the dialogical *form*. Part of what this meant for Schleiermacher was that Platonic dialectics was inherently dialogical (Socratic)—that is to say, communicative and social, as opposed to being speculative and solitary.[84] In the *Christmas Dialogue*, Schleiermacher expands the dialogue form so as to be more inclusive and democratic. Women and men are equal partners in the conversation, critiquing, challenging, and teasing one another in a good-spirited manner; even the girl Sofie is included in the dialogue. In the course of the evening, as the conversation builds, that dialogue lends real insight. For Schleiermacher, such lively communication becomes the ideal of Christian fellowship. At the same time, the particularly Christian form of dialogue makes another departure from that found in (Schleiermacher's understanding of) the Platonic dialogues, insofar as the dialogue also necessarily becomes inarticulate and nonverbal: it is found in gestures, in the exchange of gifts, in the visual arts, and in music. These he refers to as the "dialogue of love."

From a historical perspective, the *Christmas Dialogue* was groundbreaking for several reasons. It treated the topic of the incarnation not as a matter of dogma but in a literary, or "poetic-theological,"[85] manner. As Matthias Morgenroth has argued, it marked a shift in emphasis in modern Protestant piety from the cross to the incarnation, and from institutional forms of worship and theology to private forms.[86] As Kurt Nowak points out, this privatization of the Christmas celebration needs to be read against the backdrop of laws against Christmas Eve church services in the late eighteenth century due to the fact that they had taken on the character of New Year celebrations,[87] to which Schleiermacher alludes in Ernestine's story, as well as in Ernst's speech.

The life that Schleiermacher had begun to build for himself in Halle was shattered in late 1806 when the city fell to Napoleon's troops on October 17; three days later, the university was shut down. Schleiermacher's apartment was ransacked and valuables stolen, and he was forced to quarter French troops. Steffens and his family moved in with Schleiermacher for a while, since both men found themselves without income. During this time he continued to work on his Plato translation; he applied his hermeneutical theory to Scripture by undertaking a historical-critical analysis of 1 Timothy, determining that it was not authentically Pauline;[88] and he wrote a review of Fichte.

Berlin, 1807–1834

Schleiermacher moved back to Berlin in May 1807. Two years later, on May 18, 1809, he married Henriette Charlotte Sophie (von Mühlenfels) von Willich (1788–1840), the young widow of his close friend, Ehrenfried von Willich (1777–1807); he thereby also became father to her two young children, both under four years of age, and at last was the family man he had longed to be; the couple would go on to have four children together.[89] A few weeks after the wedding, he became the Reformed pastor of Trinity Church (*Dreifaltigkeitskirche*) in the center of Berlin, a position he would hold until his death in 1834.[90] Schleiermacher was a famous and influential preacher (see two examples of his sermons translated in this volume).[91] In 1810, he was given membership in the Royal Prussian Academy of Sciences, where he would deliver fifty-three addresses in twenty-four years; also in that year, together with Wilhelm von Humboldt (1767–1835), he helped to found the University of Berlin (now Humboldt-Universität zu Berlin) on the famous boulevard Unter den Linden, a short walking distance from Trinity Church.[92]

His work as pastor was demanding and, monetarily speaking, would not have supported him and his family without supplemental sources of income. In addition to his weekly sermons, which were major accomplishments of scholarship and religious insight, he had the usual demanding responsibilities of a pastor of any church, made unusual perhaps by the circumstances of time and place.[93] He had, first, to restore the church, which had been virtually destroyed by Napoleon's army. He had to see to the poor and, as he had before while chaplain at the Charité, he raised this from being a local, case-by-case matter to a larger social issue by considering the societal structures at play and proposing, for instance, some kind of system of social security. In 1829, he became a member of the Berlin Board for the Poor. He had to console and lead his congregation through the cholera epidemic of 1831, which meant, too, that he had to find cemetery plots in which to bury them. In addition to conducting baptisms, weddings, and funerals, he taught weekly confirmation classes and served as superintendent of several schools. All the while, his pastoral activities also engaged the larger world, insofar as he used his pulpit to preach against Napoleon and was instrumental in helping to bring about the Church of the Union.[94]

As a member of the Theology faculty at the University of Berlin, Schleiermacher lectured regularly on the New Testament, Christian dogmatics, ethics, hermeneutics, dialectics, church history, and practical theology. He was the first to offer academic lectures on the life of Jesus.[95] His major published works from this time of theological and philosophical maturity are *A Brief Outline on the Study of Theology* (1811, 1830), *The Christian Faith* (1821/22, 1830/31), and *On Luke's Writings*. For the purposes of understanding his spirituality, it is his magnum opus *The Christian Faith*, his great systematic work of dogmatic theology, that calls for our attention.

6. *The Christian Faith* (1830–1831)

As was true of just about everything that Schleiermacher taught and wrote, *The Christian Faith* (or *Glaubenslehre*) staked out entirely new territory and so invited criticism from many sides. When the first edition appeared in 1821–22, traditionalists (those espousing supernaturalist, confessionalist, or biblicist approaches) criticized it for being too philosophical or, even worse, pantheistic; Enlightenment philosophers and theologians, for being too subjectivist. Some of the criticisms Schleiermacher did not give much heed to, but others he found it necessary to address. He began working on his revisions in 1827; in the following two years (1828/29) he published two "Letters to Dr. Lücke,"[96] in which he sought to clarify certain issues; and in 1831/32 he published the second and final edition of *The Christian Faith*. The most significant revisions were in the famous Introduction (with respect to its organization as well as its terminology) and in the christological propositions in part 2. *The Christian Faith* marks a watershed in Christian theology. For almost two centuries now, Christian theologians have had to take it into account, whether or not they have agreed with Schleiermacher.

Here I shall offer an overview of *The Christian Faith* in order to provide some sense of its organization and basic commitments. In the next two sections of this introduction, I shall explore the method and content, especially as they relate to the matter of his spirituality, more fully: for more on his theory of religious language and methodology, see section 2, "Schleiermacher's Writing as Spiritual Exercise"; for more on his treatment of particular doctrines (for example, on God, Christ, redemption) and his notion of the *feeling of absolute dependence*, see section 3, "Five Themes in Schleiermacher's Spirituality."

While it is likely true that any theological classic would have something to reveal about the author's spirituality, this is especially true of *The Christian Faith*, inasmuch as Schleiermacher took "piety" as a starting point and a guiding principle in *The Christian Faith*, and he described Christian doctrines as "accounts of the Christian religious affections set forth in speech."[97] Schleiermacher understood Christian dogmatics to be an expression (of the "descriptively didactic type"[98]) of religious consciousness, and therewith he actively tried to hold together religious experience and theological, "scientific" formulations. As "descriptive," Schleiermacher held that Christian dogmatics belongs under "historical theology," except that it systematically and clearly presents "the knowledge of doctrine now current in the evangelical Church."[99]

The significance of Schleiermacher's choices regarding starting points, parameters, and method becomes readily apparent if we consider the options in his day and how, for him, they were not in fact real options. Approaches based on the Bible and revelation—approaches that read the Old Testament mainly as prefiguring Christ, that based their theology on literal interpretations of creation and the fall, and that prioritized miracles and put too much store in the supernatural—had been rendered implausible by the new historical consciousness and the emerging historical-critical method.[100] Rationalist approaches, he thought, were too arid and either mistook doctrine for Christian faith or, as was true for Kant, made faith a postulate of practical (ethical) reason. Speculative approaches, which often sought to derive an entire system from a single principle, ran the risk of projecting one's own system and making Christian faith conform to that. Schleiermacher contended, however, that theology cannot contradict science, whether the historical or the natural sciences, nor should it try to compete with science or with philosophy by setting up an alternate system.

According to Schleiermacher, the Introduction is not, properly speaking, a part of Christian dogmatics itself but consists instead in propositions borrowed from other fields of study. This is important because, while these "borrowed" propositions connect Christian dogmatics to other disciplines related to human sciences, and thus help to ensure that dogmatic theology is neither merely confessional nor arbitrary, they are not to be understood as a so-called foundation for theology.[101] Borrowing from ethics,[102] he puts forth a definition of *church* or religious community in terms of piety: "The piety which forms the basis of all ecclesiastical communions is, considered purely in itself, neither a knowing nor a doing, but a modification of feeling, or of immediate self-consciousness" (§3).[103] He then offers his famous definition of *piety* (§4). Borrowing from the philosophy of religion, he goes on to describe three stages of development of piety (fetishism, polytheism, and monotheism, §8), and he maps Christianity in relation to Judaism and Islam (§9). Borrowing from apologetics, he identifies the distinctive essence of Christianity: "Christianity is a monotheistic faith, belonging to the teleological type of religion, and is essentially distinguished from other such faiths by the fact that in it everything is related to the redemption accomplished by Jesus of Nazareth" (§11).[104]

In the final third of his Introduction, Schleiermacher lays out the method of Christian dogmatics. He identifies three forms of dogmatic propositions: descriptions of human states, conceptions of divine attributes and modes of action, and utterances concerning the constitution of the world (§30). Since only the first of these "can be taken from the realm of inner experience"[105] and is therefore most closely tied to the feeling of absolute dependence, it is the elementary form. The other two forms must be able to be reduced to the first form if dogmatic theology is to "be safe from the creeping in of alien and purely scientific propositions."[106] This rule for relating the three forms of propositions has several important consequences for writing a modern dogmatics, two of which I note here. First, it means the doctrine of God is not given in one location but is developed throughout *The Christian Faith*, while it limits what can be said about God. In one respect, this was a necessary move for theology after Kant's critical philosophy: one cannot prove the existence of God or claim knowledge of the divine essence. Schleiermacher thereby avoids (and actively rejects) exaggerated claims of speculative theologies. The divine attributes, he insists, do not describe "something special in God, but only something special in the manner in which the feeling of absolute dependence is to be related to God" (§50).[107] Second, it also underscores that Christian piety (hence Christian dogmatics) is not primarily a worldview; it makes no specific claims about the world that might seem to compete with scientific claims (hence with a knowing).

In part 1, under the first form of proposition, Schleiermacher treats the doctrines of creation and preservation. For him, the doctrine of creation is not a claim about *how* or *when* the world came into being; rather, negatively speaking, it is the denial that there is "anything whatever [excluded] from origination by God" (§40);[108] and, positively speaking, it affirms (through its companion doctrine of preservation) that everything that "affects or influences us" is also absolutely dependent on God and is itself also determined by the "interdependence of nature" (§46).[109] The feeling of absolute dependence, as it is expressed in the doctrines of creation and preservation, points to the absolute divine causality (§51), and for Schleiermacher that relationship is described in terms of the divine attributes (the second form of proposition) of eternity, omnipresence, omnipotence, and omniscience (§§52–55). Finally, under the third form of proposition in part 1, Schleiermacher treats of the "original perfection of the world." This is not about some remote point in time, since historical consciousness, natural science, and his own method would not allow for a literal reading of Genesis 1—3. Instead, he speaks of the "original perfection" as "the conditions necessary for the continuous existence of the God-consciousness in every human individual, and also for its communication from one to the other."[110]

Schleiermacher divides part 2 into two "aspects," the first having to do with the consciousness of sin and the second with the consciousness of grace; each aspect is then further subdivided according to the three forms of propositions. When it comes to the consciousness of sin, Walter Wyman puts it bluntly: "Schleiermacher's account of the universality of sin is dramatically revisionist."[111] It has to be because of the limits set to piety by the sciences. Because Schleiermacher does not take the Mosaic narrative literally, he cannot trace sin to a historical "fall" of two persons, nor can he presume an alteration in human nature. Sin for him is an arrest, diminishment, or disturbance of God-consciousness; it is "an arrestment of the determinative power of the spirit, due to the independence of the sensuous functions."[112] "Original" sin does not mean the "first" sin but points instead to the "the corporate act and the corporate guilt of the human race" (§71).[113] The consciousness of sin points to the divine attributes of holiness and justice.

It is in the second aspect, under the first form of proposition, that we find the "heart" of Schleiermacher's Christian dogmatics—namely, the experience of having been redeemed by Jesus of Nazareth. Here Schleiermacher gives an account of the person and work of Christ, as well as of how individuals are redeemed and reconciled to God through Christ—and he does so, he thinks, in a way that is neither supernaturalistic nor reductionistic.[114] Everything else in the dogmatic system derives from this experience of having been redeemed by Christ: sin only comes to light in its antithesis to the experience of grace; creation, divine preservation, and the original so-called perfection of humanity, all of which are treated in part 1, are further expressions of the experience of grace; the divine attributes of love and wisdom, which are treated at the end of part 2, come to light through the experience of being grasped by Christ; and finally the church, the formation of which was the direct result of Christ's activity and through which Christ's redeeming and reconciling activity continues, is treated as the third form of proposition in part 2. Indeed, the most formal expression, so to speak, of this experience of grace is the feeling of absolute dependence, described in his Introduction.

In sum, the full title of the work itself reveals much about Schleiermacher's basic commitments: *The Christian Faith presented systematically according to the Fundamental Principles of the Evangelical Church.*[115] In highlighting Christian *faith* (and in the particular way he goes about explicating that), Schleiermacher holds together theory and practice, community and individual, what is said or taught about Christian theology and what is actually believed or lived. In stressing the systematic interconnection of Christian doctrines, Schleiermacher emphasizes, in the words of Richard Crouter, that "theology is not supposed to be just an aggregate of theological insights."[116] And in specifying the fundamental propositions or principles of the Evangelical (Protestant) Church of his time, Schleiermacher underscores his understanding of religion as always being historically situated and of Christian theology as itself being a historical task. In each of these moves, he not only departs from how systematic theology had been done but also distinguishes himself from other new, modern approaches.

Death

In October 1829, Schleiermacher and his family were devastated by the sudden death of his nine-year-old son, Nathanael, from scarlet fever. The final revisions of *The Christian Faith* were made under the shadow of that terrible grief. Schleiermacher himself contracted a bad cold at the end of January 1834, which turned into pneumonia. He preached for the last time at Trinity Church on February 2. He was confined to bed by the next Sunday, surrounded by his family and close friends, with whom in his final hours he celebrated the Last Supper.[117] He died on February 12, 1834.

Schleiermacher's Writing as Spiritual Exercise

The philosopher Pierre Hadot has argued that, for the ancients, philosophy was not so much a discourse or system but *a way of life*, and therefore their act of writing is best understood as a spiritual exercise. Explaining the "fascinating power" of Marcus Aurelius's *Meditations*, Hadot writes,

We have the feeling of witnessing the practice of spiritual exercises—captured live, so to speak. There have been a great many preachers, theoreticians, spiritual directors, and censors in the history of world literature. Yet it is extremely rare to have the chance to see someone in the process of training himself to be a human being....

We feel a quite particular emotion as we catch a person in the process of doing what we are all trying to do: to give a meaning to our life, to strive to live in a state of perfect awareness and to give each of life's instants its full value. To be sure, Marcus is talking to himself, but we still get the impression that he is talking to each one of us as well.[118]

Although here, with Marcus Aurelius, he depicts spiritual exercise as a solitary activity, elsewhere Hadot stresses the importance of the dialogical character of spiritual exercises for ancient philosophers; witness Socrates: "Thus, the Socratic dialogue turns out to be a kind of communal spiritual exercise. In it, the interlocutors are invited to participate in such inner spiritual exercises as examination of conscience and attention to oneself; in other words, they are urged to comply with the famous dictum, 'Know thyself.'"[119] There is, Hadot maintains, an oral (pedagogical) dimension to ancient philosophical writing.[120]

Allow me to summarize Hadot's phrase *writing as spiritual exercise*. *Spiritual* refers as much to the goal (wisdom, the ideal good person) as to a way of life (to act justly, to live intentionally and calmly, to think rightly, to value correctly, to be aware).[121] *Exercise* refers to the discipline, concentrated effort, and continual practice this way of life requires. The act of *writing* is an exercise (a repeated, disciplined practice) that is spiritual in nature (due to its content and its result). The repetition and association of ideas that occur by means of writing serve to reactivate "a series of representations and practices."[122] And, Hadot explains,

> Whoever wishes to make progress strives, by means of dialogue with himself or with others, as well as by writing, to "carry on his reflections in due order" and finally to arrive at a complete transformation of his representation of the world, his inner climate, and his outer behavior. These methods testify to a deep knowledge of the therapeutic powers of the [word].[123]

Hadot's insights have influenced scholars from many different disciplines, so much so that any reflection on spirituality would be wanting were it not to address this aspect. And surely, for a prolific writer such as Schleiermacher, this connection cannot be ignored. Indeed, this is another way in which the study of spirituality can enhance our understanding of Schleiermacher. At the same time, it ought not to go unnoticed that it was Schleiermacher's own revolution in Plato studies—in particular, his insistence on the importance of the dialogue form, and the dialogical process, for understanding Plato—that paved the way for just such an insight as Hadot's.

I propose that we consider two of the writing styles that Schleiermacher employed—his earlier, more personal style, and his later, more academic style—as exercises in spirituality. Although it may be more readily apparent how the former can be understood in this way, I shall try to show how his later academic writings, in particular his dogmatic theology, *The Christian Faith*, might also be understood as a type of spiritual exercise. If the oral, dialogical character of ancient philosophical writing was sometimes indirect and remained in the background, Schleiermacher's writing had a manifestly social and relational dimension to it.

The Earlier Writings: *Speeches, Soliloquies,* and the *Christmas Dialogue*

Consider first the formal aspects of these three genres: speech, soliloquy, and dialogue. All three have an oral, communicative dimension to them. All three are examples of interpersonal communication that stems from self-examination and attentiveness to the other. Now consider the specific execution of these genres in the *Speeches, Soliloquies,* and *Christmas Dialogue,* respectively. All engage an audience, and a very specific audience—that is to say, they all speak to a known audience, they all seek to arouse that audience, they all try to evoke certain responses from that audience in a way that respects that audience's freedom (in other words, in a nonmanipulative way), and they are all intimately expressive of Schleiermacher himself. For Schleiermacher, form is necessarily related to content. This is pivotal in his theory in interpreting Plato, and it is integral to his practice in these Romantic writings. In these works, content cannot be taught but must be stimulated *because* that content is piety, religiosity, and inner freedom.

Schleiermacher did not address his *Speeches* to just any audience, unrelated to himself, his worldview, or his own aspirations. In the *Speeches*, there is real engagement: he *knows* whom he is addressing and with whom he is sharing himself; he addresses these "despisers" respectfully, and one might even say with love; the "despisers" are known, cherished, and understood by him. In describing to a publisher how he envisioned his *Soliloquies*, Schleiermacher insisted they were not in the manner of a lecture but in the *personal* voice of an everyday person.[124] Similarly, in the *Christmas Dialogue*, although a work of fiction, Schleiermacher purportedly based his characters on friends and acquaintances, and he made countless allusions that his friends would have recognized.[125] In short, it ought not to be forgotten who the cultured despisers were to whom Schleiermacher addressed his *Speeches on Religion*, or that the *Soliloquies* were a gift to his friends (and perhaps to Eleanore in particular), or that the *Christmas Dialogue* was also a gift to his friends in Halle, Berlin, and elsewhere dispersed.

These early writings may be said to be spiritual not just in that they are expressive of Schleiermacher himself and describe the pious heart, but also in that they set forth an ideal of how life ought to be lived and valued *and* they provide training manuals of a sort (although they are *not* programmatic). In the exercise of writing, we find the development and evocation of a sensibility that is a reasoned, deliberative, sustained, and engaged act. In these writings, Schleiermacher tries to be lucid, to work things through, to exercise clarity and truthfulness, to attract, and to shape by example. Both the act of writing and the products of that act are, potentially at least, transforming of self and of others. They are the other side of the act of understanding and interpreting. Schleiermacher attempts not only to express and articulate his own piety (and, he says, to "translate" the piety of those who are not given to reflection or gifted with words), but also to share and communicate it, which requires and presupposes that he knows, understands, and trusts his originally intended audience. In short, these earlier works are not simply outbursts of emotion but employ a kind of discipline. Although the *Soliloquies* and *Christmas Dialogue*, especially, were spontaneous and written in the span of a month or less (which resulted in their not being as polished as they could have been), they too are sustained engagements of self, of other, and of the divine operations.

Allow me to use the second *Speech* (included in this volume) as an example of how Schleiermacher's earlier writing might fairly be understood as spiritual exercise. In this *Speech*, "On the Essence of Religion," Schleiermacher invites his friends to engage in an act of contemplation, which for him means stepping back, freeing oneself of prejudices and presuppositions, looking at things from a distance, and making distinctions. They are the "despisers" of religion because they had come so to distrust the claimed authority of Christianity, its doctrines, and its rules. Schleiermacher calls for an "impartial sobriety of mind"[126] and cautions, "you do not want to have fought against a shadow";[127] along the way, he refers to the "shadows, illusions, and errors from the very same source."[128] He addresses his friends, asking them to do this, yet he is himself in the process of doing the same, and so arrives at an understanding of process. For the first portion of the *Speech*, he re-presents and critiques their mistaken views, challenging them to see their inconsistencies and inviting them, again and again, to turn to their own experience and consider what that really tells them; he offers them example after example to reflect on as an aid in opening that experience to contemplation. All of this is in a sense an apophatic move to clear a space. Then he invites them to consider nature, the forecourt of religion, and to see the mistaken associations with religion there. And *then* he proceeds to humanity: "A person must first have found humanity, and humanity is only found in love."[129] The point is that human life is relational, social, and at heart dialogical.

From that excursion throughout humanity, Schleiermacher bids his "despisers" to return to their own selves. He bids his friends to turn inward, to "the innermost sanctuary of life....I must refer you to your own selves"; "enter into that realm where you are also most properly and best at home, where your most inner life opens up to you."[130] In contemplation they are not just observing something external; they must examine their own selves, as he himself is in the process of doing. This involves admitting one's own mistakes, how one has misunderstood. Misunderstanding, as he notes in his *Hermeneutics*, can be the beginning of understanding. And, in a significant revision to the second edition, he adds a complex discussion of how the "despisers" have mixed and confused things, and how they have thus been inconsistent in their own logic. This is intended to create a kind of humility, an admission of just how complicated the matter is. According to him, religion lives in this ongoing oscillation between inner and outer, part and whole, self and other.

There is, in other words, a pattern and a rhythm to his *Speeches* that is meditative as it builds to a point, then pulls back, and repeats. Schleiermacher builds, bidding them to admit what they presently think, even though they may not be aware of it; he points to problems with that; he suggests a new movement of the mind or heart, asking them whether or not this is true to their experience; he often offers an example and explores that; he continues with this pattern by taking it further, extending and interweaving his points. The overall goal of this process is nothing less than human life, what it means to live a fully human life, which in turn is nothing less than a social life in relation to all the rest of life (meaning the full scope of the universe, not just human life) and to God. It is a way of living that resists idolatry, the dead letter, and ignorance. Yet, unlike the ancients, as it turns out, this way of life is not only for the philosopher; it is for any open, pious heart.

This is why it can be a mistake to approach Schleiermacher's *Speeches* merely as a philosophical *argument*, and why it may be instructive to read it rather as an exercise in philosophy as a way of life, reframed as *religion as a way of life*. It has to do with a transformation of attitude that results in (or rejuvenates) a different way of being in the world. Schleiermacher does not try to transform how the despisers live, but to change their attitude about religion by getting them to recognize that how they live is in many ways profoundly religious, and in seeing and naming that differently in order, perchance, to be further transformed. It is about self-knowledge: "Capture yourselves in the process," he writes.[131] Along the way, he is undergoing the process himself, coming up against problems, limitations, old ideas. The fact that he himself is engaged in a real process is evidenced by the substantial revisions he makes in the second edition: the more simplistic triad of morals, metaphysics, and religion is complexly reshaped into doing, thinking, and feeling. According to this new taxonomy, *doing* now includes *life* (as moral conduct) and *arts*; *thinking* includes *metaphysics/physics* (theories about the world) and *ethics* (as a theory of moral conduct). Reading the *Speeches* in this way might also serve to challenge the conventional thesis that revisions in the later editions were merely conservative moves on Schleiermacher's part to placate church authorities.

Scientific Writing: *The Christian Faith*

Schleiermacher's final move to Berlin also marked his departure from an earlier style of writing, wherein the connection to his spirituality was more palpable. Those earlier works—the *Speeches*, *Soliloquies*, and *Christmas Dialogue*—belong more to the poetical and rhetorical than to the descriptively didactic (to use Schleiermacher's own categories); hence, as I have just argued, they are spiritual texts in that they explore, capture, challenge, counsel, inspire, and transform. Schleiermacher, however, did try to keep true to that Socratic-Platonic ideal he had articulated in his *Occasional Thoughts on Universities in the German Sense*: "Because its first aim is to bring ideas to consciousness, university lecturing must in any case adhere in this respect to the nature of ancient dialogue, if not to its external form."[132] Even the most scientific of presentations, he insisted, is rooted in dialogue and is thus essentially communicative. In *The Christian Faith*, he carries this through in two ways that are definitive for both the content and the method of dogmatic theology.

First, he develops a theory about types of religious language and their interrelationship. In the Introduction, he expounds this theory in §§15–19, identifying three types or levels of religious language: the poetic (a more immediately expressive type "based originally on a moment of life which arises purely from within, a moment of inspiration"[133]); the rhetorical (a "stimulative" type, found for instance in sermons, which seeks to arouse moments of inspiration); and the descriptively didactic. Dawn DeVries offers a succinct account of this last type, which is the language of dogmatic theology:

> The third type of language, Schleiermacher states, arises when poetic and rhetorical language need to be understood and appropriated by hearers, and its goal is to teach and to transmit what is contained in the other two forms

of language. Schleiermacher identifies this third type as the language of confession, and alternately as didactic or descriptive instructional language. The goal of teaching and appropriating religious language demands a kind of clarity or precision, and so didactic language is disciplined by the scientific spirit. But because it is meant to be descriptive of the other two types of religious language, logical or dialectical interest can be understood only as applying to the form and not the content of didactic expression.[134]

Schleiermacher maintained that the descriptively didactic language "is made up of the two put together, as a derivative and secondary form."[135] In other words, the scientifically precise language of dogmatic theology necessarily remains connected to—indeed must remain rooted in—religious experience. Theological language that loses this connection to the poetic and rhetorical becomes arid or speculative.[136]

Second, as noted in section 1 above, Schleiermacher also identifies three forms of dogmatic propositions: descriptions of human states, conceptions of divine attributes and modes of action, and utterances concerning the constitution of the world (§30). As a result, *The Christian Faith* has a complex architecture that speaks to its method and content. It is structured *horizontally* according to the Introduction, part 1 (subdivided into three "sections"), and part 2 (subdivided into two "aspects," "sections," and several more "divisions"). It is structured *vertically* (so to speak) according to the three forms of propositions. Methodologically speaking, the "descriptions of human states," those having to do with the religious affections and the feeling of absolute dependence, are elementary or "fundamental"; hence, each main "part" of *The Christian Faith* (parts 1 and 2, as well as the two "aspects" within part 2) begins with this form. Regarding content, the most "fundamental" propositions in *The Christian Faith* are therefore those on divine preservation, the consciousness of sin, and the consciousness of having been redeemed by Christ—because these are most closely connected to the feeling of absolute dependence. The other two forms of propositions are derivative and "are permissible only in so far as they can be developed out of propositions of the first form."[137] Not only does this serve to keep theological doctrines rooted in the religious experience (both individual and corporate), but it also resists letting dogmatics be mistaken for a form of knowledge or even a philosophy, which could dislodge theology as a knowing from any relation to feeling.

In short, simultaneously interwoven throughout Schleiermacher's own scientific presentation, which is a systematic description of the Protestant Christian religious consciousness of his time and place, are ways of maintaining the connection between theory and practice, scientific precision and experience. An ongoing dialogue on many different levels is required. Once again, DeVries describes this well (in this case, with reference to preaching):

> Producing coherent religious speech involves the speaker in a "dialogue" between his life in his congregation and his immersion in the text of scripture. Schleiermacher is quite clear that both partners of this dialogue must be present for a successful outcome. The speaker must be so involved with his congregation that he can think their thoughts before them. At the same time, the speaker must also be a careful scholar whose ministry cannot be imagined "without a diligent occupation with the Bible."[138]

This connection between theory and practice was always a concern for Schleiermacher, and he developed methods and safeguards to maintain it. In his own writing, he quite self-consciously employed those methods. Writing remained a spiritual exercise for Schleiermacher.

Five Themes in Schleiermacher's Spirituality

For a thematic understanding of Schleiermacher's spirituality, a good starting point would be to take together his description of himself as "a Moravian again, only of a higher order,"[139] along with several of his favorite passages from Scripture, such as "God is love" (1 John 4:16); "It is no longer I who live, but it is Christ who lives in me" (Gal 2:20); and "So if anyone is in Christ, there is a new creation: everything old has passed away; see, everything has become new" (2 Cor 5:17). His appropriation of passages such as these latter two captures the Christomorphic[140] nature of his piety and underscores the joyousness that defined his experience of grace. His Moravian background, as we have already seen,[141] is also key to understanding Schleiermacher as a person and as a theologian. "Moravian" refers to a particular branch of Pietism, tied to Herrnhut, which was significant in his earliest religious formation. It is here that we find the roots of Schleiermacher's emphasis on an open heart turned lovingly toward neighbor and God, his emphasis on the religious affections, his emphasis on an inward devotion to Christ and on grasping and being grasped by Christ, and his inclination toward and celebration of sociability. At the same time, his qualification of a "higher order" hints at the distance he established between himself and the Moravians—by his having left the community, by his rejection of certain of their theological teachings and devotional practices,[142] and by his forward-moving embrace of the new sciences at the turn of the nineteenth century.

In more ways than this, the modifier *higher* figures prominently in Schleiermacher's spirituality. He often speaks of "higher unity," "higher joy," and lower and "higher" levels of spiritual life. By *higher* he does not mean spiritual as opposed to bodily. On the contrary, he means a life more and more integrated in every aspect of our sensible self-consciousness (our sensible, intellectual, emotional, moral, creative, and social existence), which occurs when God-consciousness increasingly informs and is integrated with our sensible self-consciousness. When that happens, Schleiermacher maintains, we are no longer so much determined by the oppositions of finite existence as we are defined by the joyful freedom of the higher unity of the Spirit.

The temptation might be to say that Schleiermacher's spirituality is christocentric, but the implied geometry of that imagery would have been too static for him. Schleiermacher's preferred geometrical image was that of the ellipse. In fact, he uses it in his letter to Jacobi (translated in this volume) to illustrate the relationship between his philosophy and his dogmatics.[143] An ellipse has two foci along the major axis, both of which are equidistant from the center; any point around the curve of the ellipse stands in relation to both foci, although at a given time the point may be closer to one focus than to the other. The imagery of the ellipse is much more dynamic than that of a circle in that it allows for novelty and change, especially when the third dimension is taken into account. Applying this to Schleiermacher's spirituality, we might therefore think of its two foci as, on the one hand, the joy of having been redeemed by Christ and, on the other hand, the trust that defines the feeling of absolute dependence on God (who is ever active in every moment in the universe). Schleiermacher consistently held these two foci in dynamic relationship.

Below, I identify five themes in Schleiermacher's spirituality: Christ and grace; the open, attuned heart (*Gemüth*); feeling (*Gefühl*); God; and mysticism. These are not meant to be exhaustive. Indeed, there are far too many themes than could be treated here. For instance, almost every text included in this volume calls attention to the distinction Schleiermacher often makes between the spirit and the letter, as he rails against the blind servitude that results from adherence to the letter. Part of the purpose of this volume is to present readers with texts that are particularly illustrative of Schleiermacher's spirituality, so that readers themselves may identify themes and pursue those further. The five themes developed here have been chosen so as to highlight an aspect important for Schleiermacher himself and distinctive in his thought. All five themes are interrelated. Except for the fact that his experience and understanding of Christ must come first—because that is where his own experience and own theology begin—the others are not listed in descending order of importance. The subsections on "Christ and Grace" and on "God" are longest because I consider them to be the two main foci that shape everything else, and because his mature thought about these is presented in *The Christian Faith*, which is not included in this volume and therefore stands in need of some explication.

Christ and Grace

If Christ had only instituted the Last Supper, I would have loved him to the point of adoration.
                                    —*Letter to Eleanor Grunow*

The starting point for this thematic treatment of Schleiermacher's spirituality can only be his faith in Christ, the experience of having been redeemed by Christ, and his way of understanding this in a modern context. This last point is almost as important as the first two for understanding his spirituality, insofar as it underscores his confidence that knowing and believing are compatible. One of the things that Schleiermacher inherited from Pietism, which he absorbed during the few years he spent with the Moravians as a youth, was an internal, personal grasping of Christ and the joyful experience of being grasped by Christ. This would always be an integral part of his Christian piety, and indeed would form the very foundation of his mature Christian dogmatics, *The Christian Faith*. At the same time, Schleiermacher unambiguously rejected major tenets of not just the Moravians', and not just the Reformed Church's, but also Western Christianity's soteriology.[144] This juxtaposition of positive appropriation and outright rejection (or heterodox reconfiguration) gets at the heart of Schleiermacher's spirituality. As he wrote to Jacobi, "The Bible is the original interpretation of the Christian feeling, and for just this reason is so established that it might always be better understood and developed. I, as a Protestant theologian, will not let anyone deprive me of this right of development."[145] Finally, because for him piety can never contradict science, his faith in Christ never shrank back from historical criticism, which was just emerging as he began his career. In fact, Schleiermacher was at the forefront of the new approach: he was the first, for instance, to offer academic lectures on the life of Jesus.[146]

As already noted, Schleiermacher had a major crisis of faith around the age of eighteen while a student at the Moravian Seminary at Barby.[147] The crisis was both religious and theological in nature, one having to do with Christ, salvation, and in particular, the Reformed Christian doctrine of penal substitutionary atonement.[148] The Pietism of the Moravian Church, in particular, emphasized a "wounds-theology"[149] (with special focus on the side wound of Christ) in its spirituality—in its musical tradition as well as its theology.[150] For other Protestants, this too closely echoed what they deemed to be the excesses of Roman Catholicism. By the time he wrote to his father in 1787 begging permission to leave the Moravian seminary, Schleiermacher had in his own mind already worked through the spiritual crisis. The real crisis for him at that later moment was more a moral one: he could no longer bear the hypocrisy of staying in the Moravian Congregation, pretending to believe what he no longer did and what was in fact offensive to his sensibilities. Such doubts and disillusionments could be attributed in part to Enlightenment thought, which Schleiermacher and his classmates were both aware of and hungry for, but his doubts also had to do with his own sensibility. His religious experience was essentially one of joy at having been redeemed by Christ, and his experience of God was not of an angry, punitive God (which he always found too anthropomorphic) but of a gracious, beneficent God who would not demand the impossible.

1. Christ and Grace in the Christmas Dialogue

Almost twenty years later, in his *Christmas Dialogue* (1806), we can see these same sensibilities and commitments still at play, although now Schleiermacher addresses the crisis of faith triggered by the new historical consciousness, by "Lessing's ditch"[151] and the problem of history, and by the threat of the new historical criticism to the continuity of the Gospel narratives, in particular, the infancy narratives in Matthew and Luke. The *Christmas Dialogue*, as noted above, marks a turn in the very treatment of Christmas as a topic. An underlying theme in this work could be said to be the affirmation of the celebration of Christmas after (educated) Christians had lost confidence in the reliability of the Gospel narrative and the continuity of history. At several points, Schleiermacher plays with the twofold meaning of *Geschichte*, "story" and "history." In the conversation that takes place earlier in the *Christmas Dialogue* (part 2), the issue of the difference between sacred history and fables and their possible collapse into each other is raised; then later in the evening, after presents had been opened, a meal served, and past Christmases recalled, the three men deliver "speeches" on Christmas—the topic having been set by the women (part 4). Although none of the speech-givers admit to any personal anxiety, the anxiety of the age is palpable. If we cannot trust the Gospels as historical accounts, if they were not written by eyewitnesses, if therefore we do not have unbroken access to Jesus of Nazareth, then what can we believe? If the infancy narratives are themselves so suspect, then why do we celebrate Christmas? What connection do we have to the birth of the Redeemer, and what significance is there to be found in the birth of the Redeemer?

The first speaker is Leonhardt, who plays the skeptic, pressing the Christmas holiday as what we might call a social construction and highlighting the discontinuity of history and the unreliability of Scripture as historical record. He avers, "But Christ as the founder of Christianity—and this is certainly the content of his life and the singular relation in which his first appearance in history can be celebrated—has only a sketchy meaning. For how little can be traced back to Christ himself, and how most of it is, by far, of another and later origin!"[152] The truth of the matter, he says, is that Christ stands closer to John the Baptist than to the apostles and the founding of the church. The Christmas holiday, Leonhardt suggests, is created and carried by tradition, especially by children: "For just as a child is the main subject of Christmas, so too children are primarily the ones who lift and carry it—and, in turn, by means of the holiday, lift and carry Christianity itself."[153] He also hints that, in this holiday, the point of most consequence about Christ—namely, his death—has escaped the average Christian.[154] The *Christmas Dialogue*, in other words, is not all nostalgia. There is a real question here, a real doubt, still relevant for Christians today.

At this point in the *Christmas Dialogue*, as B. A. Gerrish puts it, "Schleiermacher now makes his crucial move: he does not have his other characters, Ernst and Eduard, reply to Leonhardt on historical grounds but strictly on the grounds of the Christian experience of redemption. We begin from the Christmas joy shared among Christian people, and we ask, What must be its source?"[155] For Ernst, the universal nature of the joy expressed in Christmas is what distinguishes it from other festivals, and thus it points to the divine source, even if historical traces are weak. "There is no other principle of joy than redemption," Ernst says, "and for us the initial point of redemption must be the birth of a divine child."[156] Though perhaps unconvincing as a theological argument, this does reflect Schleiermacher's spirituality, both in the experience of the joy of redemption and in its grateful recognition of the divine source.

Eduard's response is more esoteric. The Christology he presents actually represents a passing, albeit not insignificant, phase in the development of Schleiermacher's own Christology. Nevertheless, the sentiment is quintessentially Schleiermacher's. Eduard takes as his starting point not the Synoptic Gospels but the Gospel of John and the Logos: "Thus I most prefer viewing the subject of this holiday not as a child formed and appearing such and so, born of this or that woman, here or there—but rather as the Word become flesh, who was God and is with God."[157] Whereas in the second *Speech* and the *Soliloquies* Schleiermacher had informed his readers that they will be able to develop their own individuality in discovering "humanity," here in Eduard's speech in the *Christmas Dialogue* that universal, perfect "humanity" is Christ, the "human-in-itself" (*Mensch an sich*) and "earth-spirit" (*Erdgeist*). Here is the identity of being and becoming, of spirit and flesh, of thought and sensuous nature.

There has been much debate about which of these three speeches comes closest to Schleiermacher's own theological views. Yet, especially here in a volume on his spirituality, which is about more than just theological doctrine, the key to understanding Schleiermacher actually lies elsewhere. As or more important is the fact that all three views are included; that they are included as a dialogue among friends; and that among those friends are a skeptical Enlightenment figure, a Reformed clergyman, a sage figure (Josef, probably a Pietist), and women, one of whom (Ernestine) admits to an earlier sense of alienation from institutional Christianity. All of this speaks to Schleiermacher's spirituality—of the centrality of community defined by openness, acceptance, and trust despite differences of opinion; and of the role of dialogue in moving toward fuller understanding.

Moreover, Schleiermacher's own sense of Christian piety and of how Christ is present in Christian community is found not so much in the men's speeches as in the entirety of the *Christmas Dialogue*, as his own interpretive theory would dictate. It is found in the joy, serenity, and loving relationships depicted throughout; it is there in Josef's unsaying and mystical kiss at the end; it is there in the music, which draws the guests together, transports them, and presents Christ; it is there in the women's stories of Christmases past. Each of the three women's stories presents a scene about the joy brought by new life in Christ. While each of these stories involves a mother with a baby, making it tempting to focus on natural life experiences of happiness, each actually says something important about the birth of Christ and what that means for Christians during times of crisis: everybody gives for the sake of the child; even in the deepest mourning can Christ's redeeming power be known. Each story contains its own form of dialogue; each in its own way (but especially the first and third) captures the fragility of human life; each mother is depicted as a prime example of the pious Christian. This joy of the coming of redemption is the impulse behind everything that happens in the *Christmas Dialogue*: the exchange of gifts, the choice of gifts for each person as an expression of the uniqueness of that relationship, the conversation (both its content and its form), and the music. Christ is felt in each person's heart, and that openness directs each heart to the others and to something "higher still." Finally, at the end, with the entrance of Josef, oppositions are again resolved and brought back into harmony.

2. *Christ and Grace in* The Christian Faith

Schleiermacher's *The Christian Faith* (second edition) was published a quarter century after the *Christmas Dialogue*. The dogmatic system he presents there, methodologically and structurally speaking, begins with the Christian's experience of having been redeemed by Christ, which experience can only take place in the context of the corporate life (the church). So already we see three elements of his spirituality carried over from his earliest years: personal experience, community, and being grasped by Christ. Schleiermacher also carries forth his deep distaste for traditional doctrines such as penal substitutionary atonement and its concomitant focus on the cross, and consequently he had to develop a revisionist account of sin and grace. Some reviews of the first edition (1821/22) charged that he presented Christ as little more than an ideal or projection of the religious consciousness. In the second edition (1830/31), therefore, Schleiermacher took even greater care to ground Christ historically, to explain the relationship between the believer and community and Christ and, finally, to connect the feeling of absolute dependence with the experience of having been redeemed by Christ.

According to Schleiermacher's complex structure of *The Christian Faith*, there are two irreducible, correlative *loci* that form the heart of his dogmatics: the propositions on the person and work of Christ (§§91–105), and the propositions on regeneration and sanctification (§§106–12).[158] This is of obvious relevance to his spirituality because, as has been fathomed too infrequently, the focal point and impetus of Schleiermacher's dogmatic theology is the Christian experience of grace. This also recasts, or should, his understanding of the feeling of absolute dependence. I offer here a discussion of certain moves that Schleiermacher makes in his treatment of Christology and grace, not so as to explicate his theology but rather to highlight his understanding of how the Christian is related to Christ, and to underscore how important that should be in shaping our understanding of his spirituality.

The challenge for Schleiermacher was to explain the person and work of Christ in a way that remained true to the religious consciousness of his time, that did not ignore or trespass the limits placed by scientific knowledge (both historical and physical), and that could explain the present-day believer's relationship to Christ. Again, part of his spirituality involves his firm confidence that these things are not contradictory. Yet to explain how Christ grasps the believer (the work of Christ) and how the believer grasps Christ (faith), we need to attend first to how he understood the person of Christ.

One problem with Schleiermacher's earlier Christology as presented in the *Christmas Dialogue* (in the men's speeches) was that Christ seemed no more than an ideal, to the point of being an abstraction—the "human-in-itself," the "earth-spirit." In the fifth *Speech*, "On the Religions," he described Christ as the "mediator"[159] between the finite and the divine. While this humanized Christ more, the rhetorical aims of the *Speeches* nevertheless created a note of distance. What is more, Schleiermacher there resorted to a *reductio* form of argument that leaves much to be desired;[160] in the end, he left unexplained how it is that Christ mediates and the effects of that mediation.[161]

In *The Christian Faith*, he is intent upon a systematic and "scientific" way of holding the ideal and the real together, or perhaps better put, the archetypal and the historical.[162] He explains, "As an historical individual [Christ] must have been at the same time ideal (i.e. the ideal must have become completely historical in Him), and each historical moment of His experience must at the same time have borne within it the ideal."[163] Schleiermacher affirms the "pure historicity of the person of the Redeemer"[164] by insisting that Christ "could develop only in a certain similarity with His surroundings,"[165] like any other person. Yet, he argues, Christ's development was free from any conflict due to his fully active God-consciousness, such that through him "the creation of human nature" is fully accomplished.[166] The constant potency of Christ's God-consciousness "was a veritable existence of God in Him."[167]

Christ redeems humanity, Schleiermacher says, by incorporating "believers into the power of his God-consciousness"[168] (his redeeming activity) and by assuming "believers into the fellowship of his unclouded blessedness"[169] (his reconciling activity). How does this happen? Schleiermacher refers to his approach, somewhat surprisingly, as "mystical."[170] He acknowledges the dangers of using this term, but thinks its use legitimate as long as he sticks to the narrower meaning of belonging to a "circle of doctrines which only a few share," because "doctrines are only expressions of inward experiences,"[171] which remain a mystery (*Geheimniß*) to those not sharing these experiences. As in so much of his thought and practice, so too in his Christology, Schleiermacher tries to stake out a third alternative between supernaturalism (the "magical" approach, that is, traditional Christologies), on the one side, and empiricism (the "empirical" approach, that is, reductive approaches of the new philosophical and so-called scientific approaches), on the other side. His mystical approach tries to explain how the *individual* is grasped by Christ—and to explain this in a way that recognizes and does not abrogate natural causality. This, as we shall see, is also true in his doctrine of God: he emphasizes again and again the *coincidence* of the absolute divine causality and natural causality.

The magical approach emphasizes a redeeming influence of Christ on an individual, but in a way unmediated by anything natural. (Here Schleiermacher includes those theories that emphasize Christ's atoning death in redemption.) The empirical approach allows a redeeming influence only in the form of teaching and example. In both cases, redemption is understood in external terms; in neither case is the vital relationship between Christ and the believer captured or explained. In contrast, Schleiermacher emphasizes the person-forming work of Christ. On this point he draws his inspiration from those scriptural passages that speak of Christ being and living within the believer[172] and of the Christian being made "a new creature."[173] For the original followers of Christ, this took place when each one was laid hold of by Christ in person; for believers now, this is "mediated by His spiritual presence in the Word," whereby "individuals are assumed into the fellowship of the new life."[174] As DeVries has phrased it, for Schleiermacher, preaching is an "incarnational event."[175] According to him, the relationship of the redeemed person with Christ is vital because it is personal and interior, but it only occurs within and because of the corporate life of the church—fellowship, worship, ministries, and especially its preaching the Word.[176] That is how and where the individual encounters Christ. There is thus a profoundly social dimension to his Christology and soteriology. The Spirit of God works in and through the corporate life of the church.[177]

So how, exactly, do Christ's redeeming and reconciling activities take effect in the life of the individual? And how is that experienced? Schleiermacher answers this in that other chief doctrinal *locus* in *The Christian Faith*, what may be called his treatise on grace.[178] His discussion in these propositions, though dense, is crucial for understanding his Christian spirituality, for it is here that he describes the experience of being redeemed by Christ, and this is at the heart of Christian piety. Under *regeneration*, he includes conversion and justification; under *sanctification*, the sins and the good works of the regenerate.[179] Schleiermacher states that the order in which he treats these matters is not meant to reflect an *ordo salutis* (order of salvation), which had been the subject of some of the fiercest debates on grace. Schleiermacher employs other organizing principles for his discussion of grace, principles that are experiential and systematic in character. Indeed, his active resistance to accepting traditional terms of the debate just may be relevant to his spirituality. I offer a brief account of his doctrine of regeneration with a view to his spirituality.

Grace. Schleiermacher's most succinct definition of *grace* is "fellowship with God, which depends on a communication from the Redeemer."[180] This, along with our awareness of alienation from God as originating from ourselves (sin), is the distinctive feature of Christian piety. Elsewhere, he describes grace as Christ's "gift" of his own "blessing" and "peace,"[181] the fruit of his all-powerful God-consciousness; as the "state of union" with Christ, "the real possession of blessedness in the consciousness that Christ in us is the centre of our life."[182] Grace takes away misery—specifically, the misery of sin.[183] It is the "divine life in us,"[184] a "special divine impartation."[185] Grace for Schleiermacher is nothing less than our redemption through Christ. Take note, however, of what grace is *not*. He restricts grace to the work and presence of Christ in the church; it is *not* about a universal divine presence or activity in creation. Further, he associates it solely with Christ's assuming believers into the power of his God-consciousness and drawing them into fellowship with him; it is *not* about the suffering and death of Christ. Again, we see here his allergic reaction to any kind of a "wounds-theology" or notion of penal substitution. According to Schleiermacher, the point about Christ's suffering and death had to do with his passive obedience to God, not a vicarious atonement. This obviously has consequences for spirituality.

Conversion. According to Schleiermacher, conversion has three elements: regret, change of heart, and faith. "Perfect and *effectual* divine grace," he argues, "is seen only in the union of all three."[186] When they all occur together in the same moment in time, there a divine act occurs, a new creation: conversion. Before this point, any of the three elements may occur alone or perhaps in sequence, but that would be only preparatory, not effectual, grace. The three elements of the grace of conversion occur simultaneously through a confrontation prompted by Christ's revelation in the Word. For Schleiermacher, in contrast to Martin Luther and so many of the Protestant confessions, that confrontation is not one of divine judgment that acts as a crushing hammer, humiliating the individual;[187] it is, rather, essentially positive. Christ's "self-imparting perfection," he writes, "confronts us in all its truth."[188] The focus is not on the self but on Christ, whose "soul-stirring exhibition of Himself to us leads us to abjure utterly our previous condition."[189] This was true of Schleiermacher since his earliest days and is a defining part of his spirituality. For him the experience of the redemptive power of Christ is an experience of beauty and attraction. Christ's goodness—his sinless perfection, blessedness, and self-impartation—arouses in us profound *regret*, whereby we abjure our past life. And this includes necessarily a *change of heart*. Conversion, then, is not necessarily (and, in his view, is not usually) a soul-shattering experience that must destroy the ego. Nor is it necessary that "every Christian…be able to point to the very time and place of his conversion."[190]

The third element of conversion is *faith*, which Schleiermacher defines as "the appropriation of the perfection and blessedness of Christ."[191] In the confrontation with Christ through the power of the Word, Christ "lays hold of us in his assimilating [*aufnehmenden*] activity"[192] and "unites [us] to Himself."[193] The Christian is thus drawn into union with Christ, which is what it means to share in his blessedness. According to Schleiermacher, union with Christ is not the goal of faith but *is* faith—it is given in faith. The Christian's "share in His blessedness" is present at the very beginning of faith and (a crucial point) increases throughout the course of a life of grace. Faith for him is "originally joyful" and "uplifting,"[194] and it is this joy of living fellowship with Christ that distinguishes conversion-regret from other forms of regret (e.g., a law-based regret). The "certainty of faith" is "an understanding of what union with Christ means" as well as a "delight in that union."[195] "Faith *alone* saves,"[196] Schleiermacher affirms, because it gives blessedness, because it is a sharing of Christ's blessedness.

Justification is "God's justifying of the one who is converted" (§109).[197] It is the transformation of an individual's relation to God that follows from faith in the Redeemer, and it includes the *forgiveness of sins* and *adoption*. Repentance, Schleiermacher explains, "comes to rest in forgiveness," and faith becomes "consciousness of being a child of God."[198] He insists on the interdependence of conversion and justification. "There is only one eternal and universal decree justifying [humans] for Christ's sake."[199] For Schleiermacher, the redeeming and reconciling activity of Christ is a continuation of God's creative activity that itself is an unbroken expression of the eternal divine decree.

In conclusion, what needs to be underscored is that Schleiermacher's view of Christ, of faith in Christ, and of the sanctified life is what can be called *incarnational*. Schleiermacher in fact draws an explicit "parallel between the beginning of the divine life in us and the incarnation of the Redeemer."[200] Both his Christology and his soteriology presuppose an anthropology that sees the human being as fundamentally living, hence "susceptible" or "receptive," and he describes Christ in the same terms.[201]

The Open, Attuned Heart

The heart for us is as much the seat of religion as its nearest world.

—*Second* Speech, *"On the Essence of Religion"*

Frequently in the *Speeches* and *Christmas Dialogue*, Schleiermacher writes of the pious "heart." More often than not, the German
term is *Gemüth* rather than *Herz*. Today, *Gemüt*[202] in this sense has
fallen out of usage and rings strangely for a native speaker. In
Schleiermacher's time, *Gemüth* carried a range of meanings similar to
Geist and *Seele* (mind, spirit, soul, heart), referring to the interior, to
the seat of one's feelings and basic disposition, and thus to the defining characteristics of the whole person. It took on a more specific
meaning in German Romanticism as a person's entire interior state, in
its depth and richness, including the emotions. In this volume,
Gemüth is translated as "heart." Whereas he usually uses *Herz* to refer
to a human capacity in a general sense or to the bodily organ, he uses
Gemüth to refer to the finely cultivated interior state of a pious person;
more particularly, *Gemüth* means for him the pious heart characterized by serenity, humility, openness, receptivity, joy, and love.[203]

In this emphasis on the heart, Schleiermacher's Moravian background merges with his Romantic values. For Pietism, the heart was
crucial as the locus of the intimate relationship between the believer
and Christ and of the loving communion among members of the
congregation; it conveyed the interior, affective dimension of faith.[204]
For the early Romantics, *Gemüth* captured the depth of emotion and
originality of the cultivated individual who was open to living nature
and resistant to the arid one-sidedness of the Enlightenment.
Schleiermacher drew these two trajectories together and developed
his notion of the pious heart, a notion that is at once broadly anthropological (it defines what it means to be fully human) and specifically Christian (it also defines the serene soul grasped by Christ). In
short, to understand Schleiermacher's spirituality, we must understand what he meant by the open, pious heart.

The cultivation of a pious heart is a key feature in
Schleiermacher's spirituality. The religious or pious person is the one
who has an open heart—a harmonious and integrated interior life

that is so because it is also finely attuned to its world and receptive to the divine activity working in and through that world. In a specifically Christian context, the open pious heart is one that lives in Christ and knows the joy of redemption, of being drawn into Christ's own blessedness and fellowship. It would be fair to say that one end of spirituality, or the ideal, is an open heart—for Christians, an open heart attached to Christ and trusting in God and fully participating in the life of the Spirit.

To say that for Schleiermacher the pious heart is finely attuned is to say in part that, though the heart is the locus of the emotions and affectivity, the pious person is neither emotional (in the sense of being unsteady, erratic, or reactionary) nor subject to the passions (for Schleiermacher, this is enthusiasm, *Begeisterung*). On the contrary, *Gemüth* denotes a "higher life" because the individual has so ordered and harmonized the emotions that he or she maintains equanimity whatever the circumstances, not letting enthusiasm or despair alter that almost Stoic demeanor. This was a theme that went back to Schleiermacher's earliest essays on moral philosophy. In "On the Highest Good" (1789), he wrote,

> Through constant attentiveness and extended practice, we can take things to the point at which, in normal cases, we avoid the excessively gripping influence of pleasant as well as unpleasant sensations, an influence that is the basis of an inner and necessary unhappiness, and this art stands in a close connection with ethics.[205]

A decade after he wrote these lines, Schleiermacher's own social and intellectual world had expanded almost exponentially, and so this "attentiveness" and "practice" was transplanted into an even more expansive theory of human nature. The human being is always and already the human-in-relation.

Sociability defines human existence for Schleiermacher, and the human heart is not only the source of that sociability, it is itself social. He writes in the *Speeches*,

> The human heart [*Gemüth*] is endowed with so effusive and accomplished a sociability that no single talent or fac-

ulty can produce its works in a self-contained manner—
however much you might, in contemplation, separate
them out. I think, rather, it realizes itself in the whole,
each talent and faculty being moved and penetrated by
the obliging love and support of the others in every performance, in such a way that you now find all of them in
every operation and must be content with discerning the
prevailing, productive power in this interconnection.[206]

In other words, the human heart and its effusive sociability is not a
particular faculty but is related to all the human faculties in that it
penetrates them all, unifies them by means of love, and holds them
in itself all as the "seat of religion." This unifying, expansive activity
of the human heart reflects (because it is part of) the unifying activity and interconnection in the universe. In fact, he says, "the universe
reproduces itself in the inner life, and only through spiritual nature,
the interior, does the corporeal first become understandable."[207]

The open, attuned heart is that living point of contact between
the universe and the self, hovering between them. But just as it does
not attach itself to a particular emotion or faculty when it comes to
the interior, so the open heart does not attach itself to particular,
finite objects exterior to it. The pious person is the one with the open
heart that recognizes the "universal existence of everything finite in
the infinite and through the infinite, of everything temporal in the
eternal and through the eternal"; Schleiermacher continues, "This
seeking and finding in all that lives and moves, in all becoming and
change, in all doing and suffering, and just having and knowing life
itself in immediate feeling as this existence—this is religion."[208] And
because an open heart is not determined by any one "object,"
whether that object be internal or external, it (again, not any heart,
but the open, attuned heart) is free:

Only the free delight of viewing and living, when it goes
into the infinite and is directed toward the infinite, places
the heart [*Gemüth*] in unrestricted freedom. Only religion
saves it from the ignominious fetters of opinion and lust.
For religion, everything that exists is necessary, and everything that can be is to it a true, indispensable image of the

infinite. It is only a matter of finding the point from which its relation to the infinite can be discovered. However reprehensible something may be in other relations or in itself, in this regard it is always worthy of existing and of being retained and contemplated. To a pious heart [*Gemüthe*], religion makes everything holy and worthy, even unholiness and baseness itself, whatever it grasps or does not grasp, whatever does or does not lie within the system of its own thoughts or conform to its particular way of action. Religion is the original and sworn enemy of all pedantry and all one-sidedness.[209]

The cultivation of the interior world of the heart must be stimulated by our relationship to the universe, but Schleiermacher also insists that the development of the religious sense does not have to do with "exterior nature" alone, which is only the "forecourt" of religion.

Only in intimate relation to other human beings—only in true sociability—does a person become fully alive and is the openness of the heart fully realized. This is the meaning of Genesis 2, as Schleiermacher interprets that in the second *Speech*. Alone, Adam cannot respond to God or appreciate his paradise. Only when he loves, only when he enters into intimate relationship with Eve, is he capable of communicating and of being in real relation to the world:

And now, for the first time, living and brilliant sounds stirred within him; now, for the first time, the world took shape before his eyes. In the flesh of his flesh and bone of his bone, he discovered humanity—anticipating all directions and forms of love already in this original love—and in humanity he found the world.[210]

To be open and fully human, a heart must be in dialogue. And this is why friendship, love, and intimate communication are so essential to Schleiermacher's spirituality, since the interior life and the human heart can only develop within the context of such intimacy. In intimate dialogue we begin to shape and expand our own hearts, in part by seeing and reflecting the beauty we recognize in others. As he writes to his friend Henriette Herz, "To whom it is granted to linger, gazing into the calm of a well-ordered heart, this person's life cannot thus remain without traces of beauty."[211] The open heart is characterized by the virtues of circumspection and equanimity, humility, modesty, forbearance, tranquility, wisdom and—above all—joy, love, and "eternal youth." These stand in contrast to what could fairly be called vices for Schleiermacher: fear, narrow-mindedness, one-sidedness, self-isolation, and a clinging to the dead letter. No one who demonstrates these latter traits can be considered pious, since she or he does not (yet) possess the disposition of an open heart. Schleiermacher stipulates, "You will never want to call anyone pious whose sense for the life of the world is not open, anyone who goes there in impenetrable obtuseness. This contemplation, however, does not attend to the essence of one finite thing in opposition to other finite things."[212]

In the *Speeches*, Schleiermacher offers three examples of the pious heart: the philosopher Spinoza, the poet Novalis, and (in general) women. In the *Christmas Dialogue*, he reinforces that last idea by portraying female characters as concrete examples of Christian piety. This ideal of piety, of the attunement of the pious heart (*Gemüth*), is embodied in all the women present, but especially so in the hostess, Ernestine, and in the women whose stories are told in the first and third "stories" (in part 3 of the *Dialogue*). Ernestine, Kornelie, and Charlotte all model a deep and generous love, an open and dignified disposition, and a tranquil resignation in the face of death. This ideal is captured in the final scene, when the sage Josef (likely a Pietist) declares, "I behold everything, even that which is deeply wounding, with joyous eyes."[213]

What is more, the distinction between an undeveloped or distorted disposition, on the one hand, and the genuinely pious disposition, on the other hand, is a recurring theme in the *Christmas Dialogue*. It is the contrast between the enthusiasm of new love (between Ernst and Friederike) and the serene happiness of a couple long married (Ernestine and Eduard) that prompts the long conversation that makes up the second part of the *Dialogue*. Developing this line of conversation, the interlocutors turn to the subject of religion and raise the question of religious enthusiasm, superstition, and eccentricity (distortion). These latter dispositions do not belong to genuine religious joy, what Karoline describes as "that higher, more universal joy [that] blossoms out in us unimpeded even next to the deepest sorrow, and it purges and soothes the sorrow without being destroyed by it—so original is this joy, and so immediately is it grounded in something imperishable."[214] The best analogy for the finely tuned heart is, in fact, music. In the words of the host, Eduard: "For piety, the individual occurrences would only be passing notes, but its true content would be the great chords of the heart—chords that, though alternating marvelously and in the most diverse melodies, nonetheless always resolve themselves into the same harmony, in which only major and minor, male and female, can be distinguished."[215] The open, attuned heart is related to *feeling* in that it is the result when feeling is exercised and allowed to hold sway in a person.

Feeling

This indeed is the one and all of religion: to feel everything moving us in feeling in its highest unity as one and all, and to feel everything individual and particular as imparted through this, and therefore to feel our existence and life as an existence and life in and through God.
—*Second* Speech, *"On the Essence of Religion"*

Arguably, no single term is more closely associated with Schleiermacher than *feeling (Gefühl)*. It was part of the revolutionary nature of his *Speeches* in 1799: "Religion's essence is neither thinking nor acting, but intuition and feeling."[216] It remained a signature term more than three decades later in his equally revolutionary *The Christian Faith*. Also arguably, no other term of his has been as misunderstood or as debated as this signature term. Considering feeling from the standpoint of Schleiermacher's spirituality may grant a fresh perspective, since it requires that we look at the role feeling plays in the pious heart, in the religious person: how it functions in practices, in processes, and in the cultivation of certain attitudes and relations. At the very least, it is fair to say that his spirituality cannot be understood apart from this term.

Due to long-standing debates and to criticisms from all sides, it may make sense to begin *apophatically*—that is, by saying what feeling is *not*, according to Schleiermacher's use of the term. Feeling is not an emotion. It is not a vague sense of something. It is not purely subjective. In fact, Schleiermacher used feeling to establish what he called a "higher realism," whereby he resisted more radical forms of idealism after Kant, insisting that humans do stand in immediate relation to a real universe, but at the same time acknowledging the inadequacy of older, naïve forms of realism. In his early essays in moral philosophy, he had developed the idea of feeling as performing an at once perceptive, unitive, and organizing function, somewhat akin to the moral sense in British thought at that time.[217] It was, of course, in his *Speeches on Religion* that he linked feeling so decisively with religion and piety.

1. Feeling in the Speeches

Schleiermacher begins his second *Speech* by distinguishing feeling from thinking and from doing (or acting). He wants to disabuse his friends, the so-called despisers of religion, of their penchant for associating religion with metaphysical claims and outmoded doctrines, on the one hand, and moral rules, on the other hand: "Piety must be something other than the instinct that craves this aggregate of metaphysical and moral crumbs, stirring them into confusion."[218] The problem with those other things is that, when separated from feeling or confused with religion, they are both ways of acting upon and trying to control the universe and of constricting the person, the result being a disconnection from reality and so from God. In contrast, feeling does not try to control, impose, or insist. Feeling is essentially receptive and passive in relation to the universe. It hears, listens, and lets itself be affected. This is one reason humility is such an important virtue for Schleiermacher.

If the pious heart is one that is open, feeling is the vehicle by which it becomes so. Feeling is that living contact with all of reality, whereby the universe acts upon us and *in* us, whereby we take up the operations of the universe into ourselves, and whereby we are aware of our oneness with all existence. There is no one, particular object (or act or idea) to which feeling stands in relation; rather, what one feels is the connectedness of all and the divine operation in and through all. In Schleiermacher's words, in *feeling* it is not the individual as such that affects us, but the whole, in and with the individual. Therefore, it is not the individual and finite that enters our life, but precisely God, in whom alone the particular is one and all. And so, too, it is not this or that individual function in us that is excited and that steps forward, but our entire being—how we confront the world and are at the same time in it—hence immediately the divine in us.[219]

As this passage indicates, he contends that God acts on individuals only in and through the universe, never apart from the universe. So, in being open and receptive to the activity and interconnectedness of the universe through feeling, the person who *feels* is the one who is open and receptive to the divine activity—and who is therefore "pious" or "religious." According to Schleiermacher, a person's "religiosity" depends not on their *concept* of God but on their *feeling*, their receptivity to the divine activity in and through all that *is*.[220]

In receiving the actions of the universe in and through feeling, the religious person apprehends diversity, change, and finitude—and *consents* to these. One of the most famous passages of the second *Speech* is this: "For to love the world-spirit and joyfully to behold its works is the aim of our religion, and in love there is no fear."[221] In feeling there is neither resentment, nor the desire to alter or refuse, nor yet the desire to cut oneself off from the rest of reality. Schleiermacher writes,

> And that would certainly be the core of all religious feelings from this side: to feel entirely one with nature and to be rooted entirely in it; and to expect, *with approval and tranquility*, nothing but the implementation of that eternal law in all changing appearances of life that we encounter—yes, even in the change between life and death itself.[222]

Feeling recognizes the oneness and connectedness of all things and assents to everything as "good and divine" in this interconnection.

It is through feeling that we "take up," "appropriate," or "assimilate" (*aufnehmen*) the constant activity of the universe and reproduce it in the self. Notice this verb. While feeling is passive in its openness and receptivity, it is not inert. For just as the universe is living and ever active, so too are we, as integral parts of that universe, living. Schleiermacher explains:

> The entire religious life consists in two elements: we surrender to the universe, letting ourselves be excited by the side of the universe turned towards the self; and then inwardly we reproduce this contact (which, as what it is and in its determinateness, is a particular feeling), taking it up into the inner unity of our own life and existence. The religious life is nothing other than the continual renewal of this process.[223]

Feeling is therefore the crucial ingredient for creativity, freedom, and individuality.[224] In fact, he argues that it is when a person lacks feeling and thus reacts to a single stimulus that "atrocious and horrible deeds"[225] result. This is also why for him "knowing" and "doing" need to stay grounded in feeling. When that connection to the universe is ignored and the unity lost sight of, "knowing" and "doing" become one-sided and dis-eased.

2. *Feeling in* The Christian Faith

In his Introduction to *The Christian Faith*, Schleiermacher famously defines *piety* as "considered purely for itself, neither a knowing nor a doing but a determination of feeling or of the immediate self-consciousness" (§3); and "the self-identical essence of piety is this: that we are conscious of ourselves as absolutely dependent or, which is the same thing, as being in relation to God" (§4).[226] In all this, we can detect a basic continuity with the commitments he had established in the *Speeches*, although those commitments were refined through almost three decades of debate, revision, and careful scholarship. As before, he insists that Christian piety is neither a thinking nor a doing but a feeling. In §3, however, he explicates the relation between feeling, knowing, and doing more systematically than he had in the *Speeches*. He allows that piety may be understood as "a state in which knowing, feeling, and doing are joined,"[227] as long as no subordination is intended. That is to say, "there is a knowing and doing that belong to piety, but these in no way constitute the essence of piety."[228] Piety is still essentially feeling. The qualifier "considered purely for itself" picks up on a point he had emphasized in the second *Speech* but had not made clear enough in the first edition of *The Christian Faith*—namely that, although feeling cannot be separated from knowing or doing except in contemplation, when we are trying to gain clarity on the matter, we can and must distinguish it from those two. Schleiermacher also specifies that he is speaking of a determination or modification of feeling, not just any feeling or emotion, and he now explains this in terms of the *immediate self-consciousness*. The modifier *immediate* here underscores that piety is not knowledge; the term *self-consciousness*, that piety is not consciousness of objects or the world.

Schleiermacher's propositions on piety, the feeling of absolute dependence, and religious self-consciousness (§§3–6) are among his most challenging, and have in turn been among the most contested, in all *The Christian Faith*. Here I shall limit myself to four comments on their relevance for understanding Schleiermacher's spirituality.

First, in order to get at what he means by the *feeling of absolute dependence*, Schleiermacher distinguishes it from a *feeling of relative dependence* and the correlative *feeling of relative freedom* (§4.2), and in so doing he lays out basic principles of his theological anthropology. According to him, we are always to some degree free and to some degree dependent because we are inescapably related, because we exist within the "nature-system." Our feeling of relative dependence is *one*, he says, with our feeling of relative freedom. In relation to other selves, to other things, and to the entire system of nature, we are always partially free and partially dependent (determined). This is the result of the interconnection of all that is, the "nature-system," since interrelatedness entails *reciprocity*, including the reciprocity between "the subject and the corresponding other."[229] Freedom for him is not being unaffected, nor is it doing whatever we want; conversely, dependence is not being unfree or totally determined, but is instead about being related. This is just as true in terms of *nature* (he insists that this is true even of our relationship to the farthest star, however minutely) as it is true in terms of *society* (he argues that every individual has some influence on society and the state, however indirectly).[230] The former point (nature) is significant insofar as Schleiermacher underscores the deep interconnection between humans and the rest of nature, since for him we are a part and product of nature. To the degree that his view of nature is an organic one according to which everything that exists is *internally related* to everything else and has *inherent value*, it is also profoundly ecological. The latter point (society) is significant insofar as it suggests both the *value* and the *responsibility* of every person in society. Here we can glimpse his democratic impulses and political commitments.

Second, Schleiermacher's notion of the feeling of absolute dependence is not unrelated to his experience and understanding of grace. He points out that we have no feeling of *absolute freedom*: "Our whole existence does not present itself to our consciousness as having proceeded from our own spontaneous activity."[231] We do, however, have a feeling of *absolute dependence*. No "object" is given in the feeling of absolute dependence—not the totality of the world, and not any idea of God (otherwise piety would be essentially a knowing). What is given is a "*Whence* of our receptive and active existence,"[232] on which we are absolutely dependent (exert no counterinfluence) and with which therefore we stand in relationship, albeit not one of reciprocity (as we do in relationship to the world).[233] "God," Schleiermacher writes, "signifies for us simply that which is the codeterminant in this feeling and to which we trace our being in such a state; and any further content of the idea must be evolved out of this fundamental import assigned to it."[234] Critics have attacked his notion of the feeling of absolute dependence on the grounds that freedom, not dependence (much less absolute dependence), would seem to define religion. But it is important to keep in mind that in *The Christian Faith* the feeling of absolute dependence (§4) is the most abstract expression of the experience of grace (§108)—of *sola gratia* (grace alone).[235] Everything comes from God. As grace establishes freedom, so the feeling of absolute dependence is the ground and precondition of the feeling of relative freedom; at the same time, without any feeling of freedom we would have no feeling of absolute dependence.

Third, the feeling of absolute dependence never occurs in isolation as a discrete moment apart from other moments. Schleiermacher explains, "Strictly speaking, [it] cannot exist in a single moment as such, because such a moment is always determined, as regards its total content, by what is *given*, and thus by objects towards which we have a feeling of freedom."[236] This is true not only for individuals but also for religious communions. In other words, just as there is no isolatable experience of the feeling of absolute dependence, so there is no religion, no piety, in general. This is the point of his fifth *Speech*, "On the Religions." So while Schleiermacher claims that religious consciousness is universal (an "essential element in human nature"[237]), it only takes shape within the particulars of history and within the particularity of a given communion. *The Christian Faith* is the attempt to present in a systematic, coherent presentation one instance of it: Protestant Christianity, specifically the Church of the Union (of Reformed and Lutheran Churches in Prussia), in his time.

Fourth and finally, Schleiermacher claims that the feeling of absolute dependence is the "highest grade of human self-consciousness," but he also argues that it never occurs apart from the sensible self-consciousness (§5). This point is absolutely vital for understanding his spirituality, since for him the religious or spiritual life is not about transcending our "sensible" experience or somehow escaping the material world. For him it is about the sustaining and heightening of God-consciousness, the feeling of absolute dependence, through every moment of our sensible self-consciousness. As we have seen, Schleiermacher thinks that Christ had realized this ideal of full God-consciousness in every moment of his existence, and that was the existence of God in him, and it is by drawing people into the blessedness of his God-consciousness that Christ redeems. In the Introduction, Schleiermacher delineates three grades of self-consciousness. The lowest is a "confused animal" consciousness, where there is no distinction of self and other, subject and object; this needs to be grown out of, otherwise our consciousness will not develop and we will not be in any way free (here he gives the example of young children before they learn to speak). The next grade is that of the "sensible self-consciousness," which emerges in relation to the accumulation of perceptions (and our "objective" consciousness), develops within that field of reciprocity of freedom and dependence, and includes "the social and moral feelings no less than the self-regarding."[238] This is human life as it becomes, ideally at least, more and more integrated and self-conscious. Yet it still operates in terms of the split of subject-object, and so it is also characterized by the "antithesis of the pleasant and the unpleasant, or of pleasure and pain."[239] The highest grade of human self-consciousness is the feeling of absolute dependence, which "bears within it no such antithesis."[240] Because, however, the God-consciousness always coexists with a person's sensible self-consciousness, the stamp of joy or of sorrow will inform any particular moment, depending on the individuality of that person. This is where particular religious emotions come into play. For instance, the greater degree of piety will mean, Schleiermacher thinks, that any feeling of suffering will be accompanied by trust in God.

God

Now, thou God who art love, let me not only resign myself to thy omnipotence, not only submit to thy impenetrable wisdom, but also know thy fatherly love! Make even this grievous trial a new blessing for me in my vocation! For me and all of mine let this communal pain become wherever possible a new bond of still more intimate love, and let it issue in a new apprehension of thy Spirit in all my household! Grant that even this grave hour may become a blessing for all who are gathered here. Let us all more and more mature to that wisdom which, looking beyond the void, sees and loves only the eternal in all things earthly and perishable, and in all thy decrees finds thy peace as well, and eternal life, to which through faith we are delivered out of death.

—*Sermon at the funeral of his son, Nathanael*[241]

Schleiermacher spoke these words at the graveside of his beloved youngest child, Nathanael, who died from scarlet fever at nine years of age. Nathanael's death struck the older Schleiermacher to the core, and he was never quite the same thereafter. Nonetheless, his understanding of God, as well as his demeanor before God, remained uncompromised. Schleiermacher stood firmly in the Calvinist tradition in that he always remembered the utter transcendence of God at the same time that he trusted unfailingly in the beneficence of God.[242] God's will is inscrutable, and yet it is to be trusted; the pious heart submits to the divine omnipotence with gratitude and acceptance. There is, however, a marked difference from Calvin, from Luther before him, and from much of the theological heritage. There is no trace of fear in Schleiermacher, because for him God is not wrathful; nor is there even a trace of a thought that God might be capricious.[243] Schleiermacher maintained that "love alone and no other attribute can be equated thus with God."[244] The experience of redemption, he thought, necessarily includes "recognition of the divine love."[245] Schleiermacher was as thoroughly consistent in his understanding of God as love and in his trusting attitude toward God as he was in his joyful devotion to Christ and in his insistence that these could not be separated.

God is love. This is "the one great fact," according to Schleiermacher.[246] It is the key to everything Schleiermacher believed and wrote about God. This is what God's Spirit reveals about the depths of the Godhead, and it is that single, fundamental conviction in the soul of the Christian that remains unwavering, however much other aspects of faith may change.[247] It is that revelation by the Spirit that leads the Christian to call out, like Christ, "Father!" Schleiermacher returns to this theme repeatedly in his sermons. Although to the casual eye it may seem that in his dogmatic theology this theme of "God is love" is eclipsed; in fact, it permeates the entire text.

In *The Christian Faith*, love and wisdom are the last two divine attributes discussed; in fact, they come at the very end of the entire work.[248] They are therefore the most significant because, according to Schleiermacher's method and organization, they are most immediately connected to the experience of being redeemed by Christ. Schleiermacher writes, "We have the sense of divine love directly in the consciousness of redemption."[249] Love alone speaks of the divine essence. For all the limits placed on language about God by Schleiermacher's own method (in a post-Kantian age), this alone can be said of the divine essence because it is given in the experience of redemption. "Love alone and no other attribute," Schleiermacher insists, "can be equated thus with God."[250] The divine wisdom is closely related but still does "not enter consciousness...directly."[251] But, given the consciousness of redemption, "we cannot possibly regard all finite being in its relation to our God-consciousness except as…an absolutely harmonious divine work of art."[252] The pious heart to whom God's Spirit has revealed that "God is love" will look on all of creation as the theater of redemption—that is to say, not with fear but with joyful trust.

Not infrequently, Schleiermacher got into trouble because of his rejection of the idea of God "as a solitary being outside of the world and behind the world."[253] Rather than being a sign of lack of piety on his part, his criticisms of traditional ideas of God arguably reflect central features of his spirituality, in that Schleiermacher thought that the divine transcendence imposes the need for humility and circumspection in talking about God, and also that talk about God must remain connected to the experience of absolute dependence on God. The first of these calls for *apophatic language* about God, which, by using negation ("God is not…"), inherently acknowledges the limits of every concept, name, or image used to describe the utterly transcendent God; the second of these calls for *cataphatic language* about God, which, by affirming something to be true about God ("God is…"), acknowledges the presence of God. In the history of Christian thought, *both* approaches have proven necessary for any meaningful talk about God; it is the dynamic, dialectical relation between cataphatic and apophatic language that deepens understanding and corrects overextensions. Schleiermacher himself developed an intricate relationship between them in his new and modern method of God-talk. Too often critics have focused on his negations without recognizing this as properly apophatic language deeply rooted in a religious awareness of the divine transcendence; critics have also failed to note Schleiermacher's affirmations of God and of how he views God as actively present in and to the world. In fact, he builds the dialectic between the apophatic and the cataphatic into the very structure of his *The Christian Faith.*

A case in point: in his theological system, Schleiermacher does not present his doctrine of God in any one place, but distributes it throughout the entire text under the third form of proposition.[254] This means that his discussion of the divine attributes in part 1 (eternity, omnipresence, omnipotence, omniscience) are necessarily grounded in, and are a certain abstraction from, what he says about the attributes of love and wisdom (as well as justice, holiness, and mercy), in part 2. Schleiermacher explains, "Indeed, an *omnipotence*, the aim and motive force of which I do not know, an *omniscience*, the structure and value of its contents I do not know, and an *omnipresence*, of which I do not know what it emits from itself and attracts to itself, are merely vague and barely living ideas."[255] One way in which this connection between these attributes and the divine love is manifest lies in Schleiermacher's emphasis on "the absolute causality" of God (§51). This, in a sense, is the connecting point of the divine love and the feeling of absolute dependence: the "ground of our feeling of absolute dependence" is the absolute causality of God,[256] and the ground of *that* is the divine love. "God cannot be represented otherwise than as living," he writes, "for in the living as such all is activity."[257]

That means for him that God is always active, but this also means for him that God is always active in and through the nature-system, never outside or apart from it. Schleiermacher rejects an understanding of miracle as a usurpation of the natural causal system. And this is also why God-consciousness does not and cannot involve some sort of escape from nature. His intricate interlinking of the divine attributes, and the way in which he has some functioning apophatically and others cataphatically, help him maintain this coincidence of opposites: the divine causality is equal in scope with natural causality, which means simultaneously that there is no natural causality that does not coincide with divine causality, and, conversely, that divine causality does not occur apart from the nature-system, nor does it ever abrogate the nature-system; at the same time, being different in kind, the divine causality cannot be reduced to natural causality.[258]

Schleiermacher was always deeply suspicious of anthropomorphic descriptions of God. In his view, the divine transcendence requires that we be careful to resist the tendency to create our own idols, that is to say, something that is more the product of our own sensible self-consciousness than it is informed by the higher religious consciousness. He also developed a kind of scale by which to judge various images and concepts of God. Toward the end of the second *Speech*, Schleiermacher finally comes to the concept of God, arguing that what is important is not the concept itself but "the divine in our feeling,"[259] and he delineated three basic ways of conceiving God depending on the development of feeling for the higher unity. The first level (idol and fetish) results when "a person's feeling is still a dim instinct"[260] and the world is only chaos and confusion to that person. The second level (polytheism) occurs when order is discerned, but it is still seen as multiplicity and is ascribed to necessity. On these first two levels especially, images of God will be anthropomorphic. The third level (monotheism) is reached when "the universe presents itself as totality, as unity in multiplicity, as system, and so for the first time it merits its name."[261] The complexity of this scale enters in when Schleiermacher notes that, on each level, there is a spectrum that runs from personalism to nonpersonalism; depending on the "direction of [a person's] imagination,"[262] God may be conceptualized as personal or not.[263] That is why he claims Spinoza is rightly placed at that third level: "The high world-spirit permeated him, the infinite was his beginning and end, the universe his sole and eternal love."[264]

Finally, when it comes to Schleiermacher's spirituality and his understanding of God, the importance of the Spirit for him must be underscored. Schleiermacher's dogmatic treatment of the Trinity does appear heterodox, and the fact that he situates the doctrine of the Trinity at the very end under "Conclusion" (§§170–72) only seems to corroborate that. Indeed, he himself maintains, "this doctrine itself, as ecclesiastically framed, is not an immediate utterance concerning the Christian self-consciousness,"[265] and he calls for "freedom for a thoroughgoing criticism of the doctrine in its older forms, so as to prepare the way for, and introduce, a reconstruction of it."[266] Despite these calls for rethinking trinitarian doctrinal formulations, the Spirit remains central to Schleiermacher's thought and piety, which is why his Sermon on Pentecost Sunday (1825) has been included in this volume.

Mysticism

Soon enough, though, they shall see that I am still the same old mystic.

—*Letter to Henriette Herz*

Only occasionally does Schleiermacher use the terms *mystic, mystical,* or *mysticism*—sometimes pejoratively, sometimes ironically, and sometimes positively. These shifting usages perhaps reflect the contested nature of *mysticism* in the modern world, and within Protestantism especially. During the Enlightenment, *mysticism* was a pejorative term designating religious fanatics and sectarians.[267] Many Protestant intellectuals had a strong antipathy to the category, associating it with Catholicism and Pietism. In 1924, in his *Mysticism and the Word*, Reformed theologian Emil Brunner (1889–1966) famously attacked Schleiermacher's so-called mysticism as antithetical to the word and to the biblical-Reformation understanding of faith.[268] The worry, which Karl Barth (1886–1968) and others shared, was that in Schleiermacher, experience and feeling necessarily implied subjectivism, and it was largely on such grounds he could be dismissed as a mystic. Such assumptions regarding Schleiermacher's supposed subjectivism and its dangers have largely fallen by the wayside, as have older Catholic-Protestant polemics—or at least they have not gone unchallenged. Many Protestants and Protestant theologians have gained a more positive attitude toward mysticism than was true even a quarter century ago, in part because of the reshaping of the understanding of mysticism as a result of extensive scholarship on the topic[269] and the production of new editions of primary texts.[270] Furthermore, the trend in theology now is toward closing the gap between religious experience and the study of theology,[271] and in many ways Schleiermacher can be seen as a precursor to, or perhaps an originator of, this trend. It is time, therefore, to approach the topic of Schleiermacher and mysticism anew, informed by the more recent scholarship.

A new approach is also necessitated by criticisms from the other side, from philosophers of religion and scholars of the study of religion, whose issues with Schleiermacher might be categorized under a different kind of negative association with "mystical" aspects of his thought. For instance, a common complaint against Schleiermacher, stemming back at least to Wayne Proudfoot's *Religious Experience* (1985), is that he develops a "protective strategy" in trying to "restrict accounts of religious experience and belief to the perspective of the subject"; in assuming "that religious experience and belief can be understood and assessed only from the inside"; and in claiming "that religious beliefs can never come into conflict with scientific or other nonreligious beliefs."[272] Although Proudfoot does not classify Schleiermacher under mysticism per se, he does link his criticisms of both: "In contexts other than the mystical, the religious object is often designated by terms or phrases that function as placeholders, or as operators that preclude all determinate predicates. Schleiermacher's use of the term *whence* to designate that towards which the feeling of absolute dependence is directed is a case in point."[273] The purpose is to "guarantee, in advance, ineffability."[274]

Here I touch on but a few aspects of what McGinn has called Schleiermacher's "mystical piety"[275] that warrant further reflection within the wider rubric of spirituality. If there is a mystical note or chord to Schleiermacher's life and thought, and I believe there are several, that does not necessarily mean that his religious thought can be categorized as a particular kind of mystic-*ism* (regardless of whether mysticism is viewed positively or negatively). Schleiermacher employs different kinds of language and imagery that might be deemed mystical, and while in the end these are all related, they ought neither to be casually confused with each other nor to be isolated from other aspects of his thought. I recommend the following four guidelines for reading Schleiermacher in this new context of new scholarship in the related subfields of the study of spirituality and the study of mysticism. First, the adjective *mystical* should be used only insofar as it is useful and genuinely illuminating in understanding Schleiermacher's thought. Second, it should not be used in any way that neglects the pluriform nature of those mystical chords. Third, Schleiermacher's own reserved willingness to employ the term *mystical*, along with his qualifications and circumspection concerning it, should be kept in mind.[276] And fourth, it should be remembered that even in those passages that some may want to designate as mystical, there is never a suspension of the natural causal system or of sensible self-consciousness.

Some of the passages from Schleiermacher's pen that sound the most mystical—insofar as they speak of a "higher unity," of a becoming one with the universe, and of a surrender of one's finite existence—are from the second *Speech*, "On the Essence of Religion." Indeed, most of the definitions he offers there of religion have this mystical tone to them. Many of these have already been quoted in this introduction, but here is another example, well known because of its erotic imagery:

You lie then immediately on the bosom of the infinite world; you are in this moment her soul, for you feel all her powers and her infinite life as your own; she is in this moment your body, for you penetrate her muscles and limbs as your own, and your sense and presentiment bestir her innermost nerves.[277]

Largely on the basis of such passages, Schleiermacher has been accused of being a pantheist.[278] By extension, his view of the universe might also be viewed by some as a form of nature mysticism, an association often made regarding worldviews that, like his, stress the divine immanence. Whatever it is called, Schleiermacher's is a profoundly ecological view of the interrelatedness of all of nature that warrants reconsideration in our own time of ecological crisis. But what exactly would be gained in labelling this as *mysticism* or even *mystical*? One of the things that Schleiermacher accomplished in redefining religion as he did was to democratize, so to speak, religion and religious authority anew. Would the importance of that be obscured or undermined by shifting the vocabulary to *mysticism* as a way to describe it?

This in turn raises the question of whether in Christianity the mystical experience is taken to be rare or eccentric or marginal—or whether it is something integral to the Christian life. Some passages from Schleiermacher might suggest that those mediators of religion are the elite few, but in fact he emphasizes in the *Speeches* and throughout his many works that this possibility holds for all. And so his distinguishing *feeling* from *knowing* can be read as a subversion of those who claim religious authority based on their knowledge or education. He chides the despisers of religion: "Yes, even when you look down your noses at them, the pious concede, gladly and ungrudgingly, that they do not possess knowledge as you do."[279] For Schleiermacher, the "predisposition to God-consciousness" is an "inner impulse"[280] of the human being. It is Christ who has realized full God-consciousness, and, according to Schleiermacher, "the constant potency of His God-consciousness…was a veritable existence of God in Him."[281] Christ redeems by drawing "believers into the power of His God-consciousness."[282] Therefore, although it may be developed to varying degrees in different people, all Christians share this God-consciousness and grow in it, and the degree to which they may differ is in the end minimal, because it is all grace.[283] Thus if it is a form of mysticism, would it be better understood as what has been called "everyday mysticism"?[284] If so, how would this differ from *faith*?

When Schleiermacher talks about God, the language he employs is not that of mystical union (*unio mystica*) between the individual and God, but is instead the language of surrender. Two points are important here. For Schleiermacher, God does not work on individuals as individuals,[285] and no individual has access to God apart from the natural causal system, apart from history, or apart from the corporate life. Schleiermacher emphasizes instead the *one eternal divine decree* that draws humanity to God, and he sees creation and the incarnation as the working out of that one eternal decree. In that sense, there is an eschatological and corporate dimension. Furthermore, if there is a union with God on the part of the individual, it is to be found in our giving up our insistence on our own isolated, finite existence and consenting to the divine decree. When Schleiermacher talks about surrendering to God, his religious language is arguably at its most powerful, as his words spoken at Nathanael's graveside (quoted earlier) attest. In earlier Christian mysticisms, mystical union was viewed as a foreglimpse of the heavenly goal of eternal life and the beatific vision. In Schleiermacher's rendition, his language of surrender does have to do with eternal life, but for him it is not an ecstatic experience or a foreglimpse; rather, the surrender occurs in an ongoing, daily way so that one lives her or his life in eternity—this is "eternal youth."[286]

In Schleiermacher, the language of union (or of something sounding like mystical union) is found more in how he describes faith in Christ and the work of the Spirit. Indeed, as we have seen, he uses the term *mystical* when explaining how Christ "unites" Christians to himself.[287] And when Schleiermacher talks about the Spirit of God, his language often sounds mystical. For instance, in the sermon given on Pentecost Sunday (1825), he declares, "Just as the Spirit weds with the human spirit within us in the most intimate way, so too the Spirit unveils the depths of our own being more thoroughly and consolingly than our own spirit does, since the Spirit opens up for us the depths of the Godhead."[288] His understanding of the Spirit is often neglected but would have to be taken into account in any consideration of mystical aspects of his thought.

In the *Christmas Dialogue*, there are two passages with arguably mystical characteristics in that they point to moments of transcendence, signal transformations of the heart, and suggest ineffability. But what is critical in both of these key passages is that the experiences being described involve music and are communal in nature. Neither fact can be ignored. In the first passage, which serves as the transition between the opening scene and the conversation, three of the characters are singing carols, which results in a kind of ecstatic moment for everyone:

> Soon they had everyone listening devoutly, and when they had finished, it happened, as it always does, that religious music effects first a silent satisfaction and retreat of the heart. There were a few silent moments in which everyone knew that each and every heart was lovingly directed towards all the rest, and towards something higher still.[289]

The second passage is found at the very end of the *Dialogue*; it is the "unsaying"[290] of Josef, who arrives late to the celebration: "All forms are too rigid to me, and all speech too tedious and cold. The speechless subject demands or generates in me a speechless joy, and in my joy I can only smile and cheer like a child."[291] Giving an account of his visits to other households on Christmas Eve, he exclaims,

> It was one long, caressing kiss that I gave to the world, and now my joy with you shall be the last impress of my lips. You know that you are the dearest to me of all. Come then, and above all, if she is not already asleep, bring the child [Sofie] along, and let me see your splendors, and let us be merry and sing something pious and joyful.[292]

It is not incidental that in both these scenes, when the limits of language have been reached, it is music that carries them in their celebration and in their communion with each other. Music was, in fact, one of Schleiermacher's favorite analogies for religion. In particular, like so many of his age, he was captivated by the new, apparently nonrepresentational music.[293] This serves as a reminder that, if we do describe Schleiermacher's piety as mystical, we must take care to note his inescapably communal understanding of that and must also take care to keep the several images he uses in mind (that is, the universe *and* music). Also, it reminds us that, for Schleiermacher, there are many other forms of communication than verbal; gestures and sounds are essential modes of real communication for him.

Caution therefore needs to be observed when treating the matter of ineffability in Schleiermacher. First, in passages such as these just quoted from the *Christmas Dialogue*, an experience may point to ineffability in the sense that it is nonverbal, but that is not to say that it is noncommunicative or asocial, at least not in a way that Schleiermacher emphasizes in his writing. Second, Schleiermacher does speak in the *Speeches* of the ineffability of religion: "For, however much I would like to show you religion in its original, singular form, it is not disposed to emerging publicly but only lets itself be seen in secrecy by those who love it. Wherever it is publicly presented and substituted, it is no longer quite itself."[294] Yet he immediately goes on to say that this is true of many things and is not unique to religion. This is but one reminder that, in considering possible mystical elements in Schleiermacher's thought, one also has to attend to the rhetorical framing of certain passages. Third and finally, for Schleiermacher piety requires not that the divine mysteries be sought out but rather that they be humbly accepted as just that. A Christian life lived "in the depths of the Godhead" is a simple one: it is one in which the Spirit of God in the person calls out, "Dear Father."[295]

Underlying all aspects of what may be deemed "mystical" in Schleiermacher's life and thought is his simple conviction that "God is love."

Texts and Translations

A Note on the Texts

The first title piece of this volume, *The Christmas Celebration: A Dialogue*, is the first English translation of the first edition of *Die*

Weihnachtsfeier: Ein Gespräch (1806); it is based on the critical edition in *KGA* 1/5: *Schriften aus der Hallenser Zeit 1804–1807.*[296]

The second title piece, "The Second *Speech*: 'On the Essence of Religion,'" is a translation of the full text of "Über das Wesen der Religion," the second of Schleiermacher's five *Speeches* in *Über die Religion. Reden an die Gebildeten unter ihren Verächtern (On Religion: Speeches to Its Cultured Despisers).* This translation is the first in English of the second edition (1806) and is based on the critical edition in *KGA* 1/12: *Über die Religion (2.-) 4. Auflage, Monologen (2.-) 4. Auflage.*[297] Inevitably, the present volume will be criticized for only including one of the five *Speeches*, since they are meant to be read as one whole; in particular, it will also likely be argued that the second *Speech* should not be read apart from the fifth *Speech*. The simple facts, however, are that any volume of works on Schleiermacher's spirituality would be incomplete without something from the *Speeches*; it would neither make sense nor be feasible to include all five *Speeches*, since there are ample translations of the *Speeches* available; and what is important is that, if not all *Speeches* can be included, what *is* included should be complete and not excerpted. Hence, this volume includes the *entire* second *Speech*, the most famous and most read of the *Speeches*. The hope is that this first translation of the second edition will make a new contribution by enabling English-speaking scholars to compare passages (and their revisions) in the first, second, and third editions.

This volume includes but two of hundreds and hundreds of sermons Schleiermacher delivered over his forty-year career. Obviously, the point is not to be exhaustive but indicative. These two particular sermons are later ones (1825, 1832) that reflect his mature theological thought and were chosen because they address his views of the Holy Spirit and his later Christology, which would otherwise not have been represented in this volume. The first sermon, delivered on Pentecost Sunday, May 1825, is from *SW* 2/2: 231–48. The second sermon, delivered on December 9, 1832, is from *SW* 2/3: 427–35. The *KGA* is currently in the midst of publishing division 3: *Predigten*, which covers his sermons. To date, four of the fourteen planned volumes have been published. When all is completed, these two sermons should be found in volumes 9 and 13, respectively.

A Note on Translating

Translating Schleiermacher is a notoriously difficult task, made all the more daunting by the fact that he himself was a master translator. Early in his career, in 1798 before he had made a name for himself, he published a translation of Londoner Joseph Fawcett's *Sermons*. Yet it was the monumental project of translating Plato's corpus, a project originally undertaken in collaboration with Friedrich Schlegel, which proved so significant for the history of Plato studies and for the development of interpretive theory. Schleiermacher's lectures on *Hermeneutics*, which he first delivered in Halle 1805, were the direct result of his work on translating, interpreting, and ordering Plato's dialogues; in turn, he applied that interpretive theory to a historical-critical study of New Testament texts. He also delivered an address, "On the Different Methods of Translating," to the Royal Academy of Sciences in 1813.

Overall, I have tried to follow Schleiermacher's own preference for bringing the reader back to the author rather than contemporizing the author too much for the reader. These remain early nineteenth-century texts. The language is more formal than ours, especially in the *Christmas Dialogue* and in the correspondence, and some terms seem either old-fashioned or their meanings have shifted, and so need some explanation. On this score, the *Deutsches Wörterbuch*, begun by Jacob and Wilhelm Grimm in 1838, has proven indispensable. I have tried to preserve certain rhythms of speech and to be consistent in translating certain key terms, so that readers might have a feel for Schleiermacher and can weigh and compare certain key terms for themselves.

At the same time, I have also tried to make the texts readable for the twenty-first-century Anglophone readers, which means I have had to shorten many sentences and sometimes have reworked more passive constructions. Schleiermacher's sentences can run for ten to twenty or more lines, held together by the declension of gendered nouns and pronouns and their agreement with verbs; English cannot always sustain that, at least not in a way that is pleasant to read. Still, I have tried not to shorten the sentences in such a way as to break the connecting flow of thought or insult the intelligence of readers. Schleiermacher expected his reader to sustain a line of thought, to wait for the cumulative point.

I have also tried to make his writing accessible to a new generation of readers by using only gender-inclusive language. I believe these to be the first translations in English to do so consistently. At points this might prove awkward, but less so, I suggest, than using *man* and *he* to stand for all human beings. There are times, however, when the context is heavily gendered in a manner integral to the meaning, and so in these places the gender-exclusive language is maintained.

Notes

1. For the history of the term *spirituality*, see Bernard McGinn, "The Letter and the Spirit: Spirituality as an Academic Discipline," in *Minding the Spirit: The Study of Christian Spirituality*, ed. Elizabeth Dreyer and Mark Burrows (Baltimore: Johns Hopkins University Press, 2005), 25–41.

2. John Calvin, *Institutes of the Christian Religion*, ed. John T. McNeill, trans. Ford Lewis Battles (Louisville: Westminster John Knox Press, 2006). 1:2:1, p. 41.

3. Schleiermacher, *Der christliche Glaube nach den Grundsätzen der evangelischen Kirche im Zusammenhange dargestellt* (Berlin, 1830/31), 2 vols. (hereafter, *Gl.*), in *KGA* 1/13:1–2, ed. Rolf Schäfer (New York: Walter de Gruyter, 2003). English translation: *The Christian Faith* (*CF*) by H. R. Mackintosh and J. S. Stewart (Edinburgh: T & T Clark, 1928). Citations will be to proposition and subparagraph number, and then to page numbers in *CF*. When translation is mine, citation will include page number in *KGA* with cross reference to *CF* (e.g., *Gl.* §108.1; *KGA* 1/13:2:172; cf. *CF* 481).

4. *CF* 5, 12, respectively.

5. McGinn, "The Letter and the Spirit," 32–33.

6. Sandra M. Schneiders, "Approaches to the Study of Christian Spirituality," in *The Blackwell Companion to Christian Spirituality*, ed. Arthur Holder (Oxford: Blackwell, 2005), 16.

7. Schneiders' definition reflects her own Catholic, ecumenical commitments: "Christian spirituality as Christian specifies the horizon of ultimate value as the triune God revealed in Jesus Christ to whom Scripture normatively witnesses and whose life is communicated to the believer by the Holy Spirit making her or him a child of God. This new life, which Paul

calls 'life in the Spirit'...is celebrated sacramentally within the believing community of the church and lived in the world as mission in and to the coming reign of God" (ibid., 17).

8. I borrow the term from Raymond Williams, *Keywords: A Vocabulary of Culture and Society* (London: Fontana Press, 1988), 15.

9. Rowan Williams, *The Wound of Knowledge: Christian Spirituality from the New Testament to St. John of the Cross*, rev. ed. (London: Darton, Longman & Todd, 1990), 2; cited by Philip F. Sheldrake, *Explorations in Spirituality: History, Theology and Social Practice* (Mahwah, NJ: Paulist Press, 2010), 62.

10. For example, Martin Riesebrodt, while he gives an appreciative reading of Schleiermacher's novelty when it comes to definitions of religion, notes in passing that the "now widespread notion of 'spirituality' continues the individualistic orientation of Romantic discourse" (*The Promise of Salvation: A Theory of Religion* [Chicago: University of Chicago Press, 2010], 5).

11. McGinn, "The Letter and the Spirit," 33.

12. Sheldrake, *Explorations*, 5.

13. *OR1* 209.

14. See Pierre Hadot, *Philosophy as a Way of Life: Spiritual Exercises from Socrates to Foucault*, ed. Arnold I. Davidson, trans. Michael Chase (Cambridge, MA: Blackwell, 1995), and *The Inner Citadel: The Meditations of Marcus Aurelius*, trans. Michael Chase (Cambridge, MA: Harvard University Press, 1998).

15. Each section also includes ample discussion of his systematic dogmatic work *The Christian Faith*, excerpts of which are not included in this volume because excerpts are unpleasant to read and hard to understand out of context, and because Schleiermacher's own interpretive theory does not allow for ripping parts out of the original whole. Still, the work is of immense importance and so relevant aspects of it are discussed in this introduction.

16. Sources: Kurt Nowak, *Schleiermacher: Leben, Werk, und Wirkung* (Göttingen: Vandenhoeck & Ruprecht, 2002); Martin Redeker, *Schleiermacher: Life and Thought*, trans. John Wallhausser (Philadelphia: Fortress Press, 1973); Schleiermacher's correspondence; and the historical introductions in relevant volumes of the *KGA*.

17. Schleiermacher to G. A. Reimer; Letter 1220, in *KGA* 5/5:392–93; full text translated below, 255.

18. A system of belief and spirituality that focuses on Christ's suffering, in particular on the wounds Christ received during the passion. See below, notes 149 and 150.

19. Schleiermacher, "Autobiography," in Rowan, *The Life of Schleiermacher as Unfolded in His Autobiography and Letters*, ed. Frederica Rowan, 2 vols. (London: Smith, Elder and Co., 1860), 1:6–7; see *Selbstbiographie*, in *ASL* 1:7.

20. Schleiermacher to his father, Barby, January 21, 1787; Letter 53, in *KGA* 5/1:49–52; full text below, 251.

21. Schleiermacher to his father, Barby, February 12, 1787; Letter 55, in *KGA* 5/1:57.

22. Immanuel Kant's *Critique of Pure Reason* had appeared in 1781, the *Critique of Practical Reason* in 1788, while Schleiermacher was a student at Halle.

23. Schleiermacher to his father, Schlobittten, August 16, 1791; Letter 160, in *KGA* 5/1:221.

24. Anthony J. La Vopa explains the significance of this project: "The virtual obsession with *Pädagogik* has been regarded, often with good reason, as symptomatic of the apolitical preference for individual moral improvement over structural change in the German Enlightenment. But in Gedike's reform thought pedagogy became the disciplinary core of a new professional ideology. In both its ambitions and its inhibitions, that ideology constituted a kind of political identity that has been relatively neglected in the current attention to a 'political' Enlightenment" ("The Politics of Enlightenment: Friedrich Gedike and German Professional Ideology," *The Journal of Modern History* 62, no. 1 [Mar. 1990]: 36).

25. See Albert L. Blackwell, *Schleiermacher's Early Philosophy of Life: Determinism, Freedom, and Phantasy* (Chico, CA: Scholars Press, 1982); Julia A. Lamm, "The Early Philosophical Roots of Schleiermacher's Notion of Gefühl, 1788–1794," *Harvard Theological Review* 87, no. 1 (1994): 67–105; and Brent W. Sockness, "Was Schleiermacher a Virtue Ethicist? *Tugend* and *Bildung* in the Early Ethical Writings," *Zeitschrift für neuere Theologiegeschichte* 8, no. 1 (2001): 1–33.

26. See Gérard Vallée, *The Spinoza Conversations between Lessing & Jacobi: Text with Excerpts from the Ensuing Controversy* (Lanham, NY: University Press of America, 1988). See also Julia A. Lamm, "Pantheism and Romanticism," in *The Nineteenth-Century Theologians*, ed. David Ferguson (Blackwell, 2010), 165–86.

27. Schleiermacher, "Spinozismus," and "Kurze Darstellung des Spinozistischen Systems," in *KGA* 1/1:511–58 and 559–82, respectively. For a discussion of these essays and their significance, see Julia A. Lamm, "Schleiermacher's Post-Kantian Spinozism: The Early Essays on Spinoza, 1793–94," *The Journal of Religion* 74, no. 4 (1994): 476–505, also published as chap. 1 in *The Living God: Schleiermacher's Theological Appropriation of*

Spinoza (University Park, PA: Pennsylvania State University Press, 1996), 13–56. An English translation of these essays is now available: Patrick D. Dinsmore, ed., *A Facing-Page Translation from German into English of Friedrich Schleiermacher's 'Kurze Darstellung des Spinozistischen Systems' and 'Spinozismus'* (Lewiston, NY: Edwin Mellen, 2013).

28. For more on Schleiermacher's work at the Charité, see Kurt Nowak, "Schleiermacher als Prediger am Charité-Krankenhaus in Berlin (1796–1802)," *Theologische Zeitschrift* 41 (1985): 391–411, and *Schleiermacher*, 74–78; and Simon Gerber, "Seelsorge ganz unten—Schleiermacher, der Charité-Prediger," in *Wissenschaft und Geselligkeit: Friedrich Schleiermacher in Berlin 1796–1802*, ed. Andrea Arndt (Berlin: Walter de Gruyter, 2009), 15–42.

29. Nowak, *Schleiermacher*, 77.

30. Sack was married to Spalding's daughter, Johanna.

31. For a full treatment of Early German Romanticism that also offers a critique of the history of interpretation, see Frederick C. Beiser, *The Romantic Imperative: The Concept of Early German Romanticism* (Cambridge, MA: Harvard University Press, 2003).

32. Friedrich Schlegel, "Athenaeum Fragments" (1798), no. 116, in *Philosophical Fragments*, trans. Peter Firchow (Minneapolis: University of Minnesota Press, 1991), 31–32.

33. See Ursula Klein, "Der Chemiekult der Frühromantik," in Arndt, *Wissenschaft und Geselligkeit*, 67–92.

34. Beiser, *Romantic Imperative*, 27.

35. They were so close and so associated with each other that a caricature of them, in which Schleiermacher was depicted as half her size and with a copy of the *Speeches* in his pocket, was published in 1800.

36. See Ruth Drucilla Richardson, *The Role of Women in the Life and Thought of the Early Schleiermacher (1768–1806): An Historical Overview* (Lewiston, NY: Edwin Mellen Press, 1991), 76–110.

37. Schleiermacher, *Über die Religion. Reden an die Gebildeten unter ihren Verächtern*, 1st ed. (1799), in *KGA* 1/2:185–325. English translation (*OR1*) by Richard Crouter, ed., *On Religion: Speeches to Its Cultured Despisers* (Cambridge: Cambridge University Press, 1988). A translation of the 2nd edition (1806) of the second *Speech* ("On the Essence of Religion") is given below in this volume.

38. For a succinct discussion of the history of reception of the *Speeches*, see Richard Crouter, "*On Religion* as a Religious Classic: Hermeneutical Musings after Two Hundred Years," chap. 11 in *Friedrich Schleiermacher: Between Enlightenment and Romanticism* (New York: Cambridge University Press, 2005), 248–70.

39. *OR1* 89.

40. Ibid.

41. Ibid., 84.

42. Schleiermacher, "On the Essence of Religion," 164. References to "On the Essence of Religion" are to pages in this volume below.

43. Ibid., 165.

44. Ibid., 162–63.

45. Ibid., 164.

46. Ibid., 183.

47. This is discussed further in sections 2 and 3 of this introduction.

48. *OR1* 144.

49. Ibid.,145.

50. Ibid., 190.

51. See ibid., 198–99.

52. Ibid., 213.

53. Ibid., 218.

54. See "On the Essence of Religion," 156; see also 154. Schleiermacher maintained a separating out of the three can only occur in contemplation or reflection; in life they remain related. In the first edition, he specified knowing as metaphysics and doing as morals. With regard to metaphysics, he was countering Fichte's philosophical idealism; with regard to morals, he was countering Kant's reduction of religion to a postulate of practical (ethical) reason as well as a bourgeois, conventional morality that conflated religion with being busy and following rules. In the second edition, in a long revision he added to the beginning of the *Speech*, he painted a much more complex view of different ways of knowing and acting. See below, 154–61.

55. Schleiermacher, "On the Essence of Religion," 167.

56. Ibid., 185.

57. Ibid., 206.

58. Ibid., 189.

59. Ibid., 172.

60. "In the flesh of his flesh and bone of his bone, he discovered humanity—anticipating all directions and forms of love already in this original love—and in humanity he found the world. From this moment onward, he became capable of hearing the voice of the deity and answering it" (ibid., 197).

61. "You lie then immediately on the bosom of the infinite world, you are in this moment her soul; for you feel all her powers and her infinite life as your own; she is in this moment your body, for you penetrate her mus-

cles and limbs as your own, and your sense and presentiment bestir her innermost nerves" (ibid., 170).

62. See ibid., 189–99.

63. Ibid., 203.

64. See ibid., especially 216–23.

65. Albert L. Blackwell, "The Antagonistic Correspondence of 1801 between Chaplain Sack and His Protégé Schleiermacher," *Harvard Theological Review* 74, no. 1 (1981): 104.

66. See Richard Crouter and Julie Klassen, eds., *A Debate on Jewish Emancipation and Christian Theology in Old Berlin* (Indianapolis: Hackett, 2004).

67. See Schleiermacher to Spener, Berlin, November, 8, 1799; Letter 717, in *KGA* 5/3:230–31.

68. Schleiermacher, "Gedanken III," (1790–1801), #34; in *KGA* 1/2:127.

69. Schleiermacher, *Monologen: Eine Neujahrsgabe*, in *KGA* 1/3:1–61. English translation: *Soliloquies: A New Year's Gift*, by Horace Leland Friess (Chicago: Open Court, 1926; reprint, Westport, CT: Hyperion, 1979). For a sustained discussion of the *Soliloquies*, see Brent W. Sockness, "Schleiermacher and the Ethics of Authenticity: The *Monologen* of 1800," *The Journal of Religious Ethics* 32, no. 3 (2004): 477–517.

70. Schleiermacher, *Soliloquies*, 28.

71. Ibid. 30–31.

72. Ibid., 31.

73. Ibid., 45.

74. Ibid., 97.

75. *Platons Werke von F. Schleiermacher* (Berlin: 1/1, 1804; 1/2 and 2/1, 1805; 2/2, 1807; 2/3, 1809; 3/1, 1828; 2nd ed., 1817). Schleiermacher's "Introductions" to the Platonic dialogues are available in *Friedrich Daniel Ernst Schleiermacher, Über die Philosophie Platons*, ed. Peter M. Steiner (Hamburg: Felix Meiner, 1996); an earlier English translation of these by William Dobson appears under the title *Introductions to the Dialogues of Plato* (Cambridge and London, 1836; reprint, New York: Arno Press, 1973). Schleiermacher's translations, now separated from his "Introductions," can be found in *Platon—Werke*, 8 volumes in Greek and German, ed. Gunther Eigler (Darmstadt: Wissenschaftliche Buchgesellschaft, 1990).

76. See Julia A. Lamm, "Schleiermacher as Plato Scholar," *The Journal of Religion* 80, no. 2 (2000): 206–39.

77. See Schleiermacher to his sister, Berlin, July 25–August 16, 1798; Letter 496, in *KGA* 5/2:371.

78. See Schleiermacher to Reimer, below, 255.

79. Schleiermacher, *Grundlinien einer Kritik der bisherigen Sittenlehre* (1803), in *KGA* 1/4: 27–357.

80. Schleiermacher to Henriette von Willich, Halle, October 18, 1805; Letter 2046, in *KGA* 5/8:335–36.

81. Schleiermacher to the von Willichs, Halle, November 26, 1805; Letter 2081, in *KGA* 5/8:375.

82. Schleiermacher, *Die Weihnachtsfeier. Ein Gespräch* (1806), in *KGA*, 1/5:43–98. For shorthand, I refer to it as the *Christmas Dialogue*.

83. For more recent accounts of these debates, see Julia A. Lamm, "Schleiermacher's *Christmas Dialogue* as Platonic Dialogue," *The Journal of Religion* 92, no. 3 (July 2012): 392–420; and Elisabeth Hartlieb, *Geschlechterdifferenz im Denken Friederich Schleiermachers* (New York: Walter de Gruyter, 2006). See also Richard R. Niebuhr, *Schleiermacher on Christ and Religion: A New Introduction* (New York: Charles Scribner's Sons, 1964; reprint, Eugene, OR: Wipf and Stock, 2009); and Ruth Drucilla Richardson, "Friedrich Schleiermacher's *Weihnachtsfeier* as 'Universal Poetry': The Impact of Friedrich Schlegel on the Intellectual Development of the Young Schleiermacher" (PhD dissertation, Drew University, 1985).

84. See Julia A. Lamm, "Reading Plato's Dialectics: Schleiermacher's Insistence on Dialectics as Dialogical," *Zeitschrift für neuere Theologiegeschichte / Journal for the History of Modern Theology* 10, no. 1 (2003): 1–25.

85. Matthias Morgenroth, *Weihnachts-Christentum. Moderner Religiosität auf der Spur* (Gütersloh: Chr. Kaiser/Gütersloher Verlagshaus, 2002), 16.

86. See ibid., 21, 36, 45, 106.

87. See Nowak, *Schleiermacher*, 164–65.

88. Schleiermacher, "Über den sogenannten ersten Brief des Paulos an den Timotheos," in *KGA* 1/5:153–242.

89. Clara, Hanna, Hildegard, and Nathanael.

90. There, in 1831, he confirmed the future chancellor of Germany, Otto von Bismarck (1815–98).

91. He was a part of, as well as a transformative figure within, a new style of preaching in the early nineteenth century. For more on his preaching, see Dawn DeVries, *Jesus Christ in the Preaching of Calvin and Schleiermacher* (Louisville: Westminster John Knox Press, 1996). Schleiermacher's influence also extended to Jewish congregations. See Alexander Altmann, "The New Style of Preaching in Nineteenth-Century German Jewry," in *Studies in Nineteenth-Century Jewish Intellectual History* (Cambridge, MA: Harvard University Press, 1964), 65–116, and "Zur Frühgeschichte der jüdischen Predigt in Deutschland: Leopold Zunz als

Prediger," in *Von der mittelalterlichen zur modernen Aufklärung: Studien zur jüdischen Geistesgeschichte* (Tübingen: J.C.B. Mohr/Paul Siebeck, 1987), 249–99.

92. He wrote an influential public essay on the modern concept of a university in 1808, entitled *Occasional Thoughts on Universities in the German Sense*, trans. Terrence N. Tice and Edwina Lawler (Lewiston, NY: Edwin Mellen, 1991). For more on this, see Crouter, "A Proposal for a New Berlin University," in *Between Enlightenment and Romanticism*, 140–68.

93. See Nowak, *Schleiermacher*, 209–15.

94. For more on his involvement in bringing about the Church of the Union, see Iain G. Nicol, ed., *Friedrich Schleiermacher on Creeds, Confessions and Church Union: That They May Be One* (Lewiston, NY: Edwin Mellen Press, 2004).

95. See Schleiermacher, *The Life of Jesus*, ed. Jack C. Verheyden, trans. S. MacLean Gilmour (Philadelphia: Fortress Press, 1975).

96. Friedrich Schleiermacher, *On the Glaubenslehre: Two Letters to Dr. Lücke*, ed. and trans. James Duke and Francis Schüssler Fiorenza (Chico, CA: Scholars Press, 1981).

97. *Gl.* §15; *CF* 76.

98. *Gl.* §16; *CF* 78.

99. *BO* §195, p. 71; see *Gl.* §19. John E. Thiel explains the significance of this: "Since its appearance in the nineteenth century, the principle of doctrinal development has contributed significantly to the interpretation of the continuity of Christian tradition. The development of doctrine has become a central presupposition of theological hermeneutics and a fixture in modern approaches to theological method. Although we associate this principle with John Henry Newman's *Essay on the Development of Doctrine* (1845), an earlier, original theory of development can be found in the work of Friedrich D. E. Schleiermacher (1768–1834). It was Schleiermacher's theory that introduced the conception of theological authorship to the Christian tradition" (*Imagination and Authority: Theological Authorship in the Modern Tradition* [Minneapolis: Fortress Press, 1991], 35).

100. For more on Schleiermacher's reading of the Old Testament, see Paul E. Capetz, "Friedrich Schleiermacher on the Old Testament," *Harvard Theological Review* 102, no. 3 (2009): 297–326, and "The Old Testament as a Witness to Jesus Christ: Historical Criticism and Theological Exegesis of the Bible according to Karl Barth," *The Journal of Religion* 90, no. 4 (2010): 475–506. For more on his reading of the New Testament, see DeVries, *Jesus Christ in the Preaching*; and Christine Helmer, "Schleiermacher's Exegetical Theology and the New Testament," chap. 12 in *The Cambridge Companion to Friedrich Schleiermacher*, ed. Jacqueline Mariña (Cambridge: Cambridge

University Press, 2005), 229–47; and Verheyden, "Introduction," in *The Life of Jesus*.

101. See John E. Thiel, *Nonfoundationalism* (Minneapolis: Fortress Press, 1994).

102. Schleiermacher understood ethics in broad terms. As Brent Sockness explains, *Sittenlehre* for Schleiermacher "becomes a comprehensive theory of the distinctively human-historical world. As such, it aims to provide a complete and systematic account of the different forms of human activity through which reason (*Vernunft*) appropriates and shapes nature (*Natur*) to its purposes" ("The Forgotten Moralist: Friedrich Schleiermacher and the Science of Spirit," *Harvard Theological Review* 96, no. 3 [2003]: 343).

103. *CF* 5.

104. *CF* 52.

105. *Gl.* §30.2, *KGA* 1/13:1:194; see *CF* 126.

106. *Gl.* §30.3; *CF* 126.

107. *CF* 194. For a sustained discussion of Schleiermacher's treatment of the divine attributes, see Lamm, *The Living God*, chaps. 5 and 6.

108. *CF* 149.

109. *CF* 170. See B. A. Gerrish, "Nature and the Theater of Redemption: Schleiermacher on Christian Dogmatics and the Creation Story," in *Continuing the Reformation: Essays on Modern Religious Thought* (Chicago: University of Chicago Press, 1993), 196–218.

110. *Gl.* §60.3; *CF* 247.

111. Walter E. Wyman, Jr., "Sin and Redemption," in Mariña, *Cambridge Companion*, 134.

112. *Gl.* §66.2; *CF* 273.

113. *CF* 285. As Wyman has also argued, Schleiermacher's is more an Irenaean than an Augustinian view of sin; see "Rethinking the Christian Doctrine of Sin: Friedrich Schleiermacher and Hick's 'Irenaean Type,'" *The Journal of Religion* 74, no. 2 (Apr., 1994): 199–217.

114. For a fuller discussion of this, see section 3 of the introduction below, under the theme of "Christ and Grace."

115. See note 3 above.

116. Richard Crouter, "Shaping an Academic Discipline: The *Brief Outline on the Study of Theology*," chap. 6 in Mariña, *Cambridge Companion*, 119.

117. For conflicting reports about this, see Nowak, *Schleiermacher*, 450.

118. Hadot, *Philosophy as a Way of Life*, 201–2.

119. Ibid., 90.

120. See ibid., 63–65.

121. Hadot writes, "For the ancients in general, but particularly for the Stoics and for Marcus Aurelius, philosophy was, above all, a way of life. This is why the *Meditations* strive, by means of an ever-renewed effort, to describe this way of life and to sketch the model that one must have constantly in view: that of the ideal good man. Ordinary people are content to think in any old way, to act haphazardly, and to undergo grudgingly whatever befalls them. The good man, however, will try, insofar as he is able, to act justly in the service of other people, to accept serenely those events which do not depend on him, and to think with rectitude and veracity" (*The Inner Citadel*, 35).

122. Ibid., 50. According to Hadot, "Marcus writes only in order to have the dogmas and rules of life always present to his mind" (ibid.).

123. Hadot, *Philosophy as a Way of Life*, 85–86. A typographical error in the English translation incorrectly renders *parole* as *world* rather than *word*. See Hadot, *Exercices spirituels et philosophie antique* (Paris: Études Augustiniennes, 1981), 35.

124. As the translator of the English edition notes, the *Soliloquies* "is one of the very few writings in the literature of German philosophic idealism, which imparts experiences and beliefs directly instead of through a medium of speculation and dialectic" (Friess, *Soliloquies*, xi).

125. See Terrence N. Tice, "Schleiermacher's Interpretation of Christmas: 'Christmas Eve,' 'The Christian Faith,' and the Christmas Sermons," *The Journal of Religion* 47, no. 2 (1967): 100–26; Hermann Patsch, "Die esoterische Kommunikationsstruktur der 'Weihnachtsfeier.' Über Anspielungen und Zitate," in *Schleiermacher in Context: Papers from the 1988 International Symposium on Schleiermacher at Hernnhut*, ed. Ruth Drucilla Richardson (Lewiston: Edwin Mellen, 1991), 132–56, and "Die zeitgenössische Rezeption der 'Weihnachtsfeier,'" in *Internationaler Schleiermacher-Kongreß Berlin 1984*, ed. Kurt-Victor Selge (Berlin: Walter de Gruyter, 1985), 1215–28.

126. Schleiermacher, "On the Essence of Religion," 152.

127. Ibid., 159.

128. Ibid., 167.

129. Ibid., 198.

130. Ibid., 168, 198, respectively.

131. Ibid., 168.

132. Schleiermacher, *Occasional Thoughts on Universities*, 29.

133. *Gl.* §16.1, *KGA* 1/13:1:130; see *CF* 78.

134. DeVries, *Jesus Christ in the Preaching*, 51–52.

135. *Gl.* §16.1, *CF* 79.

136. See, e.g., Schleiermacher's comments about Reinhold at the end of his letter to Jacobi, 265 below.

137. *Gl.* §30.2; *CF* 126.

138. DeVries, *Jesus Christ in the Preaching*, 55.

139. See note 78 above.

140. Niebuhr coined this term with respect to Schleiermacher: "His theology is Christo-morphic in two senses. First of all, it asserts that Jesus of Nazareth objectively exhibits what human nature ideally is, although Schleiermacher does not on this account counsel Christians to imitate Jesus in any naïve way....In this sense, then, the redeemer is the measure of human nature. And, in the second place, the redeemer is the historical person whose presence mediated through Scriptures, preaching and the Holy Spirit becomes the abiding occasion for the reorganization and clarifying of the Christian's consciousness of his [sic] absolute dependence, of his identity in the world, an of his appropriate actions toward and responses to others" (*Schleiermacher on Christ and Religion*, 212–13).

141. See above, 6–9, 25.

142. See above, 7–9, and below, 250–54.

143. See below, 263.

144. See Lori Pearson, "Schleiermacher and the Christologies Behind Chalcedon," *Harvard Theological Review* 96, no. 3 (2003): 349–67.

145. Schleiermacher to Jacobi, 1818; see below, 263.

146. This does not mean he was always correct in his assessment, since he stands at the very beginning of the historical-critical investigation of the New Testament. So, for instance, he still believed that the fourth Gospel was written by Jesus' disciple. See Verheyden, "Introduction" in *The Life of Jesus*, xxxi–xxxii.

147. See above, 8–9.

148. See letter to his father, below, 250–54. On penal substitution, see Calvin, *Institutes* 2.12.3–5.

149. Schleiermacher defines "wounds-theology" (*Wundentheologie*) as that "which thought to find the deep import of the suffering of Christ in its sensuous details, and hence, for the sake of allegorical trivialities, broke up into details the totality of Christ's suffering. Underlying this was a confusion of thought; what can only be attributed to Christ as a sacrifice or victim was transferred to His high-priestly dignity. The victim has no independent activity; it is completely passive in everything which happens to it" (*Gl.* §104.4; *CF* 459).

150. See Ruth Albrecht, "'We Kiss Our Dearest Redeemer through Inward Prayer': Mystical Traditions in Pietism," in *The Wiley-Blackwell*

Companion to Christian Mysticism, ed. Julia A. Lamm (Oxford: Blackwell, 2013), 473–88.

151. A reference to Gotthold Ephraim Lessing (1729–81). It refers to the unbreachable gap that Lessing saw between historical "truths" that had become subject to doubt (e.g., miracles) and certain metaphysical truths; the former, he maintained, cannot be used to establish the latter.

152. Schleiermacher, *Christmas Dialogue*, 139.

153. Ibid., 141.

154. Here he corroborates Morgenroth's thesis. See above, note 85.

155. B. A. Gerrish, *A Prince of the Church: Schleiermacher and the Beginnings of Modern Theology* (Philadelphia: Fortress Press, 1984), 47.

156. Schleiermacher, *Christmas Dialogue*, 144.

157. Ibid., 147.

158. Schleiermacher rather cumbersomely calls this division on grace "The Manner in which Fellowship with the Perfection and Blessedness of the Redeemer Expresses Itself in the Individual Soul" (*CF* 476).

159. *OR1* 219.

160. "If everything finite requires higher mediation in order not to stray even farther from the universe and become dispersed into emptiness and nothingness, in order to retain its connection with the universe and come to conscious awareness of it, then indeed what mediates cannot possibly be something merely finite that, in turn, itself requires mediation" (*OR1* 218–19).

161. See *OR1* 216–21.

162. Niebuhr notes that "the rendering of the German *Urbildlichkeit* by the English term *ideality* paves the way for misunderstanding of the text in these paragraphs, unless the reader keeps in mind that the ideality connoted by *Urbildlichkeit* is closer to the objective, normative *eidos*, or form, of Platonic philosophy than to the a priori ideas of reason in Kantian philosophy" (*Schleiermacher on Christ and Religion*, 219n12). For more on *Urbild* in that context, see Verheyden, "Introduction," in *The Life of Jesus*, xlviii–l.

163. *Gl.* §93; *CF* 377.

164. *Gl.* §93.3; *CF* 382.

165. *Gl.* §93.3; *CF* 382. See also his Sermon on the Second Sunday of Advent, 1832, below.

166. *Gl.* §101.4; *CF* 437. For an account of how Christ is like us in all things save sin, see his Sermon on the Second Sunday of Advent, 1832, 243–46 below.

167. *Gl.* §94; *CF* 385.

168. *Gl.* §100; *CF* 425.

169. *Gl.* §101; *CF* 431.

170. *Gl.* §100.3; cf. *CF* 428–29. *Mystical* and *mysticism* were largely terms of derision during the Enlightenment and through much of the nineteenth century. Furthermore, in the fierce religious polemics of the time, mysticism was usually associated with Catholicism, Pietism, and religious fanaticism, so Schleiermacher's choice here is an unusual and interesting one.

171. *Gl.* §100.3; cf. *CF* 428–29.

172. He cites, e.g., Gal 2:20, Rom 8:10, John 17:23, and 2 Cor 13:5 (see §100.1; *CF* 426).

173. He cites, e.g., Col 3:10 and Eph 4:22, 24 (see §100.1; *CF* 426).

174. *Gl.* §106.2; *CF* 477–78.

175. DeVries, *Jesus Christ in the Preaching*, 58.

176. On the importance of worship in the church and for theology, see Theodore M. Vial, "Friedrich Schleiermacher on the Central Place of Worship in Theology," *Harvard Theological Review* 91, no. 1 (1998): 59–73.

177. See Schleiermacher, Sermon on Pentecost Sunday, 1825, 224–41.

178. For a fuller and more theologically technical discussion of Schleiermacher's doctrine of grace, see Julia A. Lamm, "Schleiermacher's Treatise on Grace," *Harvard Theological Review* 101, no. 2 (2008): 133–68.

179. For descriptions of sanctification, see both of his Sermons translated below.

180. *Gl.* §106; *CF* 262.

181. *Gl.* §101.2; *CF* 433. Cf. §89.3; *CF* 368.

182. *Gl.* §101.2; *CF* 433.

183. See *Gl.* §86.2; *CF* 356.

184. *Gl.* §108.6; *CF* 495.

185. *Gl.* §80.1; *CF* 326–27.

186. *Gl.* §108.2; *KGA* 1/13:2:179; *CF* 486.

187. For example, in the Smalcald Articles (1537), Luther wrote under *Repentance*, "Now this is the thunderbolt of God, by means of which he destroys both the open sinner and the false saint and allows no one to be right but drives the whole lot of them into terror and despair. This is the hammer of which Jeremiah speaks....This is not 'active contrition,' a contrived remorse, but 'passive contrition' [torture of conscience], true affliction of the heart, suffering, and the pain of death" (pt. 3, art. 3, 2, in *The Book of Concord: The Confessions of the Evangelical Lutheran Church*, ed. Robert Kolb and Timothy J. Wengert [Minneapolis: Fortress Press, 2000], 312). Schleiermacher cites several Protestant creeds and confessions in §108. He quotes from article 12 of the *Augsburg Confession* (1530): "Now,

properly speaking, repentance consists of two parts: one is contrition or the terrors that strike the conscience when sin is recognized; the other is faith, which is brought to life by the Gospel or absolution. This faith believes that sins are forgiven on account of Christ" (12: 3–5; Kolb and Wengert, 45). *The Solid Declaration* (hereafter, *SD*) of the *Formula of Concord* (1577) carries through this emphasis on the divine wrath and the terror it causes in the soul: "Through these means (this preaching and hearing of his Word), God goes about his work and breaks our hearts and draws people, so that they recognize their sins and God's wrath through the preaching of the law and feel real terror, regret, and sorrow in their hearts" (art. 2:54; Kolb and Wengert, 554). For more on Schleiermacher's use of creeds and confessions, see Walter E. Wyman Jr., "The Role of the Protestant Confessions in Schleiermacher's *The Christian Faith*," *The Journal of Religion* 87, no. 3 (July 2007), 355–85; Lamm, "Schleiermacher's Treatise on Grace," 133–68; and Nicol, *Friedrich Schleiermacher on Creeds, Confessions and Church Union*.

188. *Gl.* §108.2; *KGA* 1/13:2:177; cf. *CF* 484.

189. *Gl.* §108.2; *CF* 484.

190. *Gl.* §108.3; *CF* 487.

191. *Gl.* §108; *CF* 481.

192. *Gl.* §108.2; *KGA* 1/13:2:177; cf. *CF* 484.

193. *Gl.* §110.3; *CF* 509.

194. *Gl.* §108.2; *CF* 485.

195. *Gl.* §110.2; *CF* 508. Note that he does not describe faith as a laying hold of Christ or of Christ's merits, but as joyfulness in having been laid hold of by Christ.

196. *Gl.* §109.4; *CF* 504.

197. *CF* 496.

198. *Gl.* §109.2; *CF* 498.

199. *Gl.* §109.3: *CF* 501.

200. *Gl.* §108.6; *CF* 495.

201. Schleiermacher is especially keen on resisting the theological anthropology in the second article of the *Solid Declaration*. He cites, for instance, paragraph 24, the full text of which reads, "But before people are enlightened, converted, reborn, renewed, and drawn back to God by the Holy Spirit, they cannot in and of themselves, out of their own natural powers, begin, effect, or accomplish anything in spiritual matters for their own conversion or rebirth, any more than a *stone or block of wood or piece of clay*...can. For although they can control their bodies and can listen to the gospel and think about it to a certain extent and even speak of it (as Pharisees and hypocrites do), they regard it as foolishness and cannot believe it. They behave in this case worse than a block of wood, for they are

rebellious against God's will and hostile to it, wherever the Holy Spirit does not exercise his powers in them and ignite and effect faith and other God-pleasing virtues and obedience in them" (art. 2: 24, emphasis added; in Kolb and Wengert, 548–49; cf. *SD* 2 paragraphs 7, 10, 20, 59, 73, 77, 89).

202. Schleiermacher's spelling, *Gemüth*, is outdated.

203. Although he usually uses it in a positive sense, he occasionally does describe the heart (*Gemüth*) of a person who is neither pious nor attuned. For an example of this, see the second Sermon translated below, from December 1832.

204. E.g., see Albrecht, "'We Kiss Our Dearest Redeemer through Inward Prayer.'" In the many examples that Albrecht gives, the term is *Herz*.

205. Friedrich Schleiermacher, *On the Highest Good*, trans. H. Victor Froese (Lewiston, NY: Edwin Mellen, 1992), 53.

206. Schleiermacher, "On the Essence of Religion," 154.

207. Ibid., 197.

208. Ibid., 162–63.

209. Ibid., 182–83.

210. Ibid., 197.

211. Schleiermacher to H. Herz; see below, 254.

212. Schleiermacher, "On the Essence of Religion," 162.

213. Schleiermacher, *Christmas Dialogue*, 150.

214. Ibid., 118.

215. Ibid., 119.

216. *ORI* 102.

217. See Lamm, "Early Philosophical Roots."

218. Schleiermacher, "On the Essence of Religion," 158.

219. Ibid., 217.

220. I will return to this point under the next theme, "God."

221. Schleiermacher, "On the Essence of Religion," 191.

222. Ibid., 196–97, emphasis added.

223. Ibid., 185.

224. For further explication of Schleiermacher's understanding of individuality and freedom in the *Speeches*, see Lamm, *The Living God*, 137–75, and Blackwell, *Schleiermacher's Early Philosophy of Life*, 109–204.

225. Schleiermacher, "On the Essence of Religion," 184.

226. *CF* 5, 12, respectively.

227. *Gl.* §3.5, *KGA* 1/13:1:30; cf. *CF* 11.

228. *Gl.* §3.4, *KGA* 1/13:1:29; cf. *CF* 10.

229. *Gl.* §4.2, *KGA* 1/13:1:35; cf. *CF* 14.

230. See *Gl.* §4.2, *KGA* 1/13:1:36–37; cf. *CF* 15.

231. *Gl.* §4.3; *CF* 16.

232. *Gl.* §4.4; *CF* 16.

233. For a more detailed discussion of the "feeling of absolute dependence" and "*Whence*," see Lamm, *The Living God*, 109–19, 189–93.

234. *Gl.* §4.4; *CF* 17.

235. One reason for this being overlooked may be that the English translation was actually made by several different translators, and the same frequently used term, *Empfänglichkeit*, was translated in §4 as "receptivity" and in §108 as "susceptibility."

236. *Gl.* §4.3; *CF* 16.

237. *Gl.* §6; *CF* 26.

238. *Gl.* §5.1; *CF* 19.

239. *Gl.* §5.4; *CF* 23.

240. Ibid.

241. Translated by Albert L. Blackwell, "Schleiermacher's Sermon at Nathanael's Grave," *The Journal of Religion* 57, no. 1 (1977): 75.

242. See B. A. Gerrish, "Theology within the Limits of Piety Alone: Schleiermacher and Calvin's Notion of God," in *The Old Protestantism and the New: Essays on the Reformation Heritage* (Chicago: University of Chicago Press, 1982), 196–207.

243. Calvin wrote, "For if it had not been clearly stated that the wrath and vengeance of God and eternal death rested upon us, we would scarcely have recognized how miserable we would have been without God's mercy, and we would have underestimated the benefit of liberation" (Calvin, *Institutes* 1:2:16:2, p. 504). See also B. A. Gerrish, "'To the Unknown God': Luther and Calvin on the Hiddenness of God," in *The Old Protestantism and the New*, 131–49.

244. *Gl.* §167.1; *CF* 730.

245. *Gl.* §166.2; *CF* 729.

246. See Schleiermacher, Sermon on Pentecost Sunday, 1825, 239.

247. See ibid., 236, 242.

248. For a more detailed discussion of his treatment of these two attributes in *The Christian Faith*, see Lamm, *The Living God*, 212–25.

249. *Gl.* §167.2; *CF* 732.

250. *Gl.* §167.1; *CF* 730.

251. Ibid.

252. *Gl.* §168.1; *CF* 732–33.

253. Schleiermacher, "On the Essence of Religion," 223.

254. See discussions of *The Christian Faith* in sections 1 and 2 of this introduction.

255. Schleiermacher, *On the Glaubenslehre*, 57, emphasis added.

256. *Gl.* §51.1; *CF* 201.

257. *Gl.* §50.3; *CF* 198.

258. "For the divine causality is only equal in compass to the finite in so far as it is opposite to it in kind" (*Gl.* §51.1; *CF* 201–2).

259. Schleiermacher, "On the Essence of Religion," 218.

260. Ibid., 219.

261. Ibid., 220.

262. Ibid., 221.

263. For further discussion of the complexity of this "scale," see Lamm, *The Living God*, 101–9.

264. Schleiermacher, "On the Essence of Religion," 167.

265. *Gl.* §170; *CF* 738.

266. *Gl.* §172.3; *CF* 749. For more on this see Francis Schüssler Fiorenza, "Schleiermacher's Understanding of God as Triune," in Mariña, *Cambridge Companion*, 171–88.

267. For more of the changes of fortune in the early history of the term *mysticism*, see Leigh Eric Schmidt, "The Making of 'Mysticism' in the Anglo-American World: From Henry Coventry to William James," in Lamm, *Companion to Christian Mysticism*, 452–72.

268. For analyses of this controversy, see B. A. Gerrish, *Tradition and the Modern World: Reformed Theology in the Nineteenth Century* (Chicago: University of Chicago Press, 1978), 22–48; and Christine Helmer, "Mysticism and Metaphysics: Schleiermacher and a Historical-Theological Trajectory," *The Journal of Religion* 83, no. 4 (2003): 517–38.

269. Instrumental here is Bernard McGinn's multivolume study, *The Presence of God: A History of Western Christian Mysticism*, 7 vols. (New York: Crossroad Publishing, 1991–). Vol. 7, tentatively entitled *Crisis and Renewal in Western Mysticism*, will include discussion of Schleiermacher.

270. The present series, Classics of Western Spirituality, has been a driving force in that.

271. See Mary Frohlich, RSCJ, "Mystics of the Twentieth Century," and Philip F. Sheldrake, "A Critical Theological Perspective," in Lamm, *Companion to Christian Mysticism*, 515–30 and 533–49, respectively.

272. Wayne Proudfoot, *Religious Experience* (Berkeley: University of California Press, 1985), 211–12. Proudfoot's main critique of Schleiermacher is given in chapter 1, "Expression," but his criticisms run throughout the book. Proudfoot is a careful reader of Schleiermacher who, although he stands by the basic contours of his earlier argument, has revised some details. The problem is that many influenced by Proudfoot's account have not themselves studied Schleiermacher, and certain caricatures have resulted.

273. Ibid., 130 (in chapter 4, "Mysticism").

274. Ibid., 131.

275. Bernard McGinn, *The Foundations of Mysticism*, vol. 1 of *The Presence of God: A History of Western Christian Mysticism* (New York: Crossroad, 1991), 267.

276. See discussion above, 53.

277. Schleiermacher, "On the Essence of Religion," 170.

278. For Schleiermacher's responses to charges of pantheism, see Lamm, *The Living God*, chapter 3.

279. Schleiermacher, "On the Essence of Religion," 162.

280. *Gl.* §60; *CF* 244.

281. *Gl.* §94; *CF* 385.

282. *Gl.* §100; *CF* 425.

283. See Schleiermacher, Sermon on Pentecost Sunday, 1825, 226–27.

284. The term is taken from a short piece by Karl Rahner, SJ, "Everyday Mysticism," in *The Practice of Faith: A Handbook of Contemporary Spirituality*, ed. Karl Lehmann and Alfred Raffelt (New York: Crossroad, 1983), 69–70.

285. For Schleiermacher's understanding of the doctrine of justification, see Lamm, *The Living God*, 201–12.

286. Schleiermacher to Eleanore, 257 below. For other passages on eternal life and immortality, see the end of "On the Essence of Religion," 216, 222–23, and Sermon on Pentecost Sunday, 1825, 240.

287. See above, 56.

288. See Schleiermacher, Sermon on Pentecost Sunday, 1825, 240–41.

289. Schleiermacher, *Christmas Dialogue*, 107–8.

290. See Lamm, "Schleiermacher's *Christmas Dialogue* as Platonic Dialogue," 418–19.

291. Schleiermacher, *Christmas Dialogue*, 151.

292. Ibid., 151.

293. See, e.g., Carl Dahlhaus, *The Idea of Absolute Music*, trans. Roger Lustig (Chicago: University of Chicago Press, 1989).

294. Schleiermacher, "On the Essence of Religion," 153.

295. See Schleiermacher, Sermon on Pentecost Sunday, 1825, 229, 231.

296. Schleiermacher, *Die Weihnachtsfeier. Ein Gespräch*, in *KGA* 1/5: *Schriften aus der Hallenser Zeit 1804–1807*, ed. Hermann Patsch (Berlin: Walter de Gruyter, 1995), 43–98. There are two published English translations of the second edition: *Christmas Eve: A Dialogue on the Celebration of Christmas*, trans. W. Hastie (Edinburgh: T & T Clark, 1890); and *Christmas*

Eve: Dialogue on the Incarnation, trans. Terrence N. Tice (Richmond, VA: John Knox Press, 1967).
297. Schleiermacher, "Über das Wesen der Religion," in KGA 1/12: *Über die Religion (2.-) 4. Auflage, Monologen (2.-) 4. Auflage*, ed. Günter Meckenstock (Berlin & N.Y.: Walter de Gruyter, 1995), 41–128. See also *Über die Religion. Reden an die Gebildeten unter ihren Verächtern 1799/1806/1821*, ed. Niklaus Peter, Frank Bestebreurtje, and Anna Büsching (Zürich: Theologischer Verlag, 2012). For a translation of the first edition of the *Speeches* (1799), see Richard Crouter, ed., *On Religion: Speeches to Its Cultured Despisers* (Cambridge: Cambridge University Press, 1988). For a translation of the third (1821), together with the "Explanations," see John Oman, *On Religion: Speeches to Its Cultured Despisers* (New York: Harper, 1958). Schleiermacher made significant changes to the second *Speech* in 1806 and made yet further changes in 1821.

2

THE CHRISTMAS CELEBRATION:
A DIALOGUE[1]

The inviting parlor was festively decorated. Flowers from all the other windows of the house had been transferred here. The drapes were not drawn so that the snow gleaming into the room might evoke the season. Engravings and paintings having to do with the holy feast[2] adorned the walls. A beautiful pair of these had been a gift from the lady of the house to her husband. Many translucent lights, positioned high up, gave off a solemn light that nevertheless played mischievously with one's curiosity. Familiar things it showed clearly enough, but anything strange or new could only be ascertained slowly, upon closer inspection. Thus had the cheerful and wise Ernestine arranged it, so that only gradually was the eagerness—aroused as it was half in jest, half in earnest—satisfied, and so that the small, colorful gifts might remain surrounded by an expanding shimmer a little while longer.

All who formed the tightly knit circle—men and women, boys and girl—had brought gifts with the hope of pleasing one another. They had given Ernestine the task of assembling these gifts and thus of arranging into a grand whole what, if left separate, would be unimpressive. Well, this she had accomplished. As in a winter garden one has to retrieve the blossoms of snowdrops[3] from between the evergreen bushes and violets from under the snow or from under the protective cover of moss, so each person was given their own area bordered by ivy, myrtle, and amaranth. The most delicate gifts lay cloaked under white coverlets or colorful kerchiefs, while the larger

---

1. Schleiermacher, *Die Weihnachtsfeier. Ein Gespräch* (1st edition, 1806), in *KGA* 1/5: *Schriften aus der Hallenser Zeit 1804–1807*, ed. Hermann Patsch (Berlin: Walter de Gruyter, 1995), 43–98.

2. *Das Fest*. Schleiermacher consistently uses this one term throughout. It has been translated variously as *feast, celebration, holiday*, or *festival*, depending on the context.

3. The first flowers of the year.

101

gifts had to be sought out around or beneath the holiday tables. Nametags found their way, written with edible trifles, on the coverlets. It fell to everyone to figure out the giver of each gift.

The company waited in the adjoining rooms. Their eagerness gave a slight sting to the practical joking going on. Under the pretext of guessing or disclosing who had given what to whom, gifts were contrived whose relation to little flaws and habits, to comical events and farcical misunderstandings or embarrassments, were unmistakable. And whoever was subjected to such pranks eagerly reciprocated right back. Only little Sofie paced up and down with the longest of her small strides, lost in thought. And she, with her restless uniformity, was almost as much in the way of the others, who were running up to each other and speaking in an unruly way, as they were in hers. Finally Anton asked her, with feigned annoyance, whether she would not now gladly give back all her presents for a crystal glass that would allow her to see through the latched doors.

"I at least would be more likely to do so than you," she said, "since you are more selfish than you are curious—and besides, you probably believe that no door could block the rays of your marvelous brilliance." With that she sat down in the darkest corner of the room and cradled her little head thoughtfully in her upturned hands.

Not long thereafter, Ernestine opened the door and remained there, leaning against it. However, instead of hastening to the trimmed tables, as might have been expected, the spirited flock, desirous though they were, turned around in the middle of the parlor, where they could survey the whole. All gazes fell on her. So beautiful was the arrangement, and so perfect an expression of her sense, that feeling and eye alike gravitated toward her, unconsciously and ineluctably. She stood there, half in the dark, intending, herself unnoticed, to take delight in the beloved figures and in their ebullient joy. Yet it was she in whom everyone first took delight. They gathered around her, as though everything else had already been enjoyed and she were the giver of it all. Sofie clasped her around the knees and beheld her with wide eyes, without a smile but infinitely sweetly; the women embraced her; Eduard kissed her beautiful downcast eye; and all of them, as it befitted each one, demonstrated their most heartfelt love and devotion. She herself had to give the signal for them to claim their gifts.

"I have appointed it to thank you, my dears," Ernestine said. "Just do not lose sight of the picture for the frame, and bear in mind that I have only paid homage to the festive day and to your joyous love, whose tokens you have entrusted to me. Come now, and see what has been brought for each person, and whoever cannot guess wisely must bear patiently with being made fun of."

And there was no lack of this here. Although the women and Sofie proclaimed with great confidence the giver of any gift, such that none could deny it, the men made many mistakes, and nothing was more comical, or more vexing, than when they had made a witty joke about their conjecture, and this was then sent back under protest like a fake coin.

"It is only fitting," Leonhardt said, "that the women so outmatch us in perspicacity in these charming little trifles—however much it annoys us, and rightly so. For inasmuch as their gifts, much more than our own, disclose the finest attentiveness through their meaning, and we relish this beautiful fruit of their talent, we must also put up with that other effect of the very same talent, even though we are put to shame by it."

"You are too kind!" retorted Friederike. "It is not completely a matter of our talent. On the contrary, if I may say so, a certain ineptitude in you men comes to our aid—and not just a little. You quite prefer the direct ways, as also befits the powers that be. Your movements give you away, even though you don't intend to say anything by them— just like the schemes on the chess board of someone who cannot refrain from touching the critical pieces of the other player while scrutinizing them, and raising his own indecisively six times before he moves once."

"Yes, yes," replied Ernst, smiling honestly and pretending to sigh. "No doubt it remains the case, as old Solomon said, 'God has created man upright, but women seek many arts.'"[4]

Karoline said, "Well, you still have the consolation of not having corrupted us with modern manners. Both ways perhaps may well be just as eternal as necessary. And if your honest simple-mindedness is the condition of our cunning, then take comfort in this: perhaps the

---

4. See Eccl 7:28–29. Schleiermacher changes some things to make a pun.

other side of it is that our narrowness[5] acts just the same way in relation to your greater talents."

The presents, meanwhile, were being looked at more closely. Above all, properly feminine works in stitching and fine needlework were being examined and praised by all those knowledgeable in the art. At first Sofie had thrown only a fleeting glance at her own treasures, and was going around to all alike—a little while here, a little while there—curiously inspecting and fervently extolling everything, but, more than anything, she was begging for sizable pieces from the destroyed nametags. For she was insatiable when it comes to sweets of all kinds, and she loved to own great stockpiles of them, the more so when she collected them in this way. Only when she had increased her wealth with one such stack did she, too, begin to look at her presents more closely, and now she made the rounds once again, displaying and rejoicing in each individual article separately, making use of each one right away, as much as could be done, in order thereby to demonstrate in no uncertain terms the excellence of the gifts.

"But you seem not to have even noticed the best gift," her mother pointed out.

"Oh, yes I have, Mother extraordinaire!" said the child. "I just don't have the heart to open it yet. If it is a book, there is no use looking inside it now. Later, I'll have to shut myself up in my little room so that I can enjoy it there. If, however, someone—not you, of course—played a serious joke on me with patterns and instructions for all kinds of knitting and embroidery and other marvels, then I promise, as surely as I can, to use them really diligently in the New Year. But right now I do not really want to know."

"Badly guessed!" her father said. "It is nothing of the sort, since you're still not old enough to deserve such things. Nor is it a book with which you could retreat to your room—*if* you want to enjoy it the way it is meant to be enjoyed."

With that, she pulled it out with the greatest desire, at the risk of spilling a large portion of her stockpile, and exclaimed with a loud cry, "Music!" and, leafing through it, "O great Music! Christmas for

---

5. *Beschränktheit* here suggests a word play between physical narrowness (i.e., women generally being restricted to the private sphere) and mental narrowness. In the *Speeches* the word carries the meaning of narrow-mindedness.

a lifetime! Sing, children, the most wondrous things." She read the titles of mostly religious compositions, all of them related to the lovely holiday. Select ones she read more loudly, and to some extent ancient, rare items as well. She ran immediately to her father and covered him with kisses in ardent gratitude.

For all the aforementioned aversion to feminine works, the child demonstrated a definite talent for music—a talent as narrow as it was great. Truly, her sense for it was in no way narrow. To the contrary, she took heartfelt joy in everything beautiful, in every aspect of this art—except she did not really like to perform by herself anything set in grand church style. When she warbled a light gay ditty in half voice, one would seldom take it as an indication of a purely joyous temper. When, however, she went to the instrument and exercised her voice properly, a voice that early on inclined toward alto, it was always only in that great genre. Here she knew how to give each note its proper value. Each emerged from the previous note lovingly, as if unable to let it go, and then nevertheless was just there, by itself, with measured strength, and then again, as with a pious kiss, it gave way to the next note. Even when she practiced her singing alone, she showed such a great attentiveness to the other voices—as if they, too, could be heard. And as much as she was often quite moved, still no sort of excess destroyed the harmony of the whole. Regardless of the subject matter, one can hardly designate it otherwise than that she sang with devotion, and she held on to and attended each note with humble love. And now, since Christmas is quite properly a children's holiday, and she lived in it in such a totally exceptional way, it followed that no more preferable present than this could have made an appearance.

She sat there for a while, absorbed in contemplating the notes on the page. She fingered the notes on top of the book and sang softly to herself without sound, but with visible movement of the muscles and with lively gestures. Then, suddenly, she sprang out of the room, but she soon returned, saying, "All right, quit looking about and chatting, and come be my guest over there. I've already lit everything up. Tea is almost ready, so this is the best time. As you know and as you have seen, I was not allowed to give you anything. Inviting you to a play, however, is not forbidden." The condition had been set that she would be included among the gift givers as soon as she could present a perfect, delicate needlework as her first gift. Not yet able to do that, she wanted nevertheless to make up for it in some way.

She owned one of those miniature play sets in which, originally, the story of this day was supposed to be presented with small, moveable, carved figurines against the appropriate backdrop. As commonly happens, however, that story was virtually displaced by a host of unseemly, tasteless additions, added to lend, as much as possible, motley functions to the simple mechanism. This she had cleaned, restored, improved here and there, and it was now in her room, quite favorably assembled and illuminated. On a fairly large table were depicted—with passable skill, in unrestrained confusion, and interrupted by a few episodes—many important moments from the external history of Christianity. You could see all interspersed the baptism of Christ; Golgotha and the mount of the ascension; the outpouring of the Holy Spirit; the destruction of the Temple; Christians battling with the Saracens around the Holy Sepulcher; the pope in a ceremonial procession to Peter's Basilica; the funeral pyre of Hus; the burning of the papal bull by Luther; the baptism of the Saxons; missionaries in Greenland and among the Africans; the cemetery in Herrnhut and the orphanage in Halle, which the maker, it seems, had considered the last great work of a religious enthusiasm. The child had, with particular diligence, used fire and water throughout, and had successfully highlighted the contending elements. The rivers really flowed and the fires really burned, and with great foresight she knew to maintain and keep watch over the lighted flames.

Among all of these obtruding objects one sought, for some time, the birth itself, but to no avail, since she had cleverly tried to hide the star. You had to follow the angels and shepherds, who were also gathered around a fire. You opened a door in the wall of the structure and caught sight of the holy family in a sort of room, which, because the house served only as decoration, really lay outside. Everything was dark in the meager hut, except for a powerful, concealed light that illumined the head of the child and formed a reflection on the downturned face of the mother. In contrast to the wild flames outside, this mild radiance acted as heavenly fire against the earthly. With obvious satisfaction, Sofie herself commended this as her highest achievement. She imagined herself thereby a second Correggio[6] and made a great mystery about how she had done it. She did say, however, that she had still not figured out how to introduce a rainbow, because after all, she said, Christ is the true guarantor that life and delight will never more perish in the world.

She knelt for a few minutes before her work, her little head only just reaching to the tabletop, peering intently into the room. Suddenly, she became aware that her mother was standing right behind her. Without changing her position, she turned toward her and said, deeply moved, "Oh, Mother! You could just as well be the blessed mother of the divine babe, and doesn't it pain you, that you're not? Isn't this why mothers prefer having sons? Just think of the holy women who accompanied Jesus, and everything that you've told me about them. Certainly, I, too, want to become one of them, just as you are." The mother, touched by this, picked her up and kissed her.

The others, meanwhile, were each examining this and that on their own. Anton stood before it, especially engaged. He had his younger brother next to him and was showing him everything he knew, explaining with the long-winded, pompous vanity of a tour guide. The younger boy seemed very attentive but understood nothing at all. He kept trying to reach between, through, and into the various bodies of water and to grab for the flames, so as to see for himself whether they were real, too, and not an illusion.

While most were still occupied here, Sofie kept pleading gently with her father. She insisted that he retire to the other room with Friederike and Karoline. Karoline sat down at the clavier, and together they sang the chorus, "Let Us Love Him," and the chorale, "Welcome to the Vale of Tears," and some other selections from Reichardt's excellent *Christmas Carols*,[7] where the joy, the feeling of salvation, and humble adoration are expressed so beautifully. Soon they had everyone listening devoutly, and when they had finished, it

---

6. The reference is to Antonio da Correggio (1489–1534), whose painting of the nativity (*Die Anbetung der Hirten*, or *Die heilige Nacht*) hung (and still does) in the Gemäldegalerie in Dresden.

7. *Weihnachts-Cantilene von Mathias Claudius, in Musik gesetzt von Johann Friederich Reichardt* (Berlin, 1786). See Hermann Patsch, "Die esoterische Kommunikationsstruktur der 'Weihnachtsfeier.' Über Anspielungen und Zitate," in *Schleiermacher in Context: Papers from the 1988 International Symposium on Schleiermacher at Hernnhut*, ed. Ruth Drucilla Richardson (Lewiston, NY: Edwin Mellen, 1991), 152–53n31; cf. 138.

happened, as it always does, that religious music effects first a silent satisfaction and retreat of the heart. There were a few silent moments in which everyone knew that each and every heart was lovingly directed toward all the rest, and toward something higher still. The call to tea soon gathered everyone together again in the parlor, though Sofie remained behind for a long while, practicing assiduously on the clavier. She came in every once in a while, albeit quickly and disinterestedly, to quench her thirst.

The others were milling about, occupying themselves once more with the presents. Only now for the first time, after something else had happened, did the presents seem to become rightly the property of their new owner, so that now they could also be observed by the giver as something extrinsic and thus praised without inhibition. Many gifts had previously been overlooked, and the special merits of some were only now being discovered.

"This Christmas," Ernst said, "we have an especially propitious year to take delight in our gifts. Many momentous changes are imminent. The cute little baby things with which Agnes has been so richly showered, the beautiful little treasures for appointing our future home, my dear Friederike, the travel gear for Leonhardt, even the school books for your Anton, dear Agnes—all of these point to progress and to beautiful events, and they make the joys of the future vividly present to us. If, after all, the holiday is itself the proclamation of new life for the world, then naturally it becomes most impressionable and joyous for us, when in our own life something new and momentous is stirring as well. I embrace you once more, beloved Friederike, as a present of this day. Such an incredible, festive feeling seizes me with deep joy—as though you were given to me together, right now, with the Redeemer. Yes, it can pain me that not everyone here is kneeling reverently, like us, before a new stage of life—that nothing great lies before you, beloved friends, that might attach itself immediately to the great subject of this holiday. And I dread that our gifts might appear insignificant compared with your gifts to us, as also your state of mind may indeed be serene and happy, albeit less moved and heightened, and indeed almost indifferent, in comparison with ours."

"How very good of you, dear friend, to look over at us so sympathetically from out of your own enthusiasm," Eduard said. "But surely it is just such enthusiasm that moves us too far away from you.

Just bear in mind that our tranquil happiness is the very same happiness you are approaching, and that every authentic enthusiasm—including that of love—is never obsolescent, but is always excitable. Or can you imagine Ernestine's feeling at the expression of childlike devotion and deep ardency in our Sofie as something indifferent? Can you imagine it without the most lively activity of the imagination, in which present, past, and future intertwine? Just see how she is moved inwardly, as if she bathes in a sea of purest happiness."

"Yes, I gladly admit it," said Ernestine. "She has captivated me before with her few words. But I do her an injustice. The words alone could have seemed more of an affectation to someone who does not know her. What captivated me was the entire, undivided intuition of the child. The angelically pure heart opened up so gloriously, and if you understand what I mean—I don't know how else to express it—in the greatest naïveté and unself-consciousness lay an understanding of feeling so deep and sound that I was overwhelmed by the fullness of the beauty and amiability that necessarily must well up for this reason. Truly, I feel that she did not say too much in one respect, when she said that I could just as well be the mother of the adored child, because I can humbly worship the pure revelation of the divine in my daughter, as Mary had in her son, without the right relationship of the child to the mother being disturbed thereby."

Agnes spoke, "Surely we all agree on this point: the so-called pampering and spoiling, which happens not out of love of the child but out of self-love, as a way of sparing oneself some unpleasantness, can have nothing to do with what you mean."

"To be sure, we women do agree on that," Ernestine responded, "but the question is, shouldn't the men be emphatically reproached for it sometimes? If it concerns their proper duty, chiefly for the boys, then it is valid for bravery and proficiency. Progress is then always bound up with struggle and denial, and it may often also be necessary to suppress the expanding self-feeling. But that could easily give them[8] a false view, were they not to take their cues assiduously from our maternal sense and activity."

"Yes, we recognize," spoke Eduard, "how you are made and destined to foster and develop the first pure seeds, before something

---

8. He clarifies in the second edition that he means the fathers.

corrupt emerges or fixes itself. It is all-around befitting for women, who devote themselves to the holy service, to live in the interior of the temple as Vestal Virgins who watch over the holy fires. We, in contrast, march around outside in strict formation, practice discipline, and preach repentance, or we stitch the cross on the pilgrims and gird them with the sword, so as to seek a lost sanctuary and win it back."

Leonhardt interrupted, "You bring me back to my earlier thoughts, which I had lost in the flow of your conversation. It concerns your Sofie, and for some time now it has hovered before me, from time to time on the tip of my tongue, but now it is especially vivid. Her childlike piety certainly touches me, too. Not infrequently, however, it also makes me shudder. When her feeling erupts, in my mind's eye I sometimes view her as a bud that, due to too strong an inner impulse, consumes itself before it opens. For heaven's sake, dear friends, do not nourish this feeling too much. Or can't you imagine her as vividly as I can, with withered colors, perhaps even wearing the veil and kneeling in front of an image of a saint, performing the fruitless rosary service, or in a meager and feeble life in a Moravian Sisters' House,[9] shrouded in the little repulsive bonnet and in the charmless dress, excluded from the free and glad enjoyment of life?

"It is a dangerous time. Many beautiful female hearts betake themselves to one of these contemptible aberrations, tearing asunder the family bond, and thus, in any event, falling short of the most beautiful form and the richest happiness of female destiny—not to mention the inner distortion, without which something like this cannot even begin to emerge. And the child, I fear, tends too much in this direction. Yes, it would be an irretrievable loss if this heart and this spirit were seized by the corruption of a time when few women maintain their honor untainted—if what Goethe says is true, that a stigma always sticks to a person who has dissolved her marriage or changed religion. If a friend harbors such a concern, it ought to be uttered—but only once. And thus perhaps it wasn't wrong for me to have been inhibited from saying it before today—how, I don't know."

---

9. Schleiermacher's own sister, Charlotte, with whom he was particularly close, lived in the Sisters' House at Hernnhut. See introduction.

Ernestine said, "I can attest that you have been inhibited. I have often noticed your uneasy feeling—and, because it was so pronounced, I thought it would certainly soon cross over into words. I didn't demand it of you, however, because I hoped that you would become suspicious of it yourself if you but saw the child more and if her interior developed more clearly before you. Look, my dear, I am only quoting you. You assume, quite rightly, wherever such a path of life is pursued, the reason for it is always an inner distortion. This is why you are concerned. And where is this easier to recognize than in a child about whom one can little doubt whether something has arisen from the inside or has attached itself from the outside? Now, can you possibly point to something distorted in her that would extend beyond childhood? Or any maladjustment through which her pious emotions otherwise suppress what befits her?

"I only know that she gives her attention fully to this as she does to each and everything that is dear and of value to her. So she gives herself over to each movement—for every wholly childish interest you will find her the same, and she carries as little vanity with this as she does with everything else. Besides, she lacks any motive for it, and as far as we are concerned, she will always be so lacking. No one pays it any special attention, and when, as is proper, she inevitably becomes aware that we count this disposition among the highest, then we simply won't make much of a fuss about the particular emotions or about their expression. We find them natural, and thus the disposition is, in fact, natural to her. Whatever appears in this way, we believe, may be left to nature undisturbed."

Practically interrupting her, Eduard continued, "And all the more certainly, the more it belongs to the most beautiful and noble. For truly, dear friend, this must be the truth of the matter: the interior, which so seizes the little one, attaches itself to the purely external, since she has no opportunity herself at all. In a few days the Christmas play will be set aside, and you know very well yourself that there is nothing formally religious in our circle—no prayer at the designated time, no proper devotional hours. Rather, everything happens only when the spirit moves us. Moreover, she often hears us speaking like that—yes, even singing, which is by far her favorite thing—without joining us. This is all well according to the manner and way of children. She doesn't even have any particular desire for church. To her, the singing there is done too poorly, and the rest she doesn't understand. It bores her. Were something coerced in her piety, or were she inclined to imitate, or to let herself be led by, alien views—wouldn't she then force herself to find beautiful and worthy of participation what it is *we* so highly esteem? If I think of this continuing in harmony with her remaining education, then I do not foresee how being Roman[10] or even Moravian could ever be attractive to her. She would, in fact, have to give up her own taste, which doesn't at all have this character, and to give up her virtually unapologetic distinctions between what is most important in all things and what is appearance or environmental."

"I will *not* tolerate this," said Karoline, before Leonhardt could have another word. "The way in which you lump together the Moravian with the Catholic. I believe one could argue about whether it would be the same in any respect whatsoever—but the last thing I will allow is uniting them both under the fine label of 'distortion.' I have two friends there,[11] you know, who are certainly not eccentric. To the contrary, their sense and understanding are just as level-headed as their piety is deep."

"Dear girl," answered Eduard, smiling, "with Leonhardt you have to attribute it to ignorance. He repeats what is sometimes heard, and has certainly never peered into a Moravian place except to buy a beautiful saddle or to have a look at some remarkable craft, or to be introduced to the beautiful children of the Sisters' House. But I would certainly have been wrong, had I conceded something like that in general. Only please be so kind as to note that the discourse was not at all about the merits or character of the different churches; rather, we are speaking only of Sofie, so the lumping together of the two should not raise your suspicion.

"Precisely because you are familiar with the matter, and irrespective of your two friends, you will acknowledge this about a girl who can satisfy her religious sense in the bosom of her family—a girl who, precisely because she has preserved innocence and naïveté, does not find the world at all dangerous and is thereby accustomed to a joyful activity in a free life. It is unimaginable, except as a strange aberration, that she should lock herself up in a monastic Sisters' House.

---

10. He means Roman Catholic.
11. She means in a Moravian Sisters' House.

"Furthermore, what I wanted to say to Leonhardt may well obtain in the same way for both kinds of crossing over,[12] when not motivated by special circumstances that you defend. Namely, these proselytes, so far as I am familiar with them, are not people who, like Sofie, have been inclined to the religious since childhood. But, as it is said, they are coquettish females and fraudulent politicians who in later life, or after certain mishaps, become pious hypocrites. These are the ones, at least for the most part, who, whatever they practiced beforehand—science, art, or marriage—did so in a completely worldly manner and entirely ignored the relation to the infinite. When this relation does somehow open up to them, they behave toward it like little children and reach for the splendor—whether an external and expanding splendor, or an interior fire that entices by means of another force and by the darkness of its surroundings. And so one could also say that in their repentance something of sin always remains behind. That is, they want to cast the blame for their previous coldness and darkening onto the church to which they used to belong, as if there alone the holy fire had not been kept safe and had been replaced with a cold formality propelled by empty words and by eviscerated, dried out customs."

"You may well be right that this is how it stands with many," replied Leonhardt. "But certainly this is not the only source of this evil. In many others, it seems to arise immediately from within, and so it seems to be the case in little Sofie. It is truly incredible, that others and I—whom, no doubt among yourselves, you call 'unbelievers'—must alert you and preach to you against unbelief. Admittedly, it is unbelief in superstition and everything associated with that. I hardly need to assure you, Eduard, that I revere and love the beauty of religiosity—but it must be, and must remain, something internal. If it should surface outwardly and form peculiar relations in life, then the most abhorrent thing results: spiritual pride, which in the end is nothing other than the strangest and craziest superstition.

"Recall, Eduard, that we discussed this recently, and that from among the entire so-called spiritual estate[13]—which because of your own position you know far and wide—you were able with effort to

---

12. That is, crossing over to either the Roman Catholic or the Moravian Churches.
13. The clergy.

muster only a couple examples of people who had not been spoiled by spiritual pride. Among the Catholics, the laity also contracts this same state of intoxication through their pious works, which only hold an external worth. And from the very same beaker, it seems, your little one has already taken a swig—and not a weak one, for a child. So indulge her, then, and nurse this ambition to become a holy woman. But where will she go with it, other than to the cloister or to the Sisters? The rest of us, after all, do not do these things well in the world. All the playful devotion with the small Christ child, and the adoration of the halo that she made for him herself—isn't that the unmistakable seed of superstition? Is it not sheer idolatry?

"See it for what it is, dear friends. It will certainly wind up being something irrational, if you do not bring a halt to it. Far from halting it, however, I have the clearest signs that you actually give the child the Bible. I can only hope that you do not give it over entirely freely, for her to use on her own. Regardless, whether you read in the Bible in her presence or her mother recounts it to her, it is all the same. The mythical will be bound to entice her imagination, and strange, sensuous images will take root. Thereafter, no sound concept can take a seat next to it. A hallowed letter sits on the throne, and into that the child, guided by unbridled free choice, puts what was never there. The miraculous directly nourishes superstition. And incoherence aids and abets every delusion of one's own fanaticism and of every deception of a half-learned system.

"Truly, in a time when preachers, even laudably in the pulpit, devote themselves to making the Bible as dispensable as possible, putting it back in the hands of children, for whom it was never made—that is the worst. It would be better for it—to use its own words against it—if it were a millstone fastened around its neck, and it were plunged into the deepest part of the sea, than that it become a stumbling block to the little ones.[14] What shall happen, if she assimilates in herself the sacred story along with other fairy tales? Whether afterward the latter count as much as the former, or the former just as little as the latter—both are equally corrupt, especially for the female sex. A boy sooner finds a way out of it. Even if it does

---

14. See Matt 18:6.

become quite serious with him, then just let him study theology for a year—that will surely cure him."

After waiting to see whether the speech had ended, Eduard said, "I must defend our Leonhardt against those of you who do not yet know him, so that his speech does not appear to you more dastardly than it was. He has not really sunk so deeply into unbelief, and he has little in common with our philosophers of the Enlightenment with whom he associates. It is only that he has not yet wholly sorted this matter out for himself, and for that reason he always mixes jest and earnestness in such a strange way that not everyone is able to separate the two. He would certainly have a good laugh at us were we to take it all seriously. I will therefore stick solely to the jest, dear friend. As for the earnest, what was said a short time ago is enough. Let me therefore recount something to you, and do not be too alarmed.

"Yes, the girl really does hear all kinds of things from the Bible exactly as it stands there. For instance, Joseph had been presented to her as only the foster father of Christ. About a year ago or more, she posed the question, 'Who then had been his real father?' Her mother answered, 'He had no other father than God.' Sofie expressed the opinion that God was indeed her father, too, but that she would not like to be without me for that reason, and that having no true father could well have belonged to Christ's suffering, for it is a splendid thing to have such a father. And with that she snuggled with me and played with my curls. From this you see how strictly she already adheres to dogmatics, and what a superior facility she has for becoming a martyr to belief in the immaculate conception.[15] What is more, she actually does accept the sacred history in some things as a tale. For just as she herself shapes the idea out of this, when in particular moments the girl gains the upper hand over the child, so she also sometimes doubts the details and facts in the sacred story and asks whether the literal is also true. You see, it is bad enough, and she is close to the allegorical interpretation of some church fathers."

"Jesting like this gives me courage to toss in a couple words of my own," Karoline said. "I'll admit, she has indeed made the halo

---

15. The Roman Catholic dogma of the immaculate conception refers to Mary's conception, not to Christ's. In the second edition, Schleiermacher changed this to "virginal conception."

around the little Christ child, and she will soon draw, paint, and if possible sculpt the infant and mother—in defiance of, and much to the annoyance of, all heathen-minded artists. For already she often doodles such sketches while at her writing and reading lessons, and she does so absentmindedly, which clearly only makes it all the more painfully Catholic. But, seriously, I just have to laugh again at Leonhardt about his concern, since even here another reason for moving toward Catholicism ceases to apply. Or don't you say that the best went over to that church[16] because of its close association with the arts? If Sofie has already made this association in her own way, then she will feel no need to attach herself to something else that appears so strange and tasteless."

Seemingly testy, Leonhardt said, "Ah, if the girls actually want to make me out to be addled, then I must become addled through and through. As far as I am concerned, she may prefer becoming Catholic, with her application of the arts to religion—for I don't like that at all. As a Christian, I am very inartistic and, as an artist, very un-Christian. I do not like the stiff church that Schlegel has portrayed in his stiff stanzas,[17] nor do I like the poor, destitute, frozen arts that are happy to find shelter. If the arts be not eternally young, living abundantly and independently for themselves, forming their own world, as they have indisputably formed ancient mythology, then I desire no part in them. Just so religion, as we take it, appears to me weak and suspicious, if it wishes to base itself principally on the arts."

"Take care, Leonhardt," Ernst said, "that they don't remind you of your own words at an inopportune moment. Haven't you recently argued that life and art would be as little a contradiction as life and science, and that a cultured life would truly be a work of art, a beautiful display, the most immediate union of the visual and musical arts? Now they will say that you therefore do not want life to find shelter with religion or to let itself be inspired by religion. They will

---

16. Schleiermacher is alluding to the fact that many prominent Protestants were converting to Catholicism. Friedrich and Dorothea Schlegel officially converted in 1808. Schleiermacher addresses this phenomenon explicitly in his epilogue to the second edition of the *Speeches* and in his explanation of that in the third edition (see *OR3* 266–74).

17. A reference to A. W. Schlegel's poem, "The Alliance of the Church with the Arts" ("Der Bund der Kirche mit den Künsten," 1800).

say that, for you, religion should be nowhere except in words, where for various reasons you occasionally need it."

Ernestine countered, "We do not want to say that. Anyway, enough already with this pointless argument, which bores the rest of us, since we simply do not share your pure enjoyment of argument for its own sake."

"And we clearly agree in this beautiful thought, which expresses itself so especially in our life today," Eduard added. "For what else is the lovely custom of exchanging gifts than that pure display of religious joy, which, as joy always does, manifests itself in unsought benevolence, giving, and serving. And here, particularly, by means of small presents, it reproduces the great gift[18] that we all equally enjoy. The more purely this disposition emerges in its entirety, the more our sense is struck. And that is why, dear Ernestine, we were so captivated by your arrangement this evening, because you expressed so well our sense of Christmas—being rejuvenated, the return to the feeling of childhood, and the serene joy in the new world—which we owe to the child being celebrated today. All of this was conveyed in the glowing light, in the setting of flowers and greens, and in the delayed desire."

"Yes, certainly," said Karoline, "what we feel in these days is so purely pious joy in the matter itself that I duly regretted what Ernst expressed earlier—that this joy could be heightened through some merry events or through expectations about our external life. But Ernst really was not being entirely earnest in saying that. As for what he said about the meaningfulness of our small presents—their value resides not at all in what they specifically refer to, but resides generally in the fact that they refer to something, that the intention of the gifts is to please. Proof of this is how definitely we have framed in our minds an image of every dear friend.

"My feeling, at least, quite definitely distinguishes that higher, more universal joy from the most spirited participation in what is happening, or is about to happen, to you all, dear friends. If anything, I would say that the particular joy is heightened by means of the universal joy. If the beautiful and joyous stand out at a time when we are most deeply conscious of the greatest and most beautiful, then the latter communicates itself to the former, and, with respect

---

18. The gift of Christ in the incarnation.

to the great salvation of the world, all love and goodness receive a greater meaning. Yes, I still feel it vividly, just as I have once experienced it. That higher, more universal joy blossoms out in us unimpeded even next to the deepest sorrow, and it purges and soothes the sorrow without being destroyed by it—so original is this joy, and so immediately is it grounded in something imperishable."[19]

Eduard said, "I, who according to Ernst's earlier assessment would easily be the least fortunate among us—I, too, feel a glad excess of pure serenity in me, which would certainly be communicated to all. It is a mood in which I could tempt fate. Or at the very least, if that sounds sacrilegious, a mood in which I might courageously face any challenge. Indeed, this kind of mood should be wished for everyone. I believe, however, that I also owe the full consciousness and proper enjoyment of it partly to our little one, who earlier led us to music. For each beautiful feeling comes forth perfectly only when we have found the sound for it. I do not mean the word but rather the sound in the strict sense, since the word can always only be a mediated expression, only a plastic element, if I may so put it. And religious feeling is most closely akin to music. People so often talk about how the corporate expression of this feeling could be again revived, but almost no one thinks about how easily the best thing might occur if singing were reset in a more appropriate relationship to the word. What the word has made clear, the sound must make alive—capturing it as harmony and carrying it over immediately into the inner being."

"Nor will anyone deny," Ernst added, "that only in the religious realm does music attain its perfection. The comical genre of music, which alone exists as pure antithesis, confirms this sooner than it disproves it, and one can hardly make an opera without a religious basis. The same might apply to every higher artwork of sounds. No one will seek the spirit of art in inferior art forms."

Eduard said, "This closer affinity probably lies in this: only in the immediate relation to the highest, to religion, and only in a definite form of the same, does music, without becoming tied to an

---

19. This sentence probably refers to Schleiermacher's own grief due to the final separation from Eleonore Grunow, and to the transforming joy he felt walking home from a concert by the virtuoso flutist Friedrich Ludwig Dülon, an experience that inspired him to write this *Dialogue*. See introduction, 26 above.

individual fact, have enough of the given to be intelligible. Christianity is a single theme presented in infinite variations, which, however, are also united by an inner law, and which fall under definite, universal types. What someone else has said is also certainly true: church music could not do without the singing, but it could probably do without the precise words. A Miserere, a Gloria, a Requiem—what are the individual words to it? It is intelligible enough through its type. No one will say they have missed something if they heard the words put to the music. That is why religion and music must hold tight to each other, because each uplifts and transfigures the other. Jesus had been received by a chorus of angels, and so we accompany him with sounds and song, up until the great hallelujah of the ascension."[20]

"Yes, indeed," said Friederike, "the most pious sound is the one that penetrates most surely into the heart."

"And the piety that sings," Karoline added, "is the one that ascends to heaven most gloriously and most directly. Nothing accidental, nothing individual restrains the two. I am reminded by what Eduard said about something he read not long ago. You will guess right away to whom it belongs. The words go something like this: 'Music never cries or laughs about individual events, only and always about life itself.'"

Eduard said, "In Jean Paul's name,[21] we should add that, for piety, the individual occurrences would only be passing notes, but its true content would be the great chords of the heart—chords that, though alternating marvelously and in the most diverse melodies, nonetheless always resolve themselves into the same harmony, in which only major and minor, male and female, can be distinguished."

"See," Agnes chimed in, "We come back here to what I was saying before. The individual, the personal—be it present or future, joy or woe—can give to or take away from a heart that stirs in pious moods just as little as passing notes, which leave behind only light traces, can affect the course of harmony."

Leonhardt abruptly interjected, "Listen here, Eduard. Your tranquility and resignation are becoming too much for me, and I

---

20. In the second edition Schleiermacher adds an explicit reference to Georg Friedrich Handel's *Messiah*, composed in 1741.

21. Jean Paul (1763–1825) was a famous German Romantic writer.

must bring a charge against you." He proceeded, half hushed, "Can you possibly bear that Agnes should say this—she, who lives in the most beautiful and blessed expectancy?"

Agnes herself replied, "Why not? Isn't the personal perishable even here? Isn't a newborn exposed to the most dangers? How easily is the still-unsteady flame blown out by the lightest wind? Mother love, however, is the eternal in us—the fundamental chord of our being."

Leonhardt asked, "And so are you indifferent as to whether you can form your child into what you envision, or whether the child is snatched away from you again in the first, defenseless period of life?"

"Indifferent?" Agnes retorted, "Who is saying that? Yet the inner life, the demeanor of the heart, will not lose thereby. And do you then believe that love revolves around what we are capable of forming the children into? What *can* we form? No, love revolves around the beautiful and the divine—which we believe already to be in them, for which every mother searches in each and every stirring, as soon as the soul of the child expresses itself."

"See!" Ernestine said, "My dears, in this sense, every mother is once again a Mary. Every mother has an eternal, divine child, and devoutly searches in that child for the stirrings of the higher spirit. No fate can bring grievous destruction into such love, nor does the corrupt weed of maternal vanity germinate in it. The old man may prophesy that a sword will pierce her soul; Mary merely ponders the words in her heart.[22] The angels might rejoice and the wise men come and pay homage; she does not exalt herself but instead remains always in devout and humble love."

"Were it not for the fact that everything you have to say is expressed so charmingly that one hesitates to offend, there would be much to say against it," spoke Leonhardt. "Otherwise, if everything held up so well, you would truly be the heroines of the time, you lovely idealistic fanatics, with your contempt for what is individual and real. It should be lamented that your congregation is not stronger and that you do not have sons who are nothing short of excellent, already able to bear arms, ready to defend. You would be the real Christian women of Sparta. But even if that is not the case, plan well for yourselves that you might withstand other trials that may be in store for you.

---

22. See Luke 2:35, 2:19, respectively.

Preparations are already made. A great fate marches back and forth in our vicinity, making earth quake with its steps, and we do not know how it is going to overtake us.[23] May reality with proud superiority not retaliate against your humble contempt!"

"Dear friend," Ernst replied, "the women will scarcely take second place to us in this matter. And the whole test is not much, it seems to me. What from afar appears to us as a great scene of misery, breaks down into many instances of pettiness when close up. The great scene dissipates, and what strikes the individual are always only some of these small details, mitigated through its similarity to everything around it. What must sway *us* in these affairs is not anything depending on proximity or distance, but precisely that which does not fall in the sphere of women."

Meanwhile, Sofie had for the most part been at the clavier, acquainting herself with her newly acquired treasures, some of which she did not yet know, and wanting just as gladly to greet the many parts she did know as her very own. At just this moment, she could be heard singing especially loudly a chorus from a cantata,

He who gave the Son that we might ever live
Shall He not with Him to us all give?[24]

This was followed by a magnificent fugue,

If I have but Thee, I ask for no more on heaven and earth.[25]

When she concluded, she closed the instrument and returned to the parlor.

"Behold!" said Leonhardt, who saw her coming, "Our little prophetess! I want to hear forthwith the extent to which she already belongs to you. Pray tell, little one," he addressed her, reaching his hand out to her. "Is it not true you prefer being merry to being sad?"

---

23. The reference is to Napoleon, who had just had a major victory over Russia and Austria at Austerlitz and who would conquer Halle on October 17, 1806. See introduction, 29–30 above.

24. See Rom 8:32.

25. This likely refers to Heinrich Schütz (1585–1672), *Musikalische exequien* Op. 7, SWV 279–81, part 2. See also Novalis's hymn, "Wenn ich nur ihn haben."

"At this very moment, I am not particularly one or the other," she replied.

"Really? Not merry after so many beautiful presents? That is certainly due to the serious music! But you have misunderstood my meaning. I asked, admittedly in an excessive manner, which of the two you would rather be in general, merry or sad?"

"That is hard to say," she answered back. "I am not exceedingly glad to be either, but I always like best being whatever I am at the time."

"I still do not understand you, little Sphinx. What do you mean by that?"

"Well," she said, "I only know that sometimes merriment and sadness get so strangely mixed up and contend with each other, and still I feel quite fine. But my mother has also told me that there is always something amiss or wrong with *that*—and that is why I don't like it."

"Therefore," he asked further, "if you are not entirely one or the other, then is it all the same to you whether you are cheerful or sad?"

"Not at all, for I am just glad to be what I am, and I am not indifferent to what I gladly am." Sofie continued, turning toward Ernestine, "Oh, Mother! Help me! He is quizzing me so strangely, and I do not understand what he really wants. Have him ask the grown-ups instead. They will understand him better."

"As a matter of fact, Leonhardt," said Ernestine, "I don't believe you will get much further with her. She simply isn't yet very adept at making comparisons about her life."

"Don't let this effort deter you," Ernst consoled him, smiling. "Catechizing always remains a fine art—one used just as well before the court as anywhere else. Besides, one always learns something thereby, unless of course it is badly begun."

Dodging Ernst and his taunts, Leonhardt turned toward Ernestine, "But should she have no feeling about whether she feels more comfortable in a merry or a sad state?"

"Who knows!" she replied. "What do you think, Sofie?"

"I truly don't know, Mother. I can be very well in both states, and now I am perfectly fine without being one or the other. Except that his questions make me anxious, and I can't stand going over all that is past, bit by bit." And with that she kissed her mother's hand and returned to her Christmas gifts in the darkness at the other end of the parlor, where only a few of the lamps shimmered.

Karoline said, in a hushed tone, "This, at least, she has clearly shown us. The childlike sense, without which one cannot enter the kingdom of God, is just this: to accept every mood and every feeling for itself, and to wish to have it purely and completely."

"Perhaps," spoke Eduard, "except she is no mere child—she is, rather, a girl—and therefore this is not entirely the childlike sense."[26]

"Well, yes," Karoline continued, "it should also hold true only for us. I was simply trying to say that one hears complaints from young and old alike, especially during these days of childlike joy, that they are not now able to be as happy as they were in their childhood years. But surely such complaints do not come from those who had such a childhood. Only yesterday I had to wonder at the astonishment of some people when I insisted that I was now still capable of such buoyant joy, even more so."

"Yes," joked Leonhardt, "and the poor thing, when she does nothing but rejoice quite childishly in something girlish, is sometimes deemed vain even by people like those. But leave it at that, fair child. These adversaries are those to whom nature has granted a second childhood at the end of life, so that when they reach this destination, they might get one last refreshing draught from the beaker of joy at the conclusion of the long, miserable, joyless time."

"I dare say, this is more serious and tragic than humorous," said Ernst. "I, for one, scarcely know something more dreadful than how the great mass of humanity must necessarily lose the first articles of childlike joy, and how, incapable of attaining the higher things, they are thoughtless about the beautiful development of life and are afflicted by boredom. I do not know if it should be said they 'watch' or 'attend,' for even that is too much for their pure idleness. Finally, out of the nothingness, a second childhood emerges again, but one that relates to the first like an undesirable runt to a fair child, or like the erratic flicker of a dying flame to the escalating, in many cases transforming, glow of a just-ignited flame."

Agnes spoke, "I'd like to take exception again, this time to only one point. Do the first childlike articles of joy have to dwindle away in order for someone to obtain the higher ones? Shouldn't there be a way

---

26. In other words, as a girl she does not represent all children since she does not represent boys. This touches on Schleiermacher's theory of gender, as the following conversation indicates.

of obtaining the latter, without relinquishing the former? For doesn't life begin with a pure illusion, in which there is no truth at all, nothing enduring? What do you really think? Do the joys of the human person—who has advanced to reflection about self and the world, who has found God—begin with conflict and war, with the obliteration not of evil but rather of innocence? For that is the way we always characterize the childlike—or the childish, too, if you will. Or must time, with what poison I know not, have slain the first original joys of life already beforehand? And did the transition from the one state into the other still go through a nothingness?"

"You probably can't call it a nothingness," Ernestine chimed in. "But it does seem, and they themselves also admit it, that men—you might even want to say the best men, most men—lead a fantastical, dissolute life between childhood and their improved existence, a life both passionate and confused. It looks like a continuation of their childhood, whose joys also indicate a boisterous and destructive nature. But, in its erratic impulses, it looks like an indecisive life, ever alternating between letting go and wanting to grasp. We women understand nothing of this. In us, both unite with one another imperceptibly. Our whole life lies in what attracts us in the games of childhood, and the higher meaning reveals itself gradually in each of our lives. Even though we understand God and the world according to our own way, we express our highest and sweetest feelings always together in those charming details, in that gentle glow that first befriended us with the world."

Eduard said, "Men and women, therefore, would also have their distinct ways in the development of the spiritual, which after all must be the same in both men and women, so that they may unite herein by means of mutual recognition. Yes, it may very well be, and it makes clear sense to me, that in *us* the opposition of what is unconscious and what is thought out emerges more strongly, and it reveals itself during the transition into that turbulent striving, that impassioned battle with the world and oneself. In contrast, in *your* calm and graceful being the consistency of both and their inner unity comes to light, and holy earnestness and charming play are one throughout."

"But then strangely enough," Leonhardt countered, smiling facetiously, "we men would be more Christian than the women. For

Christianity speaks everywhere of a turning around, of a transformation of the mind, a renewal through which the old should be cast out. None of which you women, a few Magdalenes excepted, would have any need whatsoever—if the previous speech is true."

Karoline retorted, "Yet Christ himself did not convert. Thus he has also always been the patron of women. And whereas you have only argued amongst yourselves about him, we have loved and worshiped him. Or what could you object to, if we were now to put the right meaning into the worn-out proverb that we always remain children. By contrast, do you first have to turn around in order to become a child again?"

"And thus it stands to reason," Ernst added, "what is the celebration of the infancy of Jesus but the clear recognition of the immediate union of the divine with the childlike, which thus requires no further turning around. Agnes, too, has already expressed this before, as the universal insight of all women: they presuppose the divine already from birth on and seek it in their children, as the church does in Christ."

"Yes, this holiday in particular is the nearest and best proof that our situation is really just as Ernestine described it earlier," Friederike said.

"How so?" Leonhardt asked.

She replied, "Because here, in little episodes that nevertheless are neither unrecognizable nor forgotten, one can keep track of the nature of our joy in order to see whether it has experienced multiple sudden metamorphoses. We could hardly be required to examine our consciences, since the matter really speaks for itself. It is obvious enough that women and girls everywhere are the soul of these little holidays—they are the ones most occupied with making preparations, but they also rejoice in the most purely receptive and highest way. If holidays were left just to you men, they would soon perish. Only through us do they become an undying tradition. You'll ask, 'But couldn't we also have this religious joy by itself? And wouldn't we get it, even if we hadn't found it until later on as something new?' No, because everything is still tied together just as it had been in earlier years. Already in childhood, we attached a special importance to these presents. They were more to us than they would have been had they been given at some other time. The difference is that in childhood it was a dark, mysterious presentiment, which has since then gradually emerged more clearly, but that still shows itself to us best under the same form and that does not want to abandon the familiar symbol. Indeed, the emergence of the higher life can be traced in the precision with which the small, beautiful moments of life remain in our memory."

"Truly," Leonhardt said, "if you women wanted to depict for us your Christmas joys with their noteworthy aspects—and if you carried this out as vividly and as well as you are capable of doing—it will surely give a beautiful series of small portraits. Even someone not particularly sympathetic with the intended purpose would take delight in it."

"How nicely he phrases what he really wants to say—that it would bore him!" Karoline exclaimed.

Ernestine said, "Admittedly, done in that way, it would be too trivial—as much for the man who still wants to behave more chivalrously as for the one who really has a better sense of the matter. But whoever has something noteworthy and relevant to our discussion to relate, please do so. Join it to this incident from my early childhood that I'd like to tell you about, though some of you may perhaps already be familiar with it."

Friederike rose and said, "As you know, I am not accustomed to relating in that way. There is, however, something else I'd like to do so as to bring you pleasure. I shall sit down at the instrument and accompany your stories with *Fantasias*.[27] Thus you will also be listening to something from me, but with your finer and higher ears."

Ernestine began, "At our house, the joyous holiday had been preceded by all kinds of miserable circumstances that had, only shortly beforehand, come to a somewhat happy resolution. Thus the joy of the children had been tended to with far less love and diligence than usual. This was an opportunity to satisfy a wish that I had expressed a year earlier but in vain. Back then, of course, the so-called Christmas Matins[28] were still held in the late evening hours and con-

---

27. A kind of improvisation popular in the Romantic era.

28. The earlier Catholic tradition had been that on Christmas Eve, after compline, matins were said and then the Mass itself would begin after midnight. Ernestine is referring to a former Protestant tradition of Christmas Eve worship services, before new laws were passed in German lands and the celebration of Christmas shifted to the private sphere. See Nowak, *Schleiermacher*, 164-65; and Morgenroth, *Weihnachts-Christentum*.

tinued up until midnight, alternating between lessons and carols, before a restless and not exactly reverent assembly. After some hesitation, my parents allowed me to go to church in the company of my mother's chambermaid. I am not aware of—I cannot easily recall—such mild weather in this time of year as there was on that night. The heavens were clear, and yet the evening was almost warm. In the area of the Christmas market, which was winding down, great droves of boys chased about with the last of the whistles, chirping birds, and buzzing tops—all being sold off for a cheap price. They ran noisily here and there on the way to the various churches. Not until we were very near did we hear the organ and a few voices of children and adults accompanying it in a disorderly manner.

"Despite a seeming extravagance of lamps and candles, the ancient gray pillars and walls could not be made bright, and I could only make out individual figures with difficulty—none of which were in any way pleasant. Still less could the clergyman, with his squawking voice, inspire me to participate, and, totally dissatisfied, I just wanted to ask my companion to return home. I took one last look around. There I spotted in an open choir stall, under a beautiful old monument, a woman with a small child in her lap. She appeared to pay little attention to the preacher, the songs, or anything around her; she appeared rather to be deeply lost in her own thoughts, her eyes steadfastly directed at the child.

"I was drawn irresistibly to her, and my companion was obliged to lead me over to her. Here I had found at last the sanctuary I had sought for so long in vain. I stood before the noblest picture I had ever seen. The woman was simply dressed; her pleasant, gracious deportment made the open choir stall a closed chapel. No one stopped nearby—even so, she did not seem to notice me standing right in front of her. Her countenance appeared to me at once smiling and then sorrowful, her breath at once joyfully trembling, then with difficulty suppressing happy sighs, but the most lasting impression of all was the friendly tranquility, the loving devotion—and these radiated gloriously forth from the large, dark, sunken eyes, which the eyelashes would have hidden from me completely had I been somewhat taller. The child, too, appeared to me uncommonly lovely. He moved in a lively way but was quiet and appeared to me to be grasped in a half-unconscious dialogue of love and longing with his mother.

"I now had living figures of the beautiful pictures of Mary and the Christ child, and I so lost myself in this fantasy that I half unintentionally pulled on the woman's dress and asked her with an emotional, very pleading voice, 'May I give the lovely child something?' And so I emptied out onto his coverings some little handfuls of sweets that I had taken along for comfort in case of need. The woman stared at me for a moment, then drew me kindly to herself, kissed my forehead and spoke, 'O yes, dear little one, today everyone gives, and all for the sake of a child.' I kissed her on the hand she had laid on my neck and kissed one of the outstretched hands of the little baby. I wanted to go quickly, but then she said, 'Wait, I want to give you something, too. Perhaps I shall recognize you again by it.' She searched around and drew from her hair a golden pin with a green stone that she fastened to my coat. I kissed her cloak one more time and quickly left the church with a full, overall blessed feeling.

"It was Eduard's oldest sister, the noble, tragic figure, who more than anyone—ever, anywhere—has affected my life and my inner existence. She was soon to become the friend and mentor of my youth, and though I had nothing but sorrows to share with her, I still count my connection with her among the most beautiful and important elements of my life. Eduard, a grown lad at that time, stood behind her, although I hadn't noticed him."

Friederike seemed to have been familiar with the content—so exactly did her playing accompany the charming recounting, and so exactly did each part immediately harmonize with the total impression of the whole. When Ernestine ended, Friederike transitioned from playing a few improvised passages to playing a beautiful church melody. Sofie, who guessed it, ran over to add in her voice, and they sang together the beautiful verse of Novalis:

I see thee in countless pictures,
O Mary, so lovingly portrayed;
But not one of them captures
How my soul has thee beheld.
All earthly turmoil since then
Does like a dream from me depart,

And an ineffably sweet heaven
Stands ever in my heart.[29]

"Mother," Sofie said when she returned, "now everything you have told me appears quite vividly before me—everything about Aunt Kornelie and about the handsome young man whom I have once seen, and who died so heroically and so futilely for freedom. Let me fetch the pictures. We are all, of course, familiar with them, but I think we should look at them again now."

The mother beckoned, and the child held out two paintings, not yet mounted, by Ernestine's brush. Both depicted her friend and her son of sorrows. The one, as he returned to her from the battle, wounded but crowned with fame; the other as he took his leave from her, only to fall as one of the last offerings to that bloodthirsty time.

Leonhardt interrupted the painful memories, which only gave vent to solitary, mournful words, by saying to Agnes, "Tell us something else, child, and release us both from the stabbing grief, which in no way belongs to our joy, and from the Mary worship into which the girls there have sung us."

"Well then," responded Agnes, "I want to recount something less significant, but probably for that reason quite cheerful. As you know, a year ago we were all scattered on this holiday. I had already been at my brother's for several weeks to help out around the time of Luisen's first confinement. There, too, Christmas Eve was begun according to our usual custom—with a gathering of friends. Luisen was completely recovered. Still, I had not failed to arrange everything. That cheerfulness and freshly excited love that takes place among good people everywhere on this universal day of rejoicing also reigned among us. And just as, amidst presents and attestations of joy, this clothes itself in the merry cloak of jokes and free playful childishness, so it was among us.

"Suddenly the nurse appeared in the parlor with her little charge. She moved around the table looking about, and then cried

---

29. Novalis, *Geistliche Lieder*, No. 15. "Novalis" is the pseudonym for Georg Philipp Friedrich Freiherr von Hardenberg (1772–1801), a Romantic poet. He died just short of his twenty-ninth birthday. In the second edition of the second *Speech*, Schleiermacher added a tribute to him (see below, 167–68); he also mentions him in a letter to Henriette Herz, translated below, 259.

out several times successively—half jokingly, half whiningly—'Didn't anyone give something to the baby? Have you completely forgotten about the baby?' At once we gathered around the cute, tiny creature, and all kinds of speeches ensued, in jest and in earnest, about how, even with all the love in the world, we could still not bring him joy, and how appropriate it was that we had given his mother everything that really belonged to him. We then showed the nurse everything and also held it all out before the baby—a little hat, tiny stockings, clothes, a little spoon, and small bowl. Yet neither the shine and jingle of the precious metals nor the dazzling or translucent white of the material seemed to stir his senses. 'Yes, so it is, children!' I said to the others. 'He is still completely focused on his mother, and even she can still do nothing else than arouse in him the same day-to-day feeling of satisfaction. His feeling is still joined with hers. It dwells in her, and we can only attend to it and appreciate it in her.'

"'But we are all quite narrow,' started an amiable young girl, 'in that we have only thought of the present moment. For doesn't the entire life of the child stand before the mother?' With these words she demanded my key from me. At the same time, several others scattered with the assurance that they would be back soon, and Ferdinand cajoled them into hurrying, for he too had something in store for the little one. To those of us who had stayed behind, he asked, 'Can you not guess what it is? I want to baptize him right away. I cannot think of a more beautiful moment for that than this one. Take care of what is necessary. I will be here again when our friends return.'

"So, as quickly as possible, we dressed the baby in the cutest of the presents that were on hand, and we had hardly finished when those who had gone off reappeared with all kinds of gifts. Jest and earnestness were wonderfully mixed together in this—as it can only be with any realization of the future. Material for clothes not only for his boyhood but even for his wedding day. A toothpick and a watch ribbon, so that one might say of him, in the best sense, what was said of Churchill: 'When he played with his watch band or picked his teeth, a poem came out.' Elegant paper on which he was to write his first letter to a beloved girl. Introductory textbooks for all kinds of languages and sciences, and also a Bible, to be handed over to him when he would receive his first instruction in Christianity. Yes, his uncle, who liked to draw caricatures, brought forth spectacles as the first requirement of a future dandy—as he expressed himself in a Campe-ish manner[30]—and he was not satisfied until they were held before the large bright blue eyes.

"There was a lot of laughing and joking, but Luisen insisted quite seriously that, except for the glasses—for he must surely have her and Ferdinand's good eyes—she could see him now quite vividly and, certainly genuinely prophetically, with definite form and features, in all the times and circumstances before him that the gifts anticipated. In vain they teased her about how old-fashioned he would probably appear if he really wanted to honor every present with use and how he would have to take special care lest the paper become yellowed. Finally, we all agreed to praise, most of all, the person who gave the Bible, which he would most certainly be able to make use of. I pointed out the baby's attire, but no one thought there was any special reason for it, except that he wished to accept their gifts in a right worthy manner.

"Thus they were all not a little surprised when Ferdinand entered the room in his clerical garb, and at the same time the table with the water was brought. 'Don't be so surprised, dear friends,' he said. 'With Agnes's remark earlier, the thought had naturally occurred to me to baptize the boy on this day. You shall all be witnesses to it, and in doing so you will also confirm yourselves anew as involved, lifetime friends.' After he had observed each one individually, while they were making various joyful remarks, he continued, 'You have offered him gifts that point to a life of which as yet he knows nothing, just as Christ was offered gifts that pointed to a glory of which the child knew nothing. Let us now make the most beautiful gift—Christ himself—the boy's own, even if that gift cannot yet give him any enjoyment or joy. Right now his religious feeling dwells not in his mother alone or in me, but in all of us, and from us he must one day appropriate it for himself.'

"In this way he gathered us around him and transitioned almost immediately from conversation to the sacred act. With a

---

30. A reference Joachim Heinrich Campe (1746–1818). According to Patsch, Campe's *Wörterbuch zur Erklärung* and *Verdeutschung der unserer Sprache aufgedrungenen fremden Ausdrücke* appeared in 1801. See Patsch, "Die esoterische Kommunikationsstruktur," 137 and especially 152n27, where he lists the many references to Campe.

slight allusion to the words, 'Who will prevent these from being baptized?'[31] he gushed on about how even the very fact that a Christian child is received in love and joy, and always remains embraced in them, provides the guarantee that the Spirit of God will dwell in him, how the celebration of the birth of the new world must be a day of love and joy, and how the two united together are specially ordained to initiate a child of love into the higher birth of the divine life. As we all laid hands on the child, according to the fine, old local custom, it was as if streams of heavenly love and desire converged on the head and heart of the child as a new focal point, and so would radiate again in all directions. It was certainly the shared feeling that they were there kindling a new life."

"Well now, here we have the previous story again," interrupted Leonhardt, "only, as it were, an inverted negative Christ child, with the halo flowing inward, not outward."

"You put that splendidly, dear Leonhardt," responded Agnes. "I couldn't have said it so well myself. Only the mother, whose love sees the whole person in the child—and it is just this love that calls out the angelic greeting to her—only she sees the heavenly radiance already flowing out from him, and only on her prophetic face is formed the beautiful reflection that Sofie has presented in an unconscious, childlike sense. That is why tonight I have recounted for all of you what you, Leonhardt, may well say better and more beautifully than I am able to—or even say as well as can be said. For I do not have the words to describe how deeply and inwardly I felt on that occasion that every serene joy is religion. Love, delight, and devotion are notes from one perfect harmony that can follow one another in any number of ways or can sound together. And if you want to do it really beautifully, go ahead and scoff—then the truth will surely come back to bite you, as it did before."

"Why should I?" Leonhardt answered. "You have yourself indicated how you would have it expressed—namely, not with words, but in music. But Friederike, as it appears, has herself only listened and has given us nothing to listen to—not once your symbol, by which you are now so transported: the simple cadence. Why is that?"

"Yes," Friederike said, "it is easier to accompany a story like Ernestine's directly." She added, smiling, "Especially if you know

---

31. See Acts 10:47.

something about it. "Besides, I believe that my art will be less likely to be lost on you if I follow the story first. If you want, I shall play it for you right now."

She improvised with interwoven melodies of some cheerful, bright church melodies that now, however, are seldom heard, and then she sang so as to finish once again with her favorite poet, according to one of his assorted verses of the hymn, "Where Tarriest Thou, Consolation of All the World?"[32] Naturally, she chose those verses that were most intelligible to the feminine sense. And where she came upon a break, she filled it with harmonies that expressed the inward tranquility, the profound delight that had taken hold of her and that she wanted to bring out.

"But now, Friederike," said Karoline, "You will need to forge a passage to notes of melancholy[33]—if, that is, you all do not want to end with pure joy but wish to have from me, too, a portrait set within the frame of this beautiful holiday. For I feel compelled to tell you how I celebrated Christmas last year at the home of my dear friend, Charlotte. Admittedly, there is really nothing to tell you about—it is only further input to what you know about Charlotte from other stories and from her letters, so you will have to recall everything that you already know about her.

"They have a clever custom there among the adults of giving presents anonymously. Everyone sees to it that their gifts to others are given by means of the greatest subterfuges and in the most peculiar way—for instance, hiding the gift under something less significant—so that the recipient, already happy or amazed, sometimes cannot figure out who the giver is. Many things must be devised, and the happy plan is often put in place with long, complicated preparations.

"Already for several weeks, however, Charlotte had suffered an unexplained, hence all the more wrenching, illness of her darling, her youngest child. For a long time, the doctor could give so little hope as to take away all hope. The longer the pain and agitation lasted, the more the little angel was robbed of his powers, so that

---

32. Novalis, *Geistliche Lieder*, No. 12. It is also a line in *O Heiland, reiß die Himmel auf*, an Advent hymn by a German Jesuit, Friedrich Spee (1591–1635), who was a poet, hymnist, and opponent of witch trials.

33. *Wehmuth*. For the Romantics the term conveyed an aestheticized, poetic idea of melancholy as mournfulness linked to an idea of acute longing.

nothing but his demise was expected. Her friends, with heartfelt sorrow, ceased all preparations of surprising her with a clever trick or a mischievous joke. Indeed, no one would venture, even by means of a simple gift, to wish to divert her attention from the object of her love and her pain. Everything was being put off to a more agreeable time.

"She carried the child around in her arms almost constantly. At night she would never properly lie down. Only during the day, when the child at times appeared more tranquil and when she could entrust him with me or another friend, did she permit herself a little bit of rest. Even so, she did not neglect matters related to the holiday, despite the fact that we often begged her not to exhaust herself with tasks unrelated to her cares. Admittedly, it was impossible for her to do the work herself, but she made plans and gave directions. And she often surprised me with a question, in the midst of her deepest grief, as to whether this or that had been seen to, or with a new idea about a little joy. There was no merriment or playfulness in what she said—but that is never how it is with her. Sensibility and meaningfulness, however, were never lacking. A calm gracefulness characterizes all of her actions.

"I still recall once, when I expressed almost disapprovingly my amazement at her, her saying to me, 'Dear child, there is no more beautiful nor more fitting frame for a tremendous grief than a necklace of little joys that we prepare for others. In this way everything is in the setting in which it can remain for life, and who wouldn't immediately want to be in this setting? In all that time effaces—and it does this with everything impetuous and one-sided—there is also something impure.'

"A few days before Christmas, an inner battle could be noticed in her. She, and practically she alone, had not yet been convinced of the hopeless condition of the child. Now, especially, she grasped his appearance and his weakness. All of a sudden, the image of death rose clearly before her. Deeply lost in thought, she went up and down for a good hour with the child in her arms, manifesting all the signs of innermost emotion. Then she looked at him with a mournfully serene face for a long while, as if for the last time. She bent down for a long kiss on his forehead, and then, fortified and brave, she reached her hand to me and said, 'Well, I have overcome it, dear friend. I have given the little angel back to heaven from which he came. I now calmly await his demise—calmly and certainly. I can even wish to see him pass away soon, so that the signs of pain and destruction will not darken for me the angelic image that has impressed itself deeply and forever upon my heart.'

"On the morning of Christmas Eve she gathered the children around herself and asked them whether they wanted to celebrate their holiday that day—it was all prepared, and it was entirely up to them—or whether they wanted to wait until Eduard was buried and the initial silence and the initial grief were over. They unanimously weighed in that they could take pleasure in nothing, but their little brother was still among the living and might not die.

"In the afternoon, Charlotte handed me the child and lay down for a rest, and while she slept in a long, refreshing slumber—from which I had resolved not to wake her, whatever might happen—a crisis arose. The nearly dead body underwent violent convulsions, which I took to be the last. To the doctor who had been summoned, it revealed the disease and the cure at one and the same time. After an hour, the child was noticeably better, and it was clear that he was on the road to recovery. Quickly, the children festively decked the room and the little one's bed. His mother walked in and thought that we simply wanted to enhance the appearance of the dead body for her.

"When she looked at his bed, the first smile of the child beamed back at her. Among the flowers, he appeared to her as an already half-dead bud that rises again and wants to open up after a beneficent rain. 'If this is not a deceptive hope,' she said, hugging us all after she had heard the whole story, 'then it is a different rebirth from the one I had expected. I had hoped and prayed,' she continued, 'that the child might be raised out of the earthly life at this time. It touched me poignantly and sweetly to send an angel to heaven at the time when we celebrate the sending of the greatest one to earth. Now both of them come to me at the same time, immediately given by God. On the celebration of the rebirth of the world, unto me is born to a new life the darling of my heart. Yes, he lives—there is no doubt about it,' she said, while she bent over him, hardly daring to touch him or to press his hand to her lips. 'Even so, he remains an angel,' she said after a while. 'He is purified through his pains. He is, as it were, drawn forth through death and sanctified to a higher life. He is to me a special gift of grace, a heavenly child, because I had already dedicated him to heaven."'

Karoline had to tell many more things, with more detail, about this story, and about the admirable, exceptional woman to whom she was dedicated with a special pious reverence.

Leonhardt listened with particular interest and almost became annoyed when Ernst asked him, "But do you not find here, too, the same thing again as before—as it were, an inverted Mary, who begins with the deepest sorrows of motherhood—with the Stabat Mater—and ends with the joy in the divine child?"

"Or maybe not inverted," said Ernestine. "For Mary's sorrow must have surely disappeared in the feeling of the divine greatness and glory of her son—just as, on the other end, from the beginning on, with her faith and her hopes, everything that happened to him externally could only have appeared to her as suffering, as alienation."

At this point the wider conversation was interrupted by a merry, rowdy band of acquaintances who themselves belonged to no particular circle, or who had in an erratic restless sense spent their own joy more quickly and now wandered around here and there to see how others had been celebrating and what gifts had been given. To make themselves a more welcome audience and also to find a friendly tour guide every place they went, they announced themselves as Christmas helpers[34] and distributed to the children and girls the choicest delicacies for the palate. Sofie was spared the usual ceremony of first being asked about her good behavior, and in return she gave herself over to them very readily and obligingly. She quickly renewed the illumination of her panorama, and she was ever so eloquent a castellan as she was a curious questioner, asking them about everything they had already seen elsewhere. In the meantime, a hastily made refreshment was passed around. The visitors hastened on their way but then returned, hoping to get some of the company to join their ranks. But this Eduard did not allow. He said they must stay together a while longer yet. And besides, Josef was still certainly expected and had been promised that he should find them all there.

---

34. *Weihnachtsknechte*, a reference to *Knecht Ruprecht* (Servant Rupert), a companion and servant of St. Nicholas, often associated with punishment when children are not good.

When they had again dispersed, Ernst said, "Good. If it is decided that we will spend the night here in conversation over drinks, then I think we owe the women something in return so that they will more willingly stay with us. Admittedly, storytelling is not the gift of men, and I haven't the faintest idea how I myself would carry out such a thing. But what do you think, friends, if we, in the English manner—not to mention the ancient one, which is not entirely foreign to us—were to choose a topic about which each was obliged to say something? I mean a topic and manner of speaking such that we in no sense forget the presence of the women, but rather that we would regard it as the most beautiful thing to be understood and praised by them."

They all agreed to this, and the women were happy because they had not heard such a thing for a long time.

"Well," said Leonhardt, "if you women agree to take part in this proposal, then you should also assign the topic on which we are to speak, lest our cluelessness grasp after something all too indifferent."

"If the others are of the same opinion," said Friederike, "I propose the holiday itself, that which has gathered us here—as much as I wish not to cause you too much displeasure, Leonhardt. Indeed, it has so many aspects that each speaker can exalt what he likes best."

No one objected, and Ernestine expressed the opinion that any other topic would be strange and would ruin the evening.

"Well then," said Leonhardt, "according to our custom, I, as the youngest, may not decline being the first to speak. And I prefer it that way, partly because the imperfect speech is most easily blown away by a better one, and partly because I will most surely experience the joy of anticipating the first thoughts of another." Smiling, he added, "At the same time, your arrangement doubles the number of speakers on this topic in an invisible way. For tomorrow you will undoubtedly go to church, and it would redound more to our annoyance than to those men's joy—perhaps the most to your boredom— if there you were to hear the same thing again. For this reason I will veer as far as possible away from this course and advance my speech in the following manner.

"One can exalt and commend anything in one of two ways: on the one hand, by praising it or acknowledging its kind and inner nature as good; on the other hand, by extolling it or singling out its excellence and perfection in its kind. The first way may be set aside, or it may be left to others to praise a festival[35] in general terms—insofar as it is good that the remembrance of great events is secured and preserved through certain acts recurring at appointed times. If, however, there are to be festivals, and if the first origin of Christianity is to be held in high regard as something great and important, then no one can deny that the Christmas festival is one worthy of being marveled at, so perfectly does it achieve its end and under such difficult conditions. For if someone were to say that this remembrance is preserved much more through Scripture and through instruction in Christianity, generally speaking, rather than through the festival, then I would venture to deny this. Why? I think we who are cultured might find the former sufficient, but that would never suffice for the great mass of uncultured folk. For, if we don't count the Roman church—where the Scriptures are rarely if ever placed in their hands—and if we consider only our own churches, then it is clear how little inclined the folk are to read the Bible or how little capable of understanding it in context. And what *is* impressed on their memory through instruction is not so much the story[36] as the proof of particular propositions. Then again, what would be brought to remembrance from the story in this way is the death of the Redeemer, much more than his life or first appearance in the world.[37]

"Just how much people also experience history more through festive customs than through the written tradition is illuminated in the following way. Think of how much common Catholics know about saints, about whom they have never read anything, only because of the fact that they have celebrated their feast days; and they connect the special help they ask for from each saint with a definite notion of the *person*. And think of how much from the ancient past, about which the historian and poet have little or nothing to say, was preserved throughout antiquity by means of festivals. Yes, action is

---

35. In these speeches, Schleiermacher uses one term, *das Fest*, which works well in German but not so much in English. I use "festival" when they are making more general comparisons, and "holiday," "celebration," or "feast" at other times, depending on the context.

36. *Geschichte*. It could also be translated as "history"; the English translation loses the twofold sense of "history" and "story."

37. In the second edition, a long revision of the text begins here. It includes mention of Catholic beliefs, including belief in the assumption of Mary.

so much stronger than the word that, not infrequently, false histories are fabricated out of festive activities whose true meaning has been lost. But it is never the other way around. If, therefore, people stick so much more with festivals than with words, then we must also believe that the remembrance of Christ is preserved to a greater extent through the Christmas festival than through Scripture—and this is particularly so among people who, to speak candidly and simply, have just as little enjoyment as understanding of Christ.

"Furthermore, when I said that this recollection is especially difficult to preserve, this is what I mean: the more we actually know about a topic, the more definitely and meaningfully we also let it present itself; and the more necessarily we connect it with the present, the easier becomes each performance that is supposed to recall it. With Christ, however, this seems to be almost completely missing. For I certainly grant that Christianity is a strong and powerful presence,[38] but how little this connects with Christ the actual person! I exclude from this what is taught concerning his atonement, since this is based more on an eternal decree of God than on a specific, individual fact,[39] and therefore it should not be said of a specific moment but should rather be raised beyond chronicles and be regarded as mythical.

"But Christ as the founder of Christianity—and this is certainly the content of his life and the singular relation in which his first appearance in history can be celebrated—has only a sketchy meaning. For how little can be traced back to Christ himself, and most of that is, by far, of another and later origin! So much so, that if one thinks of John the forerunner, Christ, the apostles, including the last of them,[40] and the first fathers as members in a series, then it must be admitted that Christ, as the second, does not stand in the middle between the first and the third, but is much closer to John the Baptist than to Paul. Yes, it remains doubtful whether it was his will that a separate church be formed, without which our Christianity—

---

38. In the second edition, another significant revision begins here.

39. Schleiermacher's own rejection of the traditional Reformed doctrine of vicarious atonement goes back to his days at Barby (see his letter to father, 251 below). The "specific, individual fact" refers to Christ's death, as Schleiermacher makes clear in the second edition.

40. St. Paul.

and with it also our holiday, the topic of my speech—could not be imagined.

"And how much deeper still, after time, does Christianity plunge, if you consider the persistent attempt by Christ's biographers to tie him to the ancient royalty of the Jewish people—which surely, whether it is so or not, is totally insignificant for the founder of a world religion.[41] That the birth and actual existence of Christ in history is barely connected with Christianity itself is clear. That we know virtually nothing about him is just as certain. For already at the time when the first reports were composed, opinions were so varied that those authors appear to have taken all of them into account, whereby the authors themselves were turned again to a certain extent from being witnesses and reporters to being partisans. Yes, you can say that each report and each assertion cancels the others out. For the resurrection means the death did not happen, which can be put in no other terms than that the later deed nullifies the opinion that had been held about the earlier deed. The ascension, in turn, means the life is suspect, since the life belongs to the planet, and what can be separated from the planet cannot have stood in a truly living connection with it. Just as little remains if you lump together the opinion of those who deny Christ a true body, or of those who deny him a true human soul, with the belief of those who, on the contrary, do not want to attribute true divinity to him, or anything superhuman at all. Yes, if you consider that it is disputed whether Christ is still present on earth now only in a spiritual and divine way, or is also present in a bodily and sensual way, then you can easily be led by both parties to the conclusion that their common and hidden sense of the matter is this: during his lifetime Christ was not present on earth and did not live among his own in a manner any different or any more real than right now.

"In short, the experiential, historical basis of the matter is so weak that our holiday is exalted all the more, and its power closely borders on the aforementioned—namely that sometimes, through such customs, history itself is first created. What is most amazing about this, and what can serve as a model for us and at the same time as an embarrassment for many others, is this: clearly, the holiday itself owes its high status largely to the fact that it has been estab-

---

41. In the second edition, a fairly long revision on supernatural birth begins here.

lished in the home and among the children. There we should secure many things that are worthy and sacred to us, and we should reckon it as a reproach and an evil sign that we do not do it. At the very least, therefore, we want to hang on to *this* as it has been handed down to us. And the less we know wherein lies the miraculous power, the less also will we change even the slightest detail. To me, at any rate, the smallest thing is significant. For just as a child is the main subject of Christmas, so too children are primarily the ones who lift and carry it—and, in turn, through the holiday, lift and carry Christianity itself. And just as night is the historic cradle of Christianity, so too is the festival of its birth celebrated during the night. And the candles with which it is resplendent are like to the star above the inn and the halo, without which the child would not be found in the darkness of the stable and in the otherwise starless night of history. And just as what we have received in the person of Christ, and from whom we have received it, is dark and doubtful, so too is that custom, which I learned about in Karoline's story, the most beautiful and most symbolic manner of receiving Christmas gifts.

"This is my honest opinion, to which I now invite you to toast and empty your glasses. And I am so certain of your approval that I hope thereby to make all well and to wash away what appeared somewhat sacrilegious in my speech."

"Now I realize," said Friederike, "why he put up so little resistance against our assigned topic, the unbelieving rogue, given that he had in mind to speak so completely against its genuine sense. I insist that he pay a steep penalty, all the more so since *I* proposed the assignment, and it is fair to say that he has mocked me in how he performed it."

"You are undoubtedly right," said Eduard. "But it would be difficult to get anywhere with him, since he has been careful in a quite lawyerly manner—in his explanation, and in the way in which he interwove the disparaging with the aim of elevating Christmas, which, after all, he *had* to place at the top."

"Treading warily in a lawyerly manner is certainly nothing evil," said Leonhardt. "And why shouldn't I take every opportunity to practice the legitimate and respectable aspects of my art? Besides, I could hardly have refused the women, and they could have provided nothing else or nothing better for the way of thinking to which I openly enough confess. But after all, I haven't really proceeded like a lawyer, since I have not once inserted into my speech the smallest solicitation for favoritism from our female judges."

"I can attest to the fact," said Ernst, "that you spared us from much that still might have been brought forth as evidence, whether it was because you did not have it at hand or because you refrained from it in order to save time and not to speak too learnedly and unintelligibly in front of the women."

"For my part," said Ernestine, "I would also like to praise him for how sincerely he kept his word, as he promised, to stay as much as possible away from what we could perchance hear tomorrow in places of public worship."

Karoline said, "Well then, if it is not possible to bring him to justice straightaway, then we will take our chance at refuting him. And if I am not mistaken, it is your turn, Ernst, to speak, and to rescue the honor of our assignment."

"I intend to do the last without the first," said Ernst. "Besides, I am not, for my part, capable of combining these two things together. The refutation would divert me to other topics, and then I myself could become culpable. Furthermore, nothing is more difficult for someone unaccustomed to extemporaneous speeches than to do so while following the train of thought of another."

Ernst began his speech. "Before you spoke, Leonhardt, I did not know how to distinguish what I want to say—whether it would be a praising or an extolling. Now, however, I see that it is in its own way an extolling. For I, too, want to commend the holiday as excellent in its kind. However, I do not want to let the praise—recognizing its kind and idea as good—be set aside, as you had. On the contrary, I presuppose it all the more. Except that your explanation of a festival is not adequate for me, since it was generally adapted only for your purposes and is one-sided. My purpose, however, is different, and so I need the other side. That is to say, you only looked at the fact that every festival is a commemoration of something. What interests me is, a commemoration of *what*?

"Accordingly, I say that a festival is founded only for commemoration of *that* which, through its re-presentation, excites in people a certain mood of the heart and disposition. And the excellence of any particular festival rests in this: it is carried out throughout the entire area of its influence and to a vivid degree. The mood that our holiday is supposed to bring forth is joy, and the fact that Christmas spreads this joy widely and arouses it vividly is so evident that nothing need be said about it, since people see it for themselves.

"There is just one difficulty that I have to overcome. One could say that it is not really the proper and essential part of the holiday that produces this effect, but only the accidental part—the gifts given and received. It needs to be shown just how wrong this is. If you give children the same things at another time, you will not elicit even the shadow of a Christmas joy, until perhaps you come to the opposite point—namely, when their own, personal feast day is celebrated. I believe I am right in calling this 'an opposite point,' and certainly no one will deny that birthday joy has an entirely different character from Christmas joy. The former joy is characterized entirely by the inwardness that engenders its being enclosed in a specific relation; the latter, entirely by the fire, the swift movement of a widespread universal feeling. Two things follow from this. First, it is by no means the presents themselves that are so pleasing but rather the occasion. Also, second, the distinctiveness of Christmas joy consists precisely in this total universality.

"Throughout a great part of Christendom, as far as the beautiful old custom reaches, everyone is busy preparing a gift, and this consciousness is the very magic that takes possession of us all. A present picked up incidentally from an ordinary shop, or made in idle hours without wider connection, is little or nothing. But the joint parleying; the working in the race up to the appointed festive hour; the outdoors Christmas market reflected in every present; and the illumination, which like a tiny shimmering star shines on the earth in the winter night so that the heavens reflect it—all of this is what gives the gifts their value.

"And what is so universal can never have been arbitrarily devised. It must be based on something internal, otherwise it could neither produce an effect nor even continue to exist, as we indeed have seen well enough in many recent attempts. This 'inner,' however, can be nothing other than the cause for all joy that moves in waves among people. And such an effect could not arise from anything else. That is also so in fact. I but call to mind—and at the same time accuse—those who have displaced the universal joy of this celebration to New Year's Eve, to the point when the change and contrast in the time is represented. For it is clear that those who are lacking this inner demeanor live only in this change and are only pleased with the renewal of what is fleeting.

"This, then, is the relation between the birth of the Redeemer and the universal celebration of joy—namely, for all who do not, like those others, live only in this changing of the time, there is no other principle of joy than redemption, and for us the initial point of redemption must be the birth of a divine child. For that reason, too, no specific celebration has as much a resemblance to this one as infant baptism, if one does not go about it totally senselessly. Hence the special appeal of that charming story in which both the baptism and the celebration of Christmas appeared united to us.

"Yes, Leonhardt, do what we may, here there is no escape. The life and the joy of the original nature[42]—where those oppositions between appearance and essence, time and eternity, do not occur at all—is not ours. And if we imagined this in one person, then we imagined this very one as Redeemer, and he had to, for us, start out as a divine child. We ourselves, in contrast, start out in disunity and first attain harmony through redemption, which is in fact nothing other than the lifting away[43] of those oppositions, and just for that reason can only proceed from one for whom they did not first need to be lifted. Surely, no one will deny that! This is the proper nature of this holiday: that we become conscious of the innermost ground and the uncreated power of the new untroubled life, and that we intuit its highest perfection, both in its first seeds and in its most beautiful blooms. However unconsciously it may be in many, the marvelous feeling can be resolved into nothing else except into this concentrated intuition of a new world. The feeling seizes every one, it is presented in the most diverse ways in a thousand images—as the rising and returning sun, as the spring time of the spirit, as the king of a better realm, as the most loyal emissary of the gods, as the most beloved prince of peace.

"And so, at last, I am getting around to refuting you, Leonhardt, even by agreeing with you and by comparing our different initial

---

42. Schleiermacher later regretted that, in the next three lines in particular, he did not more clearly distinguish the second and third speeches (by Ernst and Eduard, respectively).

43. *Aufhebung.*

assumptions side by side. When the matter is viewed critically—as in a lower sense[44]—the historical traces may still be weak. The holiday does not depend on that but depends instead on the necessary idea of a Redeemer,[45] and therefore those historical traces were also sufficient. The largest crystallization needs only the smallest crystal in order to trigger its formation. Whatever breaks forth from inside this joy requires only the least occasion in order to take on a definite shape. Whoever, therefore, recognizes Christianity as a powerful presence—as indeed you, too, wanted to do—and as the great form of the new life, this same person hallows this holiday, not as someone who does not dare offend something misunderstood, but rather as someone who understands it completely, every single thing in it as well—the presents and the children, the night and the light.

"And with this small amendment, which I hope might please you, I echo your proposal to a toast, Leonhardt, and I wish—or rather prophesy—this for the beautiful holiday: that it forever bear the merry childlikeness with which it always returns to us. And for all who celebrate it, that they have the proper joy in the higher life which has been regained—for only out of this joy do all its many mellifluences blossom."

"I do beg your pardon, Ernst," said Agnes. "I had feared that I wouldn't understand you at all, but that hasn't been the case, and you have quite beautifully confirmed that the essence of the holiday is really the religious. Except, according to what has already been agreed upon, it surely appears as if joy must be bestowed on us women to a lesser extent, because that troubled nature reveals itself less in us. But I can also explain that well enough for myself."

"Quite easily," said Leonhardt. "One could succinctly say, and it couldn't be clearer, that women bear all things lightly for themselves and seek little indulgence, but that just as their innermost suffering is compassion,[46] so too their joy is shared joy.[47] Let's just hope that you see how you will cope with the sacred authority, which you refuse to forsake, but which so obviously declares women as the pri-

---

44. Schleiermacher is referring to a distinction between lower and higher criticism. He first lectured on hermeneutics, or the theory of interpretation, in Halle in 1805.

45. Schleiermacher changed this to "necessity of a redeemer" in the second edition.

46. *Mitleiden.*

47. *Mitfreude.*

mary originators of all disunity—and therefore of all need for redemption.[48] But if I were Friederike, I would wage war on Ernst, because he so frivolously, without consideration of his own circumstances, grants baptism precedence over marriage, which also ought to be a beautiful and joyful sacrament, I hope."

"Don't answer him, Ernst," said Friederike. "He has already answered himself."

"How so?" asked Leonhardt.

"Why obviously," retorted Ernestine, "by speaking of your own circumstances. People like you never realize it when you mix in the beloved 'I.' Ernst, however, distinguished it well, and he will certainly tell you that marriage is closer to birthday joy than to Christmas joy."

"Or else," added Ernst, "if you want to have something Christian in it, I would tell you that it is more Good Friday and Easter than Christmas. But now let's put this all aside and listen to what Eduard has to say to us."

Eduard began his speech. "It has already been observed on a similar occasion by someone better than I that the last one to speak is in the worst position whenever a topic—whatever it may be—is addressed in this way.[49] And this is not only because the earlier speakers take away whatever there was to say—though neither of you troubled yourselves about me, perhaps by omitting some detail, in order to leave something left for me; it is also and especially because the echo of every speech remains behind in the hearers, and this forms an ever-increasing resistance that the final speaker has to overcome with the greatest difficulty. Therefore, I must look around for an aid and must rest what I will say on something known and beloved, so that it will find an easier entrée.

"As Leonhardt generally referred to the mythical biographers of Christ[50] and in them sought after the historical, so I will keep to the mystical biographer,[51] in whom almost nothing historical is to be found, not even a formal Christmas narrative, yet in whose heart reigns an eternal childlike Christmas joy. This author gives us the

---

48. A reference to Genesis and to Eve's supposed responsibility for the fall of humankind.

49. A reference to Socrates in the *Symposium*.

50. He is referring to the authors of the Synoptic Gospels—Mark, Matthew, and Luke.

51. A reference to John the Evangelist.

spiritual and higher point of view about our holiday. As you know, he commences in this way: 'In the beginning was the Word, and the Word was with God, and the Word was God. In him was life, and the life was the light of all people. And the Word became flesh and lived among us, and we have seen his glory, as of a father's only son.'[52] Thus I most prefer viewing the subject of this holiday not as a child formed and appearing such and so, born of this or that woman, here or there—but rather as the Word become flesh, who was God and is with God. The flesh, however, as we know, is nothing other than finite, limited, sensuous nature; the Word, in contrast, is thought, knowing; and the becoming flesh of the Word is therefore the coming forth of this original and divine Word in that form.

"Accordingly, what we celebrate is nothing other than our very selves, as we are collectively, or human nature—or however you want to call it—beheld and recognized from the divine principle. Why we must put forward one in whom alone human nature so presents itself, why precisely this one, and also why we attribute to him this identity of the divine and the earthly right from birth and not as a later fruit of life—all this will be cleared up in what follows.

"What else is the-human-in-itself[53] but the earth-spirit itself,[54] the knowing of the earth in its eternal existence and in its ever-changing becoming? Thus there is no corruption in it and no fall, hence no need of redemption. But individuals—insofar as we attach ourselves to the earth's other forms of education,[55] and seek our knowing in those other forms even though our knowing dwells in it alone—as individuals we are in a state of becoming only. We are in a

---

52. John 1:1, 4, 14. NRSV.

53. *Der Mensch an sich.*

54. *Der Erdgeist.* See Hermann Patsch, ed., "Introduction" to *KGA* 1/5:63; also, Patsch, "Metamorphosen des Erdgeistes. Zu einer mythologischen Metapher in der Philosophie der Goethe-Zeit," *New Athenaeum/Neues Athenaeum* 1 (1989): 248–79; and "Der 'Erdgeist' als philosophischer Topos bei Friedrich Schlegel, Schleiermacher, Schelling und Hegel," in *Schleiermacher's Philosophy and the Philosophical Tradition*, ed. Sergio Sorrentino (Lewiston, NY: Edwin Mellen, 1992), 75–90.

55. The term here is the plural *Bildungen. Bildung*, especially in the Romantic concept, is difficult to translate and depends highly on context, but it means "formation," "education," "culture," and "cultivation." Since the topic at this point is about "knowing" and how we learn to know, formation in the sense of education is probably the closest meaning, but given the plural it has been rendered "forms of education." It could also read "formations," "educations," "cultures."

state of fallenness and corruption, which is discord and confusion, and we find redemption only in the-human-in-itself.[56] That is to say, that very identity of the eternal being and becoming of the earth-spirit realizes itself in us; we contemplate and love all becoming and also our own selves only in the eternal being; and, insofar as we appear as a becoming, we want to be nothing else but a thought of eternal being and want to be grounded in no other eternal being than that which is one with ever-changing and recurring becoming.

"That is why that identity of being and becoming finds itself in humanity eternally—because it exists and becomes eternally *as* the-human-in-itself. In individuals, however, that identity—insofar as it is in the individual—must also become as their thought, and as the thought of a corporate doing and living in which the very knowing of the earth not only *is*, but also *becomes*. Only when individuals intuit and build up humanity as a living fellowship of individuals, carry its spirit and consciousness in themselves, and within it lose and find again their individual existence—only then do they have in themselves the higher life and the peace of God. This fellowship, however, through which the-human-in-itself is presented or restored, is the church. The church, therefore, is related to everything else that is becoming human around it and outside it, just as the self-consciousness of humanity in individuals is related to the unconsciousness. Everyone in whom this self-consciousness is realized, therefore, comes to the church.

"That is why no one who is not in the church can have science within them in a truthful and living way; rather, such a person can only outwardly renounce the church, but not inwardly. True, there could be people in the church who do not have science in themselves, since they could possess that higher self-consciousness in sentiment,[57] if not in cognition.[58] This is precisely the case with women, and at the same time it is the reason why they attach themselves so much more inwardly and exclusively to the church.

"Now this fellowship exists as both a becoming and a having-become, and—as a fellowship of individuals—a having-become by

56. In the second edition, a significant revision is made in the long sentence that follows; Schleiermacher specifies more clearly what takes place in each person.

57. *Empfindung.* Cf. p. 165, note 21, below.

58. *Erkenntniß.*

means of communication of the same. And therefore we also seek *one point* from which this communication proceeded, even though we know that it must proceed again spontaneously from each person—and the-human-in-itself must generate and form itself in each individual.[59] But that one point, which is regarded as the beginning point of the church, as its conception—its first fellowship of sentiment, breaking out freely and spontaneously—is at the same time the birth of the church.[60] That one point must already have been born as the-human-in-itself, as the God-man, and he must have carried the self-knowing in himself and have been, from the beginning on, the 'light of the people.' For, indeed, we are born again through the Spirit of the church. The Spirit itself, however, proceeds only from the Son, and the Son needs no rebirth but rather is born originally from God.

"That is absolutely the Son of Man. Everything earlier prefigured him, alluded to him, and was only good and divine through this relation, and in him we celebrate not only ourselves but all who will come to him. In Christ, therefore, we see the earth-spirit[61] forming itself originally in the individual toward self-consciousness. The Father and fellow human beings dwell in Christ in equal measure and are one in him. Devotion and love are his very being. That is why every mother who feels that she has borne a human being, and who knows by means of a heavenly message that the Spirit of the church—the Holy Spirit—dwells in her, and who thus offers her child in her heart right away to the church and claims this as a right—such a mother also sees Christ in her child, and this is precisely that ineffable, all-rewarding mother feeling.

"And in the same way, every one of us intuits in the birth of Christ our own higher birth, through which in us, too, nothing else now lives except devotion and love—and in us, too, the eternal Son of God appears. That is why Christmas breaks forth like a heavenly light out of the night. That is why it is a universal pulsation of joy in the

---

59. He changes this in second edition to be more causal: "In order that the-human-in-itself generate and form itself in each individual."

60. As he makes explicit in the second edition, he is referring here to Pentecost. See Sermon delivered on Pentecost Sunday, 1825, translated below.

61. In the second edition he drops *Erdgeist* and specifies the Spirit doing something in an earthly manner.

entire reborn world—a pulsation only the sick or temporarily paralyzed do not feel. And precisely this is the glory of the holiday that you wanted to hear commended by me. I see, however, that I shan't be the last speaker, for the long-awaited friend is now here, too."

Josef had arrived during Eduard's speech. Even though he had quietly entered and sat down, Eduard had in fact taken notice of him.

"No chance of that," Josef said, when Eduard addressed him in this way. "You shall indeed have been the last. I have not come to deliver speeches but to enjoy your company. And, to tell the truth, you strike me as strange and almost foolish, carrying on in such a manner, as fine as it may have been. But I notice that your bad principle is among you once again: this Leonhardt—the thinking, reflecting, dialectical, overly intellectual person. He probably talked you into it, since you certainly wouldn't have needed to do it for yourselves, nor would you have degenerated into it. But it does not help him.

"And the poor women have had to put up with it. Just consider what beautiful sounds they would have sung to you. All the piety of your speeches would have dwelt far more deeply in those sounds. Or consider how gracefully, from hearts full of love and joy, they would have chatted with you. All of this would have contented and revived you in a way different from these solemn speeches of yours.

"I, for my part, cannot help you with that today. All forms are too rigid to me, and all speech too tedious and cold. The speechless subject demands or generates in me a speechless joy, and in my joy I can only smile and cheer like a child. This day, all people are children to me, and for that very reason they are dear. For once the serious wrinkles are smoothed out, for once age and worries are not written on the forehead, for once the eyes sparkle and live, and it is the presentiment of a beautiful and graceful existence in them. I myself have also become a child again to my good fortune. As a child stifles childish grief, holds back sighs, and draws in the tears when a childish joy is given, so on this day the long, deep, undying grief of my life is soothed for me as never before. I feel myself at home and as if newly born in the better world, in which grief and lament have no sense and no space.

"I behold everything, even that which is deeply wounding, with joyous eyes. As Christ had no bride but the church, no children but his friends, no house but the temple and the world, and yet had a heart filled with heavenly love and joy, so I too seem to be born to aspire to the same things. Thus I have gone around the entire evening, everywhere heartily taking part in all the trifles and games, and have loved everything and have laughed. It was one long, caressing kiss that I gave to the world, and now my joy with you shall be the last impress of my lips. You know that you are the dearest to me of all. Come then, and above all, if she is not already asleep, bring the child along, and let me see your splendors, and let us be merry and sing something pious and joyful."

3

THE SECOND SPEECH:
"ON THE ESSENCE OF RELIGION"[1]

You know how the old Simonides, through oft repeated and prolonged hesitation, reduced to silence the person who had pestered him with the question, "What are the gods?"[2] I would like to begin with a similar hesitation for our question, just as appropriate as and no less comprehensive than that one: "What is religion?"

Naturally I do this not with the aim of silencing you or, as he did, leaving you embarrassed, but so that you might try something for yourselves, so that you might for a while direct your gaze intently on the point that we are seeking, entirely putting all other thoughts aside. Is not the first demand of those who summon mere common spirits that the spectators wishing to see their apparitions and wishing to be initiated into their mysteries prepare themselves through holy silence and through abstinence from earthly things, and then, without being distracted by the sight of foreign objects, look with undivided minds at the place where the apparition is to appear? How much more such compliance will I be allowed to request? It is a rare spirit that I am to call forth, one that you will have to observe with intense concentration for a long time in order to recognize it as that for which you seek and to understand its significant traits. For truly, only if you stand before the holy circles with that impartial sobriety

---

1. This is the full text of "Über das Wesen der Religion," the second of Schleiermacher's five *Speeches* in *Über die Religion. Reden an die Gebildeten unter ihren Verächtern (On Religion: Speeches to Its Cultured Despisers)*. This translation is the first in English of the second edition (1806) and is based on *KGA* 1/12: *Über die Religion (2.-) 4. Auflage, Monologen (2.-) 4. Auflage*, ed. Günter Meckenstock (New York: Walter de Gruyter, 1995): 41–128. For a German edition with the first three editions given side by side, see Friedrich Schleiermacher, *Über die Religion. Reden an die Gebildeten unter ihren Verächtern 1799/1806/1821*, ed. Niklaus Peter, Frank Bestebreurtje, and Anna Büsching (Zürich: Theologischer Verlag, 2012).

2. A reference to Cicero's *De natura deorum (On the Nature of the Gods)* 1:22.

of mind that regards every adumbration clearly and properly, and only if you, being neither seduced by old memories nor bribed by preconceived presentiments, aspire to understand what is presented on its own terms—only then can I hope that you will recognize the religion I want to show you. Even if you do not grow fond of it, I hope that, at the very least, you will acknowledge its higher nature and come to terms with its significance.

What I would like to do is present religion to you under some well-known form, so that—having seen it here and there in life—you might instantly call to mind its traits, its tenor and manner. But this won't happen. For, however much I would like to show you religion in its original, singular form, it is not disposed to emerging publicly but only lets itself be seen in secrecy by those who love it. Wherever it is publicly presented and substituted, it is no longer quite itself. This does not apply only to religion. It also applies to anything you may accept as distinctive and particular according to its inner essence. It can rightly be said that whatever also presents itself as something external is no longer quite its own, nor does that external presentation correspond exactly to it. Not even speech is the pure operation of cognition,[3] nor custom the pure operation of disposition. For us, at this particular time, this is all the more true, since part of the ever-increasing opposition between the modern age and

---

3. *Erkenntniß*. Although this term has often been translated as "knowledge," the more precise meaning is "cognition." In the context of Kantian epistemology (as understood by the first post-Kantian generation), "cognition" differs from "knowledge" or "knowing" (*Wissen*) in that it is a preliminary concept that is not necessarily justified. Like knowledge, a cognition is intersubjective in that it has to do with the relation between the subject and an object (or objects), which is to say that it is a representation that relates to an object; it makes a truth claim that can be right or wrong and that can be debated and discussed; it can refer both to intuitions (a singular relation to a given object) and concepts (a general relation to a class of objects). It does not, however, necessarily reflect the unifying function found in concepts, and therefore cognition falls short of a knowing. Although "cognition" may sound strange to our ears, the distinction is an important one for understanding what Schleiermacher is doing in this speech, "On the Essence of Religion," since it underscores that often what is claimed to be a "knowledge" about God or about nature is in fact an unjustified representation, the result of arbitrariness or what he calls "free choice" (*Willkühr*), and religion as he understands it does not get caught up in such debates. Schleiermacher also sometimes uses the verb *Erkennen* as a noun, which I sometimes translate as "cognizing" or "knowing," depending on the context; when translated as "knowing," I give the German in a note, so readers can see it is not *Wissen*.

past ages is that one person is nowhere and no longer one thing; rather, every person is all.

And that is why, just as cultured people have opened up an intercourse among themselves so multifaceted that their distinctive temperament in the particular moments of life no more emerges as unalloyed, so too the human heart is endowed with so effusive and accomplished a sociability that no single talent or faculty can produce its works in a self-contained manner—however much you might, in contemplation, separate them out. I think, rather, it realizes itself in the whole, each talent and faculty being moved and penetrated by the obliging love and support of the others in every performance, in such a way that you now find all of them in every operation and must be content with discerning the prevailing, productive power[4] in this interconnection. That is why we can understand every activity of the spirit only insofar as we can find and intuit that activity in ourselves. And since you claim not to know religion in this way, what is more incumbent upon me than warning you especially about those mistakes that arise so naturally from the current situation of things? Let us, therefore, raise your own point of view properly at the chief moments and see whether it be somewhat right or, if not, how we can perhaps arrive at what is right from this insight.[5]

Religion is to you, in one moment, a kind of thinking, a faith,[6] a distinct manner of observing the world and of connecting whatever we encounter in it; in another moment, it is a manner of acting, a particular desire and love, a special kind of conducting and moving oneself inwardly. Without this separation of the theoretical and the practical, you can hardly think, and although religion belongs to both sides, you are nevertheless accustomed, every time, to looking at it selectively from one of the two sides. We shall therefore consider religion from both points.

First, acting. You set acting as twofold, *life* and *art*. With the poet, you like to ascribe seriousness to life and bliss to art, or to oppose both

---

4. *Kraft*. Depending on context, this is translated either as "power" or as "force."

5. Here begins a significant revision of the first edition. Schleiermacher now describes the essence of religion through sharper dialectical moves than he had before.

6. *Glaube*. In this particular context, *Glaube* carries the meaning of a belief or set of beliefs, but to remain consistent with his use of *Glaube* later in this *Speech*, it has been translated here as "faith."

in some way or another. In any case, you will certainly separate one from the other. On the one hand, when it comes to *life*, duty ought to be the motto, your moral law ought to regulate it, and virtue ought to demonstrate itself in life as the ruling principle by means of which the individual harmonizes with the universal orderings of the world, without ever acting in a disruptive or bewildering manner. And so, you believe, people could prove their worth without having at all noticed something of art in life; in fact, this must be attained through strong rules that would have nothing at all in common with the free, versatile regulations of art. Yes, you regard it yourself almost as a rule that, for those who prove themselves most exactingly in the ordering of life, art has receded and they manage without it.

On the other hand, when it comes to *art*, the imagination[7] ought to animate the artist, genius ought to rule overall in the artist, and to you this is something completely different from virtue and ethics. You are of the opinion that the highest measure of the former can probably exist with a lesser amount by far of the latter. Yes, you are inclined to loosen the artist somewhat from strong demands in life, because the sober-minded power very often gets crowded out by that fiery power of genius.

What about that which you call *piety*? To what extent do you regard it as a distinct manner of action? Does it fall in that former sphere of *life*, and there is it something of its own, therefore also something good and commendable? But, all the same, is it something distinct from ethics, since you do not want to pretend the two are one? Thus, ethics would not exhaust the sphere it ought to govern, if yet another, albeit not hostile, power is alongside it. Or do you want to retreat to the position that piety is an individual virtue, and religion an individual duty, or a branch of duties, thus annexed and subordinated to ethics, as the particular to the universal? But—if I understand your speeches correctly, as I am accustomed to hearing them and as I also have now reproduced them for you—you do not believe this, since you want so to sound as if the pious, always and everywhere, would still have something of their own in their doing and permitting.

---

7. *Fantasie.* On the significance of this term for Schleiermacher and the Romantics, see Albert L. Blackwell, *Schleiermacher's Early Philosophy of Life: Determinism, Freedom, and Phantasy*, Harvard Theological Studies 33 (Chico, CA: Scholars Press, 1982).

And how are *art* and *religion* related to each other? Surely not barely so, in the sense that they would be completely alien to each other, since from time immemorial what is greatest in art has had a religious imprint. And if you call the artist pious, do you then also grant the artist that relaxation of virtue's strong demands? Of course not. The artist is subject to these like everyone else. Then again, you will also probably—otherwise I cannot see how consistency would result—bar those who belong to life, should they be pious, from remaining completely artless; rather, they will have to take up something from this other sphere into their life, and out of this perhaps emerges the form of its own that life obtains. But please, if this is the way it is, and if anything at all is to result with your view (and no other conclusion presents itself)—if religion as a manner of action is a mixture of those two, clouded as mixtures are wont to be, and the two are somewhat assailed and diluted through each other—then it explains to me your discontent, but not your conception. For how is it you call something its own when it is accidentally being affected by two other elements? When the result would be the most thorough-going mediocrity of both, as long as both indeed endure unchanged alongside each other?

If, however, this is not the case, and if piety is, rather, a true inner permeation of those, then you may well appreciate that my analogy forsakes me and that such a permeation cannot have come into being by adding one to the other, but it must be an original unity of both. I feel, however, the need to warn you myself: be careful not to admit this to me. For if it were the case, then ethics and genius in their singling out would only be the one-sided ruins of religion, what is left standing when it dies off; *that* religion, however, would in fact be higher in relation to both, and the true divine life itself. In return for this warning, if you accept it, be so kind also to communicate to me, if you find another way out, how your opinion about religion cannot appear as nothing. Until then, there is nothing left for me to do than accept that you have not yet rightly examined, and you your-selves have not understood, this side of religion.

Perhaps it would go much more pleasantly for us with the other side—that is to say, religion considered as a kind of *thinking* and *faith*.

You will grant, I believe, that your insights, though they may appear so multifaceted, all in all fall for you into two antagonistic sciences. I do not want to argue with you about the way you further divide it or about the names you attach to it, since that belongs in the debates of your schools, with which I have nothing to do. For that reason you should not quibble with me about the words I shall use as labels—words that come from here and there. We might call the one *physics* or *metaphysics*, with one name, or then again divided with two names, and the other *ethics* or *deontology* or *practical philosophy*. We are agreed, I believe, about the contrast between them—namely, that the one science describes the nature of things or, if you wish to know nothing about that, human nature as determined through the relations of the universe, what this is for a person, and how we necessarily discover it. Conversely, the other science teaches what a human nature in itself is, and what a person ought to do.

To the extent religion is now a kind of thinking about something, and a knowing comes forth in it, does it not share the same object with these sciences? What else does faith know but the relation of human beings to God and to the world, the purpose for which God has made them, and the harm the world can do, or not do, to them? Yet again, faith does not know and establish something out of this sphere alone, but it must do so out of that other sphere as well, since it distinguishes between a good action and a bad action according to its manner of proceeding.

So then, is religion one and the same thing with both sciences? You are certainly not of that opinion, for you will never grant that religion's faith would be so grounded and so secure as to stand on the same level of certainty as the knowledge[8] of your philosophy. Rather, you accuse faith of not knowing how to distinguish what is demonstrable from what is apparent. Likewise, you never fail to note that exceedingly strange regulations of what to do and what to permit have often come out of religion. You may well be right; except do not forget that it is just the same with what you call "science" and that you believe yourselves to have rectified much and to be superior to your fathers.

And now what should we say religion is? Again, as before, a mixture—that is, theoretical and practical knowledge mingled together? But this is, if anything, more forbidden in the sphere of

8. *Wissen.*

157

knowledge, most of all when, as it indeed seems, each of these two branches has its distinctive procedure in the construction of its knowledge. Only a compilation could have originated in the most arbitrary manner—yes, indeed could be something—without resting all of its own cause entirely in the other; a method, perhaps, of teaching. something to beginners about the results of knowledge and to make them desire for the matter itself. If this is what you mean, why do you struggle against religion? As long as there are beginners, you could, without compromise, let it peacefully be. You could smile about the strange delusion if perhaps it tried to arrogate something to itself in order to be more than you. For you know quite assuredly that it is behind you and that it can always only proceed from you, the "Knowing Ones." And you would do wrong to shed even one serious word over it. I think, however, that is not how it stands. For, unless I am completely wrong, for some time you have already been working on teaching a similar summary of your knowledge to the masses, whether you call it *religion* or *enlightenment* or something else, it applies equally. In doing this, you even find it necessary first to cast out some other preexisting thing, or where that something might not be, to prevent its entrance. And this something is exactly what you call *religion*—the object of your polemic, not the goods that you yourselves want to distribute.

Therefore, dear friends, faith must be something other than this kind of mixture of opinions about God and the world, about commandments for one life or two. Piety must be something other than the instinct that craves this aggregate of metaphysical and moral crumbs, stirring them into confusion. Otherwise you would hardly be arguing against it, and it would probably not cross your mind to speak of religion, too, only from a distance, as though you were speaking of something that could be distinguished from your knowledge. For then the dispute of those who are cultured and knowing against the pious would only be the dispute of the profound and thorough versus superficiality, the master versus apprentices who want to be released to spend wasteful hours. If this is your opinion, I would fancy pestering you with all kinds of Socratic questions so as eventually to coerce some of you to answer explicitly this question: Could a person, by some means or another, possibly be wise and pious at the same time? And I would fancy submitting to everyone the question: Is it not perhaps the case that you, too, know the principles in other common things according to which similar is placed next to similar, and the particular subordinated to the universal? Or is it only here, regarding religion, where you do not want to apply these principles, in order to joke with the world about a serious subject?

But how should it be, if it is not thus? By what means will that in religious faith, which you separate in science and divide into two spheres, be linked with each other and be bound so indissolubly that one cannot be thought of without the other? For the religious person is not of the opinion that anybody can discern the right action, except insofar as he or she knows, at the same time, the relations of the person to God, and so too the reverse. Does this binding principle lie in the theoretical? Is this why you still contrast a practical philosophy over against that, rather than viewing practical philosophy as just a subset of the theoretical? And likewise, if it were the other way around, with the binding principle lying in the practical? It may be so—or it may be that both of those, which you are accustomed to contrasting, simply exist in a yet higher knowledge. You cannot believe that religion is this highest restored unity of knowledge— religion, which you most dearly want to detect in and to deny to those who are far enough removed from science. I myself do not want to hold you to this, since I do not want to take a position I would not be able to argue. You will probably admit, however, that for the first time you have to deal with this part of religion in order to discover what religion really means.

Let's deal honestly with one another. You do not like religion. On that we have already agreed. But in waging an honest war against it, a war indeed not wholly without struggle, you do not want to have fought against a shadow, like this with which we have struggled. Religion must be something of its own that could have fashioned itself so especially in the human heart—something thinkable, the essence of which can have been established for itself—that one can speak and argue about it. And I find it very unjust when, out of things so disparate, you stitch together something indefensible that you call *religion*, and then you make so many pointless conjectures with it. You will deny that you have gone to work so insidiously. Because I have already dismissed systems, commentaries, and apologies, you will call upon me to unroll all the original sources of religion, from the beautiful poems of the Greeks to the sacred scriptures of Christians, asking whether I will not find everywhere the nature of the gods and their will, and whether everywhere those who know the former and those who perform the latter are not praised as holy and blessed.

But that is just what I have already told you. Religion never appears pure; rather, its external form is also still determined through something else. And this is precisely our task: to describe religion's essence out of this, without taking the form for the essence as glibly and well-nigh as you seem to do. After all, does the physical world provide you with any primary matter presented as pure product of nature? —You would then have to, as you have fared here in the intellectual world, perceive very coarse things as something elementary. Yet to be able to describe something so elementary is precisely the infinite aim of the analytical art. It is the same in spiritual things: to create the original in no other way than producing it by means of an original creation in you, even then only for the moment when you produce it. Pray understand yourselves in this matter, and you will always be remembered for this.

As for the original sources and the autographs: attaching them to your sciences of being[9] and of acting is not merely an inevitable fate but an essential necessity inseparable from their very existence[10] itself. For what appears as the first and last in a work is not always what is true and highest. If only you but knew to read between the lines! All sacred scriptures are like the humble books that were customary in our humble fatherland and that treated important things under a diminutive cover. Admittedly, where they do not rise immediately to the more poetical (and, for you, this tends to be the least palatable), they attach themselves to metaphysical and moral concepts, and they almost appear to complete their entire enterprise in this circle. You, however, are expected to penetrate through this appearance. In the same way, nature educes fine metals alloyed with lesser substances, and our sense[11] knows to discover them and to reconstitute them in their glorious splendor.

---

9. *Sein.* He uses this term to refer to "being" or "existence" in general.

10. *Dasein.* Schleiermacher uses this to refer to concrete existence, or one's own existence.

11. *Sinn.* "Sense" broadly understood; mind.

THE SECOND SPEECH

The sacred scriptures were not for perfected believers alone but principally for the children in the faith, for the newly dedicated, for those standing on the threshold and wanting to be invited in. How could they do it otherwise than exactly as I have just done it with you? They had to attach themselves to the given, seeking in it the means toward a kind of spark by which, out of dark presentiments, the new sense could then be excited. And do you not recognize the aspiration to break through from a lower sphere to a higher sphere in the way in which those concepts are treated in the educational deepening—even if often in the sphere of a paltry and ingrate language? As you well see, this kind of communication could not be other than poetic or rhetorical. And what lies closer to the rhetorical than the dialectical? What, since time immemorial, has been utilized more magnificently and successfully in revealing the higher nature of knowing[12] and of the inner feeling? But certainly this objective will not be reached if you remain fixated on its outward dress[13] alone. This is why it is time to grasp the matter once from the other end, and to advance with the cutting opposition in which faith stands against your morals and metaphysics, and piety against what you care to call your ethics. That was what I intended to do, but I digressed from this so as first to illuminate your spiteful conception. Having done that, I now turn back.[14]

In order, therefore, to reveal to you and to state, as specifically as possible, its original and characteristic assets, religion provisionally renounces all claims on whatever belongs to science and ethics, and wishes to give back all that it has borrowed from them, or what those have burdened it with. For what does your science of being strive after—your natural science, in which everything real must

---

12. *Erkennen.*

13. The term is *Einkleidung*—clothing, covering, or accoutrement. This was an important part of Schleiermacher's breakthrough in the interpretation of Plato's dialogues. He accused previous interpreters of too quickly dismissing the dialogue form as mere *Einkleidung*, while he himself insisted that the content of Plato's philosophy could not be separated from its form. Here in the second *Speech*, he accuses the cultured despisers of dismissing religion too quickly because of its seemingly simplistic or coarse forms.

14. Here ends the first major revision in the second edition, where he describes the essence of religion through polemics—not just by contrasting it to metaphysics and morals, but by iterating the many mistaken ways in which the despisers have defined it. He now turns to offering a more positive definition of the essence of religion.

unite itself to your theoretical philosophy? To know things, I imagine, each in its distinctive essence; to identify the specific relations through which each one is what it is; to determine its place in the whole and to distinguish it from others; to situate every actual thing in its reciprocal, contingent necessity; and to state the unity between all appearances and their eternal laws. This is truly beautiful and divine, and I have no intention of disparaging it. On the contrary, if my account does not satisfy you, thrown together and suggestive as it is, then I gladly concede to you the highest and most exhaustive of what you are able to say about knowledge and about science. I maintain, however, that religion has nothing to do with knowledge and that its essence is perceived quite apart from any association with knowledge. For the measure of knowledge is not the measure of piety. Piety, rather, can also reveal itself magnificently and distinctively in those who do not have that knowledge originally in themselves but who, on the contrary, like everyone, know what is individual only through the connection with everything else. Yes, even when you look down your noses at them, the pious concede, gladly and ungrudgingly, that they do not possess knowledge as you do.

What I actually want to do is to translate for you, with clear words, what most of them only suspect but do not know themselves how to express. When you place God at the apex of your science as the ground of all knowing,[15] they do honor and respect this, but this is not the same as their way of having and knowing[16] about God— nay, neither science nor knowing[17] arises out of their way. For, indeed, religion is essentially contemplation. You will never want to call anyone pious whose sense for the life of the world is not open, anyone who goes there in impenetrable obtuseness. This contemplation, however, does not attend to the essence of one finite thing in opposition to other finite things. It is, rather, simply the immediate perceiving of the universal existence of everything finite in the infinite and through the infinite, of everything temporal in the eternal and through the eternal. This seeking and finding in all that lives and moves, in all becoming and change, in all doing and suffering, and just having and

---

15. *Erkennen.*

16. *Zu wissen.*

17. *Erkennen.*

162

knowing life itself in immediate feeling as this existence—this is religion. Religion is satisfied wherever it finds this. Wherever this lies hidden, there is for religion inhibition and anxiety, necessity and death. And so religion is certainly a life in the infinite nature of the whole, in the one and all, and it sees everything in God and God in everything. It is not, however, knowledge and knowing,[18] neither of the world nor of God—but it simply recognizes this without being it. To religion, knowledge is also a stirring and revelation of the infinite in the finite, which religion also sees in God and God in it.

Likewise, what does your *ethics* strive after, your science of acting? It, too, wants to hold the individual instances of human acting and producing separated, in their definiteness, and also to shape this into a whole, grounded and ordered in itself. But the pious admit to you, that they, qua pious, know nothing of this as well. They certainly contemplate human action, but their contemplation is simply not the kind that results in such a system. On the contrary, they seek, and they see one and the same thing in everything—namely, acting from God, the efficaciousness of God in human beings. Truly, if your doctrine of ethics is right, the pious will appreciate no other acting as divine than that which is accepted in your system. But to know and to form this system itself is your (the Knowing Ones') affair, not theirs. And if you are reluctant to believe this, then consider women, to whom you yourselves not only allow religion as attire and adornment, but from whom you also even demand the finest feeling for distinguishing godly acting from other types, whether or not you expect them to understand your doctrine of ethics as science.

And it is the same with *acting* as well, as I have been saying since the start. Artists form what is given to them to form by virtue of their own special talent. And so diversified are these talents that what one artist possesses, another lacks—unless one artist, against heaven's will, would possess all. But you never bother to ask, when some are praised as pious, which of these gifts perhaps dwell in them by virtue of their piety. Average citizens[19]—I take this in the sense of the ancients, not in the more meager sense disparaged today—order, lead, and move by virtue of their ethics. But this is something other than piety. For piety also has a passive side, it appears also as a sur-

18. *Wissen und Erkennen.*
19. *Der bürgerliche Mensch.*

163

render, a letting oneself be moved by the whole that the person faces, while ethics always and only shows itself as an intervention in the whole, as a self-moving. And that is why ethics depends on the consciousness of freedom, in whose sphere also falls everything that ethics produces. Piety, in contrast, is not at all bound up with this side of life but stirs in the opposite sphere of necessity, where no particular acting of an individual appears. Hence the two are indeed different from each other. If, in fact, religion lingers with pleasure on every acting from God, on every activity through which the infinite reveals itself in the finite, then it is not itself this activity.

Thus religion maintains its own sphere and its own character only by totally leaving both the sphere of science and the sphere of praxis. And only by its situating itself next to those two is the common field completely filled in and human nature completed from this side. Religion appears to you as the necessary and indispensable third to those two, as their natural counterpart, no less in worth or magnificence than what you want from them.

Please do not get the idea that I am merely being fanciful, as though I meant that one of these could perhaps exist without the other, or that a person could have religion and be pious, but at the same time be unethical. Such a thing is impossible. But bear in mind that, in my opinion, it is just as impossible for a person to be ethical without religion, or be scientific without religion. From what I have already said, you might want to conclude, not incorrectly, that for all I care a person could indeed have religion without science. And if so, haven't I myself instigated the separation? Please remember that, on this point, I merely meant that piety is not the measure of science. Yet just as a person can hardly be truly scientific without being pious, so as certainly the pious person can be truly ignorant, but never false-knowing. For the pious person's own existence is not of that subordinated kind, which (according to the ancient principle that like can only be known by like) would have nothing recognizable except non-being under the deceptive appearance of existence. On the contrary, it is a true existence that also recognizes true existence. And where this is not encountered, the pious person also believes there is nothing to see. In my opinion, for someone still entangled by that false appearance, ignorance is a priceless nugget of science. You know this from my speeches, and if you have not yet figured it out for yourselves, then go and learn it from your Socrates. Grant, therefore, at the very least, that I am being consistent, and that the greatest internal opposition of knowledge is also lifted away through piety, so that piety cannot endure together with this.[20]

Do not, therefore, blame me for establishing such a separation. You cannot do this without undeservedly foisting onto me your own view and your own confusion, which is as familiar as it is unavoidable. To show you this very confusion in the mirror of my speech has been my paramount desire. Because you do not recognize religion as the third, the other two—knowledge and action—are so fractured from one another that you cannot catch sight of their unity, but you think instead that someone could have right knowledge without right action, and *vice versa.* I allow the separation only in contemplation, where it is necessary. You disdain it there and, in contrast to me, transfer it to life, as though what we are speaking about could itself exist in life separated and independently, one from the other. That is why you do not have a living intuition of any of these activities; rather, to you, each is an abstraction, something torn away. Hence your conception is a meager one—the impression of nothingness bearing in on itself, because it does not engage with the living in a living way.

True science is perfected intuition; true praxis is self-generated cultivation and art; true religion is sensation[21] and taste for the infinite. To want to have one of the former two without the latter, or to let it be thought one could so have them, is an overly bold, wanton delusion, an outrageous error. It arose from the unholy sense that we preferred to pilfer imprudently and in a craven-hearted way what we could have asked for and expected in confident tranquility, in order then to possess it only as pretence. What can the human person possibly want to cultivate in life and in art that is worthy of speech other

---

20. Schleiermacher clarifies his point in the third edition: not ignorance but the conceit of knowing is the opposite of knowledge.

21. *Empfindung.* In the first, third, and fourth editions, the term is *Sinn* ("sense"). *Empfindung* also carried the meaning of sense, feeling, perception, and sentiment. To signal the switch in terminology, it is translated here as "sensation," which also ties it to later discussions in this speech. Later in this same paragraph, he goes back to using *Sinn.* In this post-Kantian philosophical context, *Empfindung* is considered more subjective in nature, while *Gefühl* is considered more objective; at the same time, *Empfindung* hints at the "matter" or "stuff" being received through the senses, the effect of some objective reality on us. Cf. p. 148 above.

than what has come to be in the self through the excitations of that former sense?[22] Or how, without that sense, can a person wish to comprehend the world scientifically? Or yet how, without that sense, when the cognition presses itself upon that person in a definite talent, can this talent be exercised? For what is all science, other than the existence of things in you, in your reason? What is all art and culture, other than your existence in things, in its measure and its form? And how can both flourish and come to life in you, other than insofar as the eternal unity of reason and nature—and insofar as the universal existence of everything finite in the infinite—lives immediately in you?

This is why you will find every truly knowing person also devout and pious. And where you see science without religion, be assured that either it has only been transferred there and is only superficially acquired, or if it does not itself belong completely to that empty appearance, it is diseased in itself. What else do you reckon this to be—this deducing and interweaving of concepts, which neither lives nor corresponds to that which is living? In the sphere of the doctrine of ethics, what else do you reckon this pathetic uniformity to be, which intends to conceive the highest human life in one single, dead formula? How can this latter way of conceiving even arise? Because it lacks the fundamental feeling of the living nature that everywhere establishes diversity and singularity. How can the former way of conceiving arise? Because it lacks the sense that defines the essence and the limits of the finite only out of the infinite, thereby being itself infinite within these limits. Hence the sovereignty of the pure concept! Hence, instead of the organic structure, the mechanical stunts[23] of your system! Hence the empty game with analytical formulas, whether categorical or hypothetical, in whose fetters life refuses to rest comfortably!

If you want to disdain religion, if you are afraid of abandoning yourself to the yearning for the infinite and to being in awe of it, then science does not seem to be your vocation, since it must either have become as base as your life is, or it must have so detached itself from it that it stands alone. Science cannot flourish in such dichotomy. The person who does not become one with the universe in the

---

22. That is, the sense for the infinite, not the "unholy sense."

23. *Kunststükk* carries a double meaning of "work of art" and "stunt."

immediate unity of intuition and feeling remains eternally separated from it, in the derived unity of consciousness.

What, then, is to become of the highest expression of speculation in our day, the perfected and rounded idealism, if it does not immerse itself again in this unity, so that the humility of religion is a portent of another realism to its pride—a realism other than the one that idealism so audaciously and with perfect right subordinates to itself? It will annihilate the universe by seeming to want to form it. It will reduce the universe to a mere allegory, to a negligible silhouette of the one-sided narrow-mindedness of its empty consciousness. Respectfully offer up with me a lock from the mane of the holy, repudiated Spinoza![24] The high world-spirit permeated him, the infinite was his beginning and end, the universe his sole and eternal love. In holy innocence and deep humility, he was mirrored in the eternal world, and he also beheld how he himself was a most genial mirror to it. He was filled with religion and full of holy spirit. And for that reason he also stands there alone and unsurpassed, master in his art, yet exalted beyond the profane guild, without apprentices and without citizenship.

Why need I show you how the same thing applies to art as well? How here you also have a thousand shadows, illusions, and errors from the very same source? Above all else, I want to suggest to you a magnificent example that you should all know as well as those others—only I shall do so silently, since sorrow new and deep has no words. I refer to the divine youth who passed away too early,[25] to how everything his spirit touched became art and how his entire contemplation of the world immediately turned into one great poem. Even though he had really barely articulated the first sounds, you must add him to the company of the most prolific poets, the rare ones who are just as profound as they are clear and

---

24. The reference is to the philosopher Benedict de Spinoza (1632–77), who was at the heart of the so-called Pantheist Controversy (*Pantheismusstreit*) at the end of the eighteenth century. His Jewish congregation in Amsterdam had issued a writ of expulsion against him. Schleiermacher had written two early essays on Spinoza (see introduction, 11 above).

25. The reference here is to Novalis (see a few lines down), whom he also mentions in the *Christmas Dialogue* and in two letters included in this volume. *Novalis* was the pseudonym for the poet Georg Philipp Friedrich Freiherr von Hardenberg (1772–1801), a key figure in early German Romanticism.

vivid. Behold in him the power of enthusiasm and the circumspection of a pious heart, and confess that when the philosophers, like Spinoza, will be religious and seek God, and when the artists, like Novalis, will be pious and love Christ, then the great resurrection will be celebrated for both worlds.

So that you understand, however, what I mean by this unity of science, religion, and art—and, at the same time, what I mean by their distinction—try to descend with me into the innermost sanctuary of life. Perhaps there we may find some common bearings. Only there will you find the original relation of feeling and intuition, and only out of this relation will their being-one and their separation be understood. But I must refer you to your own selves, to the apprehension of a living moment. You must understand it by eavesdropping on your own selves before your consciousness, or at the very least by reconstituting this condition for yourselves out of that consciousness. What you should notice is the coming-to-be of your consciousness, but you shouldn't reflect on some already-having-become. As soon as you try to turn a given, definite activity of your soul into an object of communication or contemplation, you are already within the divorce, and your thought can only comprehend that which is disjoined. That is why my speech cannot lead you by any definite example. Precisely because what I want to point out in my speech is one, it is also already past. And here I could point out to you only a faint trace of the original being-one of that which is disjoined. Yet even this I wish not to scorn preliminarily.

Capture yourselves in the process. How do you sketch an image of some one object? Do you not still find bound up with it a being-stimulated and being-determined, as it were, of your very selves by the object? And that this even forms your existence in a particular moment? The more definitely your image distinguishes itself and the more in this way you become the object, the more you lose yourselves. But just because you can trace the ascendancy of the former and the decline of the latter in its becoming, mustn't both have been one and the same in the first and original instant, that instant that has evaded you? Or, immersed in yourselves, do you find everything that you might otherwise consider as multiplicity, as divided in yourselves—that this now, in this present moment, is connected inseparably to a distinctive content of your existence? Yet, paying close attention as it escapes, do you not see the image of an object—that object from whose effect on you, from whose magical touch, this consciousness has proceeded? The more your excitement and your being caught up in it expands and permeates your entire existence, the more it leaves behind at the very least an everlasting trace in the memory—momentarily, as it must be—so that whatever new captures you initially must also carry that memory's color and imprint, and thus two moments unite into one length of time. The more your state dominates you in this way, the more faded and less recognizable that form becomes. But precisely because it fades and escapes, it was nearer and clearer beforehand; it was originally one and the same with your feeling. After all, as has already been said, these are only traces, and you can scarcely understand them if you refuse to go back to the first beginning of that consciousness.

And should you not be able to do this? Tell me, then, if you consider it completely in general and completely originally, what is every act of your life in and of itself, without distinction from the others? It couldn't possibly be something other than what the whole also is—only as act, as moment. Therefore, to be sure, it is a becoming of an existence for itself and a becoming of an existence in the whole, both at the same time; it is a striving to return to the whole, and a striving to exist on its own, both at the same time. The whole chain is put together out of these rings. How is it you now exist in the whole? Through your senses, I hope, if indeed you must exist with the senses in order to exist in the whole. And how is it you exist for yourselves? Through the unity of your consciousness, which unity you initially have in sensation, in the contrast and change of its varying degrees. It is easy to see how one can only come to be at the same time with the other, if both together form that act of life. You become sense and the universe becomes object, and this coalescence and having-become-one of sense and object, before each returns to its place, this is what I mean: it is that moment that you always experience yet also do not experience, for the appearance of your life is only the result of its constant cessation and recurrence. Precisely for that reason it is barely in time, it hurries so; and it can barely be described, so little is it actually there for us. Would, however, that you could hold it fast—and hold fast every kind of your activity, the most common just as much as the highest, since they are all the same therein, they all lead back to it.

If I might at least be permitted to compare it, I would say that it would be as fleeting and translucent as that fragrance that the dew breathes onto blossoms and fruits, that it would be as bashful and tender as a maiden's kiss, and as holy and fertile as a bridal embrace. Not only is it *like* this, it can be fairly said to be the *same* as all of this. For it is the first meeting of the universal life with a particular. It fills no time and forms nothing that can be grasped. Over and above all error and misunderstanding, it is the immediate, holy marriage of the universe with incarnate reason for the purpose of a generative, begetting embrace. You lie then immediately on the bosom of the infinite world; you are in this moment her soul, for you feel all her powers and her infinite life as your own; in this moment, she is your body, for you penetrate her muscles and limbs as your own, and your sense and presentiment bestir her innermost nerves.[26] This is how the first conception of everything living in your life—in every sphere of your life, including, therefore, that of religion—is brought about. But, as I said, it is not even a moment when consciousness comes to be and the penetration of existence dissolves in this immediate union.

And now either the intuition comes up before you, living and ever clearer, as it were the figure before the young man's eye of the beloved who has wrested herself away; or the consciousness issues forth the feeling out of your interior and, spreading, takes up your entire being, as the blush of shame and love spreads over the face of the maiden. And when your consciousness has first established itself as either one, as intuition or as feeling,[27] then—if you are not wholly self-conscious in this separation, if you have not wholly lost the true intuition of your life in the individual—what remains to you is nothing other than the knowledge of the original unity of both separated things, about their identical emergence out of the fundamental relationship of your existence. For that reason, then, what you have learned from an ancient sage is also true in this sense: every know-

---

26. Here, in the second edition, Schleiermacher changed the subject from first person singular ("I") to second person plural ("you"). The gender specificity of the pronouns for *world* (*Welt*, fem.) has been kept here to better capture the explicit sexual imagery.

27. In this second edition, he begins to distinguish feeling and intuition in a way he had not in the first edition, although they still often appear in tandem.

ing is a remembering of what is outside time and is thus justifiably placed at the apex of all that is temporal.[28]

As it is on the one side with intuition and feeling, so it is too on the other side with knowing, when it encompasses both intuition and feeling in itself, and with acting. For these latter two, knowing and acting, are the opposites through whose continual play and reciprocal stimulation your life expands and attains composure over time. That is to say, one of the two, from the beginning on, is always already in your wanting-to-become-one with the universe through an object. Either the sway of objects over you predominates, so that they try to draw you into the circle of their existence, whether you tend toward intuition or toward feeling; this always becomes a knowing. Or the predominant sway is from your side, so that you want to impress your existence on objects and to imagine yourself in them; then it is what you typically call acting, or operating on the external. But you can only communicate your existence to them if it is an excited and determined existence. Therefore, you only give back, confirm, and relinquish in the world what has been formed and effected through that kind of common existence, and only in the very same way can what they imagine in you be such an existence. For that reason, each must excite the other in a reciprocal way, and only in the exchange of knowing and acting can your life persist. For a calm existence—wherein one did not actively excite the other but rather both effectually canceled each other out—such a life would not be yours, but instead would be that out of which yours develops and into which it would again disappear.

You have here before you, therefore, these three: knowing,[29] feeling, and acting. Up to this point, my speech has revolved around them. And you can understand what I mean when I say that they are not all the same and yet they are inseparable. For if you simply gather together all that is similar together and contemplate it for yourselves, you will find that all those moments in which you exercise your sway over things and reproduce yourself in them—these moments will form what you call your "practical life," or your "ethical life" in the narrower sense. And, in turn, those introspective moments in which things generate their existence in you as intuition—these moments,

---

28. A reference to Plato.
29. *Erkennen.*

whether there be many or few, you surely call your "scientific life." Now, can one of these series of moments alone, without the other, possibly form a human life? Or wouldn't that be death? If every activity weren't excited and renewed through the other, wouldn't it have to consume itself? But for that reason is one also itself the other, or must you distinguish them, if you want to understand your life and want to speak clearly about it? Now, what holds for these two regarding each other must also hold for the third in relation to those two. And what do you want to call this third, the series of the feeling? What kind of a life ought it to form for the two others? The religious, I think, and you surely will not be able to say otherwise.

So then, the main point of my speech is uttered. For this is the distinctive sphere that I want to assign to religion—entirely and on its own—and that you certainly must also grant to it. Otherwise, you must prefer the old obscurity to clear argument or plead some other fanciful thing—what, I do not know. Your feeling—insofar as it expresses, in the way described, the existence and life common to you and to the universe, and insofar as you hold the individual moments of this existence and life as an operating of God in you by means of the universe—is your piety. Whatever individual things may come forward as belonging in this series, these are not your cognitions or the objects of your cognition, nor are they your operations and actions or the different spheres of your acting; they are, rather, merely your sensations, and the influences or ways of acting of the universe on these. These exclusively are the elements of religion, but these elements belong also in all. There is no sensation that would not be pious unless it points to a diseased and corrupted condition of life, in which case it must also communicate itself to the other spheres of life. From this it follows that, by contrast, concepts and precepts[30]—all and each, absolutely—are foreign to religion in itself. This is the second time this point has risen before us. For these, if they are to be anything, appertain to knowing,[31] and what belongs to this lies in another sphere of life than the religious.

Now that we have some ground beneath us, it stands to reason that we should investigate where the confusion may come from. Has

---

30. *Grundsä[t]ze*. Elsewhere this word is translated as "principles," but "precepts" works better in English when referring directly to the ethical life.
31. *Erkennen*.

it something to do with a person associating precepts and concepts with religion? Does the same association hold for acting? Well, in any case, it would be fanciful to speak further, since you convert what I say into your concepts and seek precepts in them, and thus the misunderstanding has become ever more deeply rooted. Who knows whether you will follow me if I explain the cause of the confusion in this way? If you still have in mind the different functions of life that I have identified, what would prevent any of those functions from becoming an object for the others, on which these others exercise and with which they are engaged? Or does this not also rather clearly belong to their inner unity and consistency—that they strive in such a way as to pass over into one another? At least it seems so to me. In this way, therefore, as feeling persons, you can become objects to yourselves and can contemplate your feeling. Yes, you could so become an object to yourself as a "feeling you" that you have a formative effect on that "object" and impress your inner existence on it more and more.

If you now want to call the product of that contemplation, the general description of your feeling according to its essence, *principle*[32] and call the description of each individual feeling emerging in it *concept*—indeed, *religious principle* and *religious concept*—you are quite at liberty to do so, and you would be right in doing so. Only do not forget that this is really the scientific treatment of religion—it is knowledge about religion, not religion itself. And do not forget that the description of piety cannot therefore possibly stand at an equal level with the described feeling itself. In fact, this feeling can dwell in some people in its full health and strength without it being given special consideration—almost all women being an example. Hence you won't be allowed to say that piety or religion is lacking, only that knowledge about these is lacking. Do not forget that contemplation already presupposes the original activity and rests entirely on it, and that those concepts and principles, if they are not the reflection of your own feeling, are nothing other than an empty essence, superficially taught from the outside.

What, therefore, are you to be told? If you understand these principles and concepts still so perfectly, if you believe yourself to possess

---

32. *Grundsa[t]z.*

them in the clearest consciousness, but you do not know and cannot point to how they have arisen in you out of the expressions of your feeling itself and how they are originally your own, then do not plead with yourselves or with me that you are pious, for it is not the case. Your soul has never conceived in the sphere of religion, and your concepts are only children foisted upon you, the products of other souls that you have adopted in the furtive feeling of your own infirmness.

I designate as unholy and as remote from all divine life those who circulate about, preening themselves with religion. Some have a concept of the ordering of the world and formulas that ought to express it, and others have regulations according to which they keep themselves in order as well as inner experiences through which they document them. The former braid their formulas one over another into a system of belief, and the latter weave a sacred order out of their regulations. And because both notice that these possess no real stature without feeling, conflict ensues over how many concepts and explanations must be retained or how many regulations and practices, and under how many and what kind of emotions and sentiments, in order to *assemble*[33] out of this an efficient religion that would be neither cold nor fanatical, neither dry nor superficial.

You fools and slow of heart![34] Are you not aware that all of those things, if they are to mean anything at all, are only decompositions of the religious sense that you yourselves had to have created? And if you are not now conscious of yourself having had something that you were able to decompose, whence do you have these?[35] You have memory, and you have imitation—but not religion. If you have not generated the concepts, how do you know the formulas? These are, rather, learned by rote and are stored away. And what you want to

---

33. *Zusammense[t]zen.* Emphasis in original.

34. See Luke 24:25.

35. In the third edition, Schleiermacher clarifies that *these* refers to concepts and precepts. The biological imagery here is typical of Schleiermacher. *Decompose* here is transitive; *Zerse[t]zung* and *zerse[t]zen* also carry the connotation of "analysis" and "to analyze," respectively, in the sense of breaking something down. Part of his theory of interpretation, as he developed that in his interpretation of Plato's works (drawing his cues from Socrates in the *Phaedrus*), is that only a "living body" is worthy of analysis; if it is to be understood, it must not only be broken down according to its natural parts and connections, but it also needs to be able to be restored and recomposed. In the next paragraph, he continues the theme of an organic body.

incorporate of the feelings—well, that you can certainly only replicate mimetically, like strange physiognomies,[36] and for this reason you only replicate them as caricature. And out of these dead, corrupted parts you want to assemble a religion? Suppose one were to dissect the vital fluids of an organic body into its nearest components and then take these separate elements, combine them in every relation, and treat them in every way. Will you be able to make a beating heart out of them again? Will something once dead ever again be able to move within a living body, to be one with it? Every human art fails in reconstituting the products of living nature out of their severed components, and therefore you will not succeed in doing it with religion, when you have imaged and imagined their individual, transmuted elements still so completely from outside. They must emerge from inside, in their original, distinctive form, and therefore indisputably as your own feelings, not as stale, more foreign description, which can only lead to a piteous imitation.

For the original cognition can be like that and does not want to be religion. Therefore what you feel and perceive through them is not the nature of things, but their acting on you. What you know or believe about the former lies far beneath the sphere of religion. The universe exists in uninterrupted activity, revealing itself to us every moment. Every form that it brings forth, every being to which it gives a discrete existence according to the fullness of life, every event that it pours forth out of its abundant ever-fruitful womb is an acting of the same upon us. And so to take up into our life all that is individual as a part of the whole, all that is limited as a presentation of the infinite, and let ourselves be moved by this—this is religion. Whatever, however, wants to encroach beyond that and perhaps more deeply into the nature and substance of things—this is no longer religion but is, rather, science. And, in turn, to want to regard what ought only to indicate and represent our feelings as science, as revealed and as having emerged out of religion, or also to regard science and religion together—this sinks inevitably into mysticism and empty mythology.

Hence, it was religion when the ancients, obliterating the constraints of time and space, regarded every distinctive kind of life throughout the whole world as the work and domain of an

---

36. Physiognomy is the study of appearances or facial features as indicative of character.

omnipresent being; they had taken up a distinctive manner of the universe's dealings as a definite feeling in themselves, and they designated it in this way. It was religion when, for every beneficial event whereby the world's eternal laws revealed themselves plausibly in the coincidental, they endowed the god responsible for it with a surname and built that god a temple; they had grasped a deed of the universe and thusly designated its individuality and its character. It was religion when they rose above the harsh iron age, full of fissures and roughness, and sought afresh the golden age on Mount Olympus among the joyous life of the gods; thus did they feel in themselves the ever-active, ever-living, and serene activity of the world and of its spirit, beyond all change and all apparent evil, which only emerges from the conflict of finite forms. When, however, they had an incredible chronicle about the lineage of these gods, or when a later belief demonstrated a long series of emanations and creations—that was empty mythology.

Let me summarize everything that belongs to my speech thus far. This indeed is the one and all of religion: to feel everything moving us in feeling in its highest unity as one and all, and to feel everything individual and particular as imparted through this, and therefore to feel our existence and life as an existence and life in and through God. But then to make divinity out to be something again isolated and individual, when it is only a designation (to some an indispensable one, to many a welcome one, albeit always an imperfect one) of the common language—this is perhaps inevitable. To treat this, however, as a cognition and so, whether through religion or in religion, to develop and present the isolated existence of God before the world and outside of the world, but for the world, as science—that is, as far as religion is concerned, certainly only empty mythology. It is a further development of taking what is only a means of presenting something as though it itself were the essential thing, an outright departure from the distinctive foundation.

From this you can also see at once how it stands with the matter of whether or not religion is a system—a question to which the answer is totally in the negative, but one that also absolutely allows an answer in the affirmative, as you perhaps hardly expect. If you mean by *system* that it fashions itself according to an inner necessary connection, so that the manner in which one person is stirred one

way in a religious sense and another person in another way constitutes a whole; and it is not just accidental how in each person the
same object stimulates first this, then that—if this is what you mean,
then religion is certainly a system. What anywhere appears, whether
among many or few, as a distinct manner and determination of feeling is also closed in itself and isolated by its nature.

What you find with the Turks and the Indians could probably
not occur just as well among Christians. But in a great succession of
steps, this inner unity of religiosity expands outward and contracts,
always taking up into itself more particularity as necessary, eliminating us from itself as incompatible. For example, as Christianity is a
whole in itself, so too is each of the oppositions that have cropped up
in it at different times, including the most recent one between
Protestantism and Catholicism, each one self-contained. And so,
finally, the piety of each individual, by which that person is rooted in
that greater unity, is again one in itself and rounded out as a whole,
grounded in what you call its distinctiveness or its character, one side
of which it even constitutes. And so there is in religion an infinite
forming and shaping of itself, down to the individual personality, and
each of these is again something infinite. For you would have none of
it, if the individual were to get defined, constituted, and specified
through the rest, and if the characteristics in the concept were exactly
defined, as if the existence and becoming of the individual were to
proceed in a finite way at defined distances out of the whole.

Were I to compare religion in this respect, I know nothing
more beautiful to place next to it than that which, in any case, is
internally bound up with it—I mean, the musical arts. For consider
how music indeed forms a great whole, a particular revelation of the
world contained in itself, and in turn the music of each and every
people is for itself a whole, this in turn being divided into different
forms peculiar to it, down to the genius and style of the individual
musician. Then consider how every living emergence of this inner
revelation in the individual, truly each and every one, contains
smaller musical units within itself and even presents itself in and
through the units,[37] but with all the delight and gladness of unbounded

---

37. By units or unities here, he doubtless means musical units that make up a whole:
notes, measures, phrases, sections, movements, and symphony. He makes a similar
analogy in the *Christmas Dialogue*.

free choice.[38] Consider how even, in the magic of sounds, the individual musician's life stirs and the world touches that musician. So, too, religion—in its individual expressions, as it steps out immediately into life—could not be any farther removed from any semblance of coercion and boundedness, regardless of what is necessary in its living composition. For everything necessary is assimilated into life and consequently also into freedom. And everything individual occurs as free imagination in which the momentary mood of the world reflects itself. Only someone unholy would claim here something held in coercion, something bounded and determined from outside. If something like this lies within your concept of system, then you must completely eliminate it here.

A system of perceptions and feelings—are you able to imagine anything more fantastical? Or is this perhaps how it is with you: that by feeling something, at the same time you feel along with it or think along with it (choose whichever you prefer) the necessity? That, in accordance with that feeling, you would have to feel in this way and no other in relation to whatever (this or that) does not now directly move you at this very moment? Or, as soon as you were to get caught in this kind of contemplation, wouldn't it be all up with your feeling, and would it have to be something completely different in you, a cold calculation and shrewdness? It is, therefore, clearly an error to hold that it belongs to religion to appreciate this connection of its individual expressions and not just to have this connection in itself and to develop itself out of it, but also to see it described before itself and thus to consider it from the outside. And it is arrogance to hold whatever is lacking in this as a deficient piety. Besides, the truly pious do not let themselves be disturbed in religion's simple goings,

---

38. *Willkühr*. This term can mean "arbitrariness" or "caprice," but these (especially the latter) can carry a more negative connotation than Schleiermacher sometimes intends. Here, for example, he means it in a very positive way: the creative process of a musician. In his ethical thought, *Willkühr* means free choice in a fairly traditional and neutral way: that we are free (to a degree) to choose among certain options, but this is different from *Freiheit* (freedom). In this second *Speech*, Schleiermacher usually indicates by *Willkühr* how different people might assemble the same things differently or might form different kinds of representations about the same objects or groups of objects; some of these more than others will stand up to reality. Here *Willkühr* has been consistently translated as "free choice" so as to allow the reader to interpret what Schleiermacher means in each context.

and they take little notice of those systems of religion that have been erected from this viewpoint.

Truly, such systems are awful enough and do not begin to approximate theories about the musical arts, however much these too may be lacking. For with these systematizers there is less than anywhere else a devout attending and listening in religion, the kind that eavesdrops on what they should be describing in their own inner being. Are they really less interested in this than in merely accounting for the symbols or merely finalizing and perfecting the designation, which is exactly what is most accidental? This is almost as accidental as that designation of the stars, in which you discover the most playful free choice but that never suffices because something new is always being seen and discovered, and what is new does not want to conform itself to something else. Or do you want to find a system in this? Something or another abiding and secure, something that would exist according to its nature and not purely through the power of free choice or the tradition? The same is true here. For however much every configuration of religion is grounded internally through itself, the designation always depends directly on the external. Thousands could be excited religiously in this same way, yet each person would perhaps make different markers in order to designate their own feeling, guided not by their heart but by external relations.

These systematizers are much less interested in presenting what is individual in religion than in subordinating what is one to the others and in deducing it from what is higher. Nothing, however, is lower than this in the sense of religion, which knows nothing of deduction and tying together. In religion there is not just one individual matter of fact that someone could call original and primary. Rather, in religion anything and everything is immediately true only for itself, each one an existing for itself without dependence on another. Admittedly, every specifically configured religion is what it is only by virtue of a definite type and manner of feeling, but how preposterous to want to treat this as a principle, as you call it, from which the other gets deduced. What is true for this definite form of a religion is just as true for each individual element of religion: that special imprint bears every expression of feeling immediately in itself and, severed from this, cannot appear anywhere and cannot be possessed. Yes, this also means that religion cannot be comprehended if it is not comprehended in this way. Nothing in religion[40] can or may be demonstrated out of the other, and everything general under which the individual is supposed to be treated—all combination and interconnection of this type—either lies in a foreign sphere, if it is to correspond to the inner and essential, or is only a work of playful imagination and the freest free choice. Everyone may have their own arrangement and rubrics—the essential can neither gain nor lose thereby. Those who truthfully know about their own religion and its essence will far subordinate that apparent connection to the individual and will not sacrifice even the smallest individual to it.

In this way, that fanciful idea has come about of a universality of one religion and of a single form to which all others ought conform, as the false to the true.[39] Yes, were I not so concerned that you would misunderstand it, I would fain say that it generally amounts to just such a comparison as true and false, which is not particularly suitable for religion. For really all this belongs together, and it applies only when it comes to concepts and when the negative laws of your logic can bring something into line—otherwise it applies nowhere. Everything true exists immediately in religion. How could it otherwise have become? Yet "immediately" is only what has not yet gone through the concept but has instead grown up purely in the feeling. Moreover, everything that has anywhere formed itself religiously is good, since it has formed itself because it proclaims a common higher life.

The entire scope of religion is something infinite and is not to be treated under any one particular form but only under the totality of all forms. Religion is infinite, not only because each particular religious organization has a circumscribed horizon within which it cannot encompass everything, and therefore it can also not believe there is nothing beyond that to perceive, but principally because each one is different and thus is only excitable in its own way, so that, inside of each one's most distinctive sphere, the elements of religion have been formed differently. Religion is infinite, not only because the relation of acting and suffering,[40] between the same circumscribed matter and the human heart, is endlessly changing, and thus also because it is always born anew in time. Religion is infinite, not

---

39. A reference to Deism and the notion of a natural religion.
40. *Leiden*; being acted upon.

only because it is incompletable as composition and thus is always developing anew, always reproducing itself more beautifully, always imagining human nature more profoundly. Religion is infinite also because it is infinite on all sides.

This consciousness is given together and immediately with religion, just as with knowledge is given the knowledge of its eternal truth and unmistakableness. This consciousness is the feeling of religion itself, and for that reason must accompany each person who really has religion. Every person must be conscious that theirs is only a part of the whole, that with regard to those very same relations that affect them religiously there are completely different views and sentiments that are just as pious, and that perceptions and feelings for which they perhaps have no sense whatsoever flow out from other elements of religion.

You see how immediately this beautiful modesty, this friendly and inviting forbearance, springs up out of the essence of religion, and how rarely it gets separated from religion. How wrongly you turn to religion with your reproaches that it is invidious and obsessed with persecution, that it subverts society and lets blood flow like water. Accuse those who corrupt religion, who inundate it with a host of concepts and want to slap it into the fetters of a so-called system. What is it in religion, then, that has been argued over, has created camps and ignited wars? Over definitions—sometimes practical, always theoretical—neither of which, however, belong in religion. Philosophy no doubt strives to bring those who want to know under a common knowledge. As you see every day, even with philosophy, the better it understands itself, the more easily it leaves room for variety. Yet religion does not seek, not even once, to bring those who believe and feel under one belief and one feeling. Religion strives, of course, to open the eyes of those not yet capable of intuiting the universe, since every person who sees is a new priest, a new organ. But for just this reason religion flees with aversion from the bleak uniformity that would again destroy this divine superabundance.

That miserable obsession with system certainly thrusts what is foreign from itself, often without properly looking into its claims, because it already corrupts the closed series of particulars and, by asking for a place, could disturb the beautiful connection. The seat of disputation and contentiousness lies in this obsession with system. It must carry on and pursue warfare, since insofar as the individual is again referred to as individual and finite, the one can certainly destroy the other through its existence. In the immediate relation to the infinite, however, everything finite stands undisturbed next to one other. All is one and all is true. It is these systematizers who have wrecked all this. Modern Rome, godless but consistent, hurls anathemas and expels heretics. Ancient Rome, truly pious and religious in a high style, was hospitable to every god, and so it came to be full of gods. Adherents of the dead letter, who throw religion out, have saturated the world with screams and turmoil. True beholders of the eternal were always quiet souls—either alone with themselves and the infinite or, when they looked around, gladly granting to everyone who understood the great word their own way. With this broad view and this feeling of the infinite, however, religion also looks at what lies outside its own sphere and contains within itself the facility for unlimited versatility in judgment and in contemplation, which in fact is not to be had anywhere else.

I do not mean to eliminate ethics and philosophy, since so much of those can remain when you separate out religion. But I do, for your sake, refer you to your own experience. Let something else animate the human being—thinking or striving. Whatever it may also be aimed at, draw a narrow circle around a person, inside of which lies what is highest to that person and outside of which all that appears base and unworthy to that same person. Those who think only in accordance with a school, who act only according to precept and purpose, and who wish to line up this or that in the world—such people inevitably circumscribe themselves and constantly oppose objects of aversion that do not promote their doing and advancing.

Only the free delight of viewing and living, when it goes into the infinite and is directed toward the infinite, places the heart in unrestricted freedom. Only religion saves it from the ignominious fetters of opinion and lust. For religion, everything that exists is necessary, and everything that can be is to it a true, indispensable image of the infinite. It is only a matter of finding the point from which its relation to the infinite can be discovered. However reprehensible something may be in other relations or in itself, in this regard it is always worthy of existing and of being retained and contemplated.

To a pious heart, religion makes everything holy and worthy, even unholiness and baseness itself, whatever it grasps or does not grasp, whatever does or does not lie within the system of its own thoughts or conform to its particular way of action. Religion is the original and sworn enemy of all pedantry and all one-sidedness.

So then, the reproaches do not really strike at religion itself, since they are only based on its contamination with that knowledge, however worthy or not it may be. But knowledge always wants to be something that does not really belong to religion. Nor, for the same reasons, do the reproaches made from the other side—from acting—reach religion. True, I have already touched on this in a way, but let us also consider this in general, so that we might completely dispose of it, and you might rightly come to experience what it is I mean.

We need to make two distinctions, properly and precisely. First, you accuse religion of not infrequently provoking abominable, horrible, and indeed unnatural actions in the sphere of common, civil, and moral life. I will not begin by imposing on you the burden of proving that pious people caused such deeds; for the time being, I grant you this. Good. By issuing your accusations, however, you yourselves separate religion and ethics from each other. Do you mean that religion is immorality itself, or a branch of it? Hardly. For then you would have to wage a completely different kind of war against it, and you would have to regard the extent to which it has already vanquished piety to be a gauge of ethics. And thus you have still not taken a stand against religion—except for the few who have admittedly shown themselves almost crazy in their mistaken fervor over against a misunderstanding. Or do you perhaps only mean that piety is something other than ethics, indifferent to it, and thus capable, probably unintentionally, of becoming unethical? On the first point you are in fact right—that is to say, insofar as one can separate piety and ethics in contemplation, they are also distinct. As I have already said and conceded, the one has its essence in feeling, but the other in acting. Except how do you get from this opposition to the position of holding religion responsible for acting? Wouldn't it be more correct to say that such people would just not have been ethical enough and, if this were the case, then they could have remained just as pious without defect? For if you want us to move forward—and that is indeed what you want—then it is not advisable, when two things that should really be equal in us have become unequal, to pull back the one that is hurrying forward; it is better instead to push forward the one that lags, so we make further progress.

Before you accuse me of splitting hairs, let me call your attention to the fact that religion in itself does not push people toward acting and that, if you could imagine religion alone implanted in the human person, this person would thereupon generate neither such deeds nor any other deeds, but would produce none whatsoever, because such a person—if you keep in mind what has been said previously, without again overturning it—would simply not act at all, but would only feel. That is why many of the most religious people— in whom the ethical was repressed too much and who were lacking in the real stimulus for acting—renounced the world and in solitude gave themselves up to idle meditation. You have complained plenty about this, and rightly so. Mark me well: religion, if it isolates itself and thus becomes diseased, can provoke *this*—but *not* atrocious and horrible deeds. In this way, the reproach to religion you intend to make is turned right around and transformed into a verdict of praise. In other words, the actions that you criticize, however else they may have been uniquely supplied, agree in this: they seem to have arisen immediately out of one solitary stirring of feeling.

You always criticize it, whether or not you call this definite feeling religious. And I, deviating quite far from you in this matter, praise you all the more, the more thoroughly and impartially you criticize this. Pray criticize it not just when the action clearly seems to be an evil, but also when it enjoys a good reputation. For acting, when it arises from a single source, gets into an unseemly dependency, coming under an almost too-much-determined influence by external objects. Feeling is impetuous according to its nature, whatever its content may be, and when it is not sleep-inducing. It is a tremor, a violence to which acting should not be subject and out of which acting should not arise. Acting should, rather, arise out of calm and circumspection, incorporating this character into itself. This is similarly required in common life as in politics and in art. But the former aberration can only happen when people—in order to act, and in order for the ethical to act in them—have not let piety do what it likes enough or entirely. Consequently, it must in fact seem that, had they only been pious, they also would have acted more ethically.

The entire religious life consists in two elements: we surrender to the universe, letting ourselves be excited by the side of the universe turned toward the self; and then inwardly we reproduce this contact (which, as what it is and in its determinateness, is a particular feeling), taking it up into the inner unity of our own life and existence. The religious life is nothing other than the continual renewal of this process. When, therefore, we have been stimulated by the world in one determinate way, is it then our piety that drives us outward straightaway with this stimulation into an effecting and acting, which then certainly carries the traces of the tremor and which must cloud the rich connection of the ethical life? Impossible. Instead, our piety invites us inward to the enjoyment of what has been acquired, to take it up into the innermost being of our spirit, to merge into one with it, thus stripping the temporal, so that it dwells in us no more as an individual, not as a tremor, but as something eternal, pure, and tranquil. And then, out of this inner unity, acting rises by itself—as a separate branch of life and, as we have indeed already agreed, as a retroactive effect of feeling. But the total acting, the details of which in their connection and their consequence depend on something else entirely, can only be called feeling when each individual presents the entire inner unity of their spirit in a free and unique way in this connection and at a particular point—*not* when it arises dependent on or subject to some one individual stimulation.

Therefore, if you are not speaking of a diseased state, your criticism certainly does not reach religion. Just as certainly, this diseased state is not based originally in the religious system or on its own but is something quite general; hence, from it nothing particular against religion can be inferred. Finally, it certainly cannot escape you that, in a healthy state, insofar as we wish to contemplate piety and ethics separately, a person cannot be viewed as acting out of religion, or as being impelled to action by religion. Rather, piety forms its series for itself, and ethics its own series as well, as two different functions of one and the same life. That is why a person should not act or perform anything out of religion, but should do everything with religion. Religious feelings should accompany the

185

active life continuously like a holy music, and no one should ever or anywhere be found without it.

If you pay close attention, you will surely be able to tell that in my presentation I have deceived neither you nor myself. Does every feeling, the more you yourselves attach the character of piety to it, exhibit a stronger inclination to turn back inward, rather than erupting outwardly in deeds? Don't pious people, whom you may rightly find inwardly moved, stand in the greatest state of embarrassment, or perhaps fail to understand you, were you to ask what kind of particular action they would be disposed to perform in order to authenticate and vent their feeling? Only evil spirits, not good ones, possess and drive human beings. The legion of angels with which the heavenly father provided for his son exerted no force over him, nor did they help him in his particular doing and forbearing—nor should they have. Instead they poured serenity and calm into the soul fatigued from doing and thinking. Perhaps he lost sight of them at times, in moments when his entire power was geared toward acting, but then they hovered back around him again in a joyous throng and ministered to him.

Why do I direct your attention to such details, and why do I speak in images? My justification in doing so appears most clearly when, with you, I take as my starting point the separation that you establish between religion and ethics, and only in pursuing this correctly and precisely have we, on our own accord, returned to their essential union in true life—and have we seen that what appears as a corruption in the one also implies a weakness in the other, and that neither of the two can be complete if the other is not entirely what it should be.

This, therefore, is how it stands with regard to the first distinction, between feeling and acting. You still often speak, however, about other actions that religion must certainly produce, since they have nothing to do with ethics and, therefore, could not possibly have arisen from it. For the same reasons, they could not have arisen out of sensuality, contrasted as it is to ethics, with which they also have nothing to do. Nevertheless, they were indeed corrupt because they accustomed humans to abide by what is empty and to value what is nought, and because all too often they had to act as a substitute for ethical action, inane and meaningless though they were. I know what you mean. Spare me the long inventory of outward discipline, spiritual practices, privations, mortifications, and whatever else you accuse of being religion's product, in this sense of religion. But do not lose sight of the fact that the greatest heroes of religion, the church's founders and reformers, also judge these things with much indifference.

Admittedly, it stands somewhat differently with regard to the second distinction, between feeling and knowing, but I also think that the case I am defending will explain itself. That knowledge we were speaking about earlier—those doctrines and opinions that tried to attach themselves more closely to religion when it approached them and were thus only designations and descriptions of feeling— is a knowledge about feeling. It is not in any way, however, an immediate knowledge about the actions of the universe through which the feeling was stimulated, or about how that necessarily must have swung toward evil, when it had to substitute either for feeling or for the actual and original cognition. In the same way, too, this acting, undertaken as exercise and conduit of feeling and so often swinging out in an empty and trivial way (for we are not speaking of another kind of symbolic and signifying acting, which is not exercise but is itself presentation of feeling), is likewise secondhand acting, so to speak, which in its own way makes feeling into an object, wanting to operate on it for educative purposes.

I do not want to decide here how much value the latter might have in itself, and whether it is not just as unessential as the former knowledge, as it is difficult to grasp rightly. In what sense can we *will* to handle ourselves and, above all, our feeling? Doesn't that seem to be more the affair of the whole? Or is it a product of our life resulting from our intentions? Is it our own? All this needs to be carefully weighed. But, as I have said, this does not belong here. I would prefer discussing this with the friends of religion rather than with you. One thing, however, is certain, and I confess it unconditionally: few errors are so corruptive as when those educative exercises of feeling should substitute for the original feeling. This, however, is clearly an error religious people are not able to make. You will perhaps readily grant this to me if I only remind you that there is something quite similar on the side of ethics. For there is also this kind of acting on one's own acting: ethical exercises that people, as they express themselves, fall into line with so as to become better. What happens is that this is substituted for immediate ethical acting, for being good—but you will not want to grant that this is done by ethical people.

Take this into consideration. You speak about human beings doing all kinds of things: one adopting something from another and transmitting it to those who come later, something that does not allow itself to be understood by many and means nothing to them, yet that always allows itself to be grasped in such a way that it stimulates and supports their religious feeling, steering it toward this or that side. Wherever, therefore, this acting is a self-generating one and really has this meaning, it clearly relates to the person's own feeling and presupposes a determinate state of that person, and this state is felt along with the acting, and the person becomes aware of their own self and inner life, with its weaknesses and coarseness. Yes, it presupposes an interest in a higher self-love whose object is the person as the ethically feeling and self-formed part of the universe. And clearly, just as this love ceased, that acting too had to cease. Can it thus ever substitute, in this perverse and foolhardy way, for feeling, and can it try to displace this feeling without annulling itself at the same time? This error can only arise among the irreligious. It is an exterior side onto which they can fasten what is hidden and what they might mimic—whether they are doing it or not—in order to deceive others or themselves with the appearance of a higher life that is not really in them.

What you criticize is, in fact, as bad as you say in this sense: it is always either base hypocrisy or abject superstition. I willingly divulge it to you and have no desire to defend it. Nothing that is exercised in this sense is essential, and we want to discard both what regarded for itself is empty, unnatural, or perverse and also everything that emerges in the same way that has a good look about it. Wild mortifications, tasteless renunciation of the beautiful, empty words and customs, charitable donation—it is all the same to us, every superstition is to us equally unholy. At the same time, we never want to confuse this with the well-meant striving of pious hearts. The two are truly quite easy to distinguish. For religious people form their own ascetics according to particular need and do not look about for some single norm, once their own ascetics is acquired. The superstitious and the hypocrites, however, adhere strongly to what is given and conventional, and agitate for it as though for something universal and holy. Naturally! For if they were all expected to devise for themselves their external discipline and practice, their calisthenics of feeling, in relation to their personal situation, they would be nasty and their inner poverty could no longer lay hidden.

I have dwelt for a long time on what is most general, what is all but provisional, and what should have been self-evident. But because it has not jelled—either for you or for those many wanting to be counted among you—how religion relates itself to the other branches of life, it was necessary to deflect the sources of the most commonplace misunderstandings, so that they would not hereafter hinder us on our way. I have now done this according to my ability, and I hope we have firm ground beneath us. Now let us take up that moment that itself is never immediately intuited yet in which all various expressions of life constantly form. Let us ask, how many plants germinate already in the closed bud and, as it were, bring the fruit already to the blossom? And further, where preeminently among all life's products is religion to be sought? I hope we are convinced that no other answer can be right and can remain than this: wherever the living contacts of the person with the world prove preeminently to be feelings, these are the beautiful and richly scented blossoms of religion. True, as they have opened themselves according to that hidden action, they also soon drop away again. But the divine plant, out of the abundance of life, always bursts forth anew, creating a paradisiacal climate around itself in which no meager change disturbs the development, nor does a harsh environment harm the gentle light and the fine texture of the flowers, to which I want now to lead your purified and prepared contemplation.

Follow me first to exterior nature, which so many take for the first or sole temple of divinity, and which, by virtue of the distinctive way it touches the heart, is taken to be the innermost sanctuary of religion. But this, although it should be more, is almost exclusively the forecourt of religion. For the view you first confront me with is wholly objectionable, as if fear of the powers that rule in nature, and how they spare life nothing and threaten human works—as if this had given human beings the first feeling of the infinite or were the sole basis of all religion. Or wouldn't you have to admit that if it were not the case, and if piety had come with fear, then piety would also have to have left with fear? You certainly would. But perhaps this really is how it seems to you, so let's have a look. This is clearly the great objective of all effort put into cultivating the earth: to annihilate the domination natural forces hold over humans and to end all fear of them.

And in fact much that is worthy of admiration has already been done on this score. Jupiter's lightning no longer terrorizes ever since Vulcan has made us a shield against it; Vesta protects what she has won from Neptune, even against the most wrathful blows of his trident; and the sons of Mars unite with those of Aesculapius to fend off the deadly-quick arrows of Apollo on our behalf. Humans are always learning to bribe or addle one of these gods by means of the others and are preparing soon to watch the games, smiling as victor and lord. If, being mutually destructive, they would thus destroy one another, and if fear had been the ground of their veneration, then they would have gradually appeared as ordinary and common, for what humans have vanquished or endeavored to vanquish they can also measure, and it can no longer stand over against them frightfully as the infinite. Hence, the objects of religion must thus become, ever more and more, untrue.

But did this really occur? Were the gods not just as much fervently venerated insofar as they held and supported one another as brothers and as kin? And also insofar as they support and look after human beings, the youngest offspring of the same father? Yes, you yourselves, when you can still be awestruck before the great powers of nature, does this depend on your security or your insecurity? And have you levity enough to be poised to mock the thunder, while standing under your lightning rods? And whatever in nature preserves and protects—is this not just as much an object of adoration? Ponder whether it is so. Is it, then, only the great and the infinite that defy and threaten human existence and works, or don't the small and the trifling also do the same? And because you cannot definitively grasp and construe this into something great, you call it *chance* and *accidental*? And is this now an object of religion, or has it even been adored as such? Or, in case you wanted to form so trifling a representation of the Fate of the ancients, you must have understood little of their poeticizing piety. For under this sublime Fate, the ancients dealt as much with the preserving powers of nature as with the destructive. Hence, the holy awe of Fate—the denial of which, in the most beautiful and most cultured times of antiquity, was taken for complete villainy—was something other than that servile fear that reputation and virtue were to banish. If you can understand it, I gladly admit to you that that holy awe is the first element of religion. Yet the fear that you mean is not only not religion, it cannot even be preparatory for religion, it cannot even lead toward religion. On the contrary, if something of fear is to be extolled, then it must only be that it coerces the person inward into worldly society, into the state, in order there to become rid of it. Piety, however, depends primarily on whether one has already laid aside that fear.

For to love the world-spirit and joyfully to behold its works is the aim of our religion, and in love there is no fear.[41] Just as little, though, can that joy in nature that so many praise be truly religious. It is almost abhorrent to me to speak of how they chase it, rushing out into the great, glorious world in order to grab hold of little emotions there, and how they look inside into the delicate designs and tints of flowers, or into the magical play of colors in a glowing evening sky; or when they marvel at the song of the birds and beautiful surroundings. They are certainly quite full of admiration and rapture, and they opine that no instrument could conjure up these sounds, nor could any paintbrush accomplish this design.

Suppose, however, one were to engage them, completely in their own manner, and reason subtly with them—then they would have to condemn their own joy. What is it, then, one can ask, that you marvel at? Raise the plant in the dark cellar. Then, if it is successful, you can rob them of all these beauties without changing their nature in the least. Or imagine the mists over us storing something else, so instead of that magnificence you have only gray, unpleasant gauze before you, and the event that you are really contemplating remains completely one and the same. Yes, try once to picture for yourselves how the same midday rays, whose glare you do not tolerate, appear to those in the east already as glimmering sunsets. You must indeed bear this in mind. If you want to consider these things on the whole, and if you then do not obviously have this same sensation, then you must become aware that you have pursued only an

---

41. See 1 John 4:18.

empty appearance. They do not only believe that, but it is also actually true for them because they are prejudiced in a conflict between appearances and existence, and what falls within this can certainly neither be a religious perception nor stimulate any authentic feeling. Yes, were they children who actually take up the light and the brilliance into themselves without pondering or wanting something else without collation and reflection,[42] thus letting themselves be open for the world through the soul of the world and feeling this devoutly and being always only excited to this through individual objects; or were they sages to whom all conflict between appearance and existence is dissolved in living intuition, which precisely for this reason can be stirred once again in a childlike manner,[43] and for whom those subtleties that could disturb them were nothing—then their joy would be a truthful and pure feeling, a moment of living contact between them and the world gladly announcing itself.

If you understand this more beautiful feeling, let yourselves say that this is an original and indispensable element of religion. But do not serve me that empty, factitious essence passed off as emotion of piety, since it applies so loosely and is only a poor mask for its cold, unfeeling education—or miseducation. In contesting religion, therefore, do not ascribe to it what does not belong to it. And do not jeer, as though a person most easily came to this so-called sanctuary by means of humiliation to the point of fear of the irrational or by means of empty gimmicks; do not jeer, as though piety could arise in none so easily—or could suit none so well—as fainthearted, feeble, and sentimental souls.

What we next come across in corporeal nature is its material infinitude, its enormous masses, disseminated in that inestimable space, traversing those immeasurable orbits. If the imagination is defeated in the occupation of expanding the reduced images to their natural greatness, then many think that this prostration is the feeling of the greatness and majesty of the universe. You are right to find this arithmetical astonishment to be something childish, and you are right to attach no great importance to what is easiest to excite in those

---

42. *Reflexion.* The meaning is specular reflection (not intellectual, self-conscious reflection), thus carrying through the light imagery.

43. The example here would be Josef, the sage at the end of the *Christmas Dialogue* who becomes a child again due to the Christmas festival.

who are immature and unwitting, owing to their ignorance. But the misunderstanding is also easy to elevate, as though that feeling were religious in this meaning. But would those who are themselves accustomed to viewing it in this way concede to us that—when those great movements had not yet been calculated, when half of the world was not yet discovered, when it was not yet even known that shining points were celestial bodies[44]—religiosity would then have been necessarily lesser, because it would have been lacking in an essential element? Just as little will they be able to deny that the infinity of size and number is really only something finite, that the intellect can concentrate their entire infinitude in small formulas and can count them, as it does the most insignificant things. They will, however, certainly deny the conclusion that through progressive education and skill something can get lost of their awe before the magnitude and majesty of the world. But that magic would necessarily vanish as soon as we compare the units by which we measure our magnitude and our movements with those great world units.

That is why, as long as the feeling is still only a feeling of a personal incapacity, it is assuredly a religious feeling, except of an entirely different kind. The former awe, however, that magnificent feeling of our relation to the whole, which is just as uplifting as it is humbling, must be entirely the same—not only where the size of a world action is too great for our ability to organize it, but also where it is too small for it, and also yet where it is equal and appropriate to it. But can it then really be the opposition between small and great that stirs us so marvelously? Or is it not, in fact, the essence of the magnitude that stirs us—that eternal law by virtue of which magnitude and number first come into being and exist, and by virtue of which we, too, become and exist as such. Thus it is only life that can operate on us in a distinctive way, not what is encumbered by weight and to that degree extinguished. And what in fact addresses the religious sense in the external world are not its masses, but its eternal laws.

Elevate yourself to the sight of how these laws encompass everything—the greatest and the smallest, the world system and the particle that flutters about unsteadily in the air—and then say whether you do not intuit the divine unity and the eternal immutability of the

---

44. *Weltkörper*: Material and measurable bodies, in contrast to heavenly bodies.

world. But what most continually and repeatedly strikes us about these laws, and thus does not escape the common perception, is the order in all the movements recurring in heaven and on earth, the determined coming and going of all organic forces, the perpetual unmistakableness in the regulation of the mechanism, and the eternal uniformity in the striving of plastic nature. This is what also confers the less vivid and great religious feeling, if and insofar as it be allowed so to compare one with the other.

If you consider but a single section of a great work of art, and in the individual parts of this section perceive in turn contours and relations that are beautiful entirely in themselves and that are self-contained in it, and whose definiteness can be understood entirely from this one section—then will that section not appear to you to be a work of art in itself, more than just a part of a work? Will you not judge that the whole, were it fashioned in this style throughout, must be lacking in sweep, in boldness, and in all that intimates a great mind? Wherever you should have a sense of a sublime unity, a magnificent connectedness, here too, along with the common tendency toward order and harmony, there must necessarily be relationships in the particular—relationships that won't be fully understood from it. The world, too, is a work of art of which you can only survey a part, and if this perfect part were ordered and perfected in itself, then you would become aware of the greatness of the whole only in a narrow way. You see that the irregularity, which should often serve to repudiate religion, has on the contrary a greater value for religion than the order that first presents itself to us in the intuition of the world and lets itself be surveyed from a smaller part. The perturbations in the course of the stars indicate a higher unity, a bolder combination, than that which we become aware of from the regularity of their orbits. And the anomalies, the idle games of plastic nature, force us to see that it treats its most definite forms with a free choice, with an imagination, so to speak, whose rule we would only be able to discover from a higher standpoint. That is why, in the religion of the ancients, only the lower gods and ministering virgins had oversight over what uniformly recurs, the order of which was already found. Yet the aberrations that could not be conceived, the revolutions for which there were no laws—these were the work of the father of the gods.

And thus in our feeling we also easily distinguish between, on the one hand, the calm and mature consciousness as a higher consciousness wherein the intricate existence of the individual in the farthest combinations of the whole, the determinate existence of the particular, reveals itself through the yet-uncharted universal life; and, on the other hand, the marvelous, dreadful, arcane stimuli that take possession of us when the imagination reminds us that what has already formed in us as cognition of nature does not at all conform to nature's operations on us, and that are the same in all, even if it is only in the Knowing Ones that they pass over into a more living activity of cognition, while in the others, often gripped by ignorance and misunderstanding, they set up a delusion, which we too unconditionally call *superstition*, since a pious shiver, of which we ourselves are not ashamed, underlies it.

Give further attention to how you yourselves feel moved by the universal opposition of all living things against what, in view of that, is taken as dead; how you feel saturated by this preserving, victorious power by virtue of which everything nurtures itself and forcibly raises the dead again, so to speak, by pulling it into its own life, thereby beginning anew the cycle; how the provision disposed to all that is living presses toward us on all sides, provision that does not lie there dead but is itself living and thus regenerates itself everywhere in new ways; how, for all diversity of life forms and of the immense amount of matter that each uses up in various ways, each nevertheless has enough to run through the circle of its own existence, subject only to an inner fate, not to an external deficiency. What infinite abundance and what overflowing riches this feeling contains in itself! How, by the stamp of the maternal forethought and by childlike confidence, we are deeply moved to play away the sweet life carefree in the full and rich world.

Behold the lilies in the field. They neither sow nor reap; yet your heavenly father feeds them. Do not worry, therefore. This gladsome view, this serene easy sense, was for one of the greatest heroes of religion the beautiful harvest from an association with nature that was quite restricted and paltry. How much more, therefore, should we not gain through those whom a richer age has allowed to penetrate more deeply into nature's innermost being, so that we become acquainted with the all-diffusive powers, the eternal laws according to which all individual things are formed and destroyed—including those things that isolate themselves into a more defined perimeter and have their souls in themselves, what we call bodies. Behold how affinity and antagonism, everywhere active without ceasing, determine everything; how all difference and all opposition dissolve again into higher, inner unity; and how something finite can brag about an entirely isolated existence only by pretence. Behold how everything strives to distribute and hide itself equally in a thousand different shapes, and how you nowhere find anything simple, but everything is interwoven and connected in an artful way.

More than just beholding, however, we may also call upon all those who share in the cultivation of the age to observe how the spirit of the world in this sense reveals itself, visibly and completely, in the smallest as much as in the greatest. This is not a perception of the universe. It develops out of everything and grasps the heart, as it had already been realized by the most ancient sages of an earlier time, despite the fact that all the knowledge that glorifies our century was then lacking. In them it had not only developed, in the intuition, into the first pure and convincing image of the world, but it had also ignited, in their hearts, into a joy and love for nature, still enjoyable and loveable to us. Had this penetrated through to the people, who knows what powerful and lofty course religion would have taken from the beginning on? Except now this actually has happened. Through the gradually effective association between cognition and feeling, all those who want to be called cultivated already have this in immediate feeling, and they find in their existence itself nothing other than an operation of this spirit and a presentation and implementation of these laws. And, by virtue of this feeling, everything that impinges on their life is to them also really world—formed and steeped in divinity, and one. Perhaps consequently that love and joy should also exist in them all, that inward devotion to nature through which the art and life of the ancients becomes holy to us and out of which first developed that wisdom which we, returning through its late fruits, laud and glorify. And that would certainly be the core of all religious feelings from this side: to feel entirely one with nature and to be rooted entirely in it; and to expect, with approval and tranquility, nothing but the implementation of that eternal law in all changing appearances of life that we encounter—yes, even in the change between life and death itself.

But what must this feeling excite in us? Love and striving? Singularity and unity in nature, through which for us it first becomes that whole? Do we find this so easily and originally in nature? This, rather, is how it is and why there is so little true religious enjoyment of nature: our sense inclines entirely toward the other side, and we perceive this immediately and principally in the interior of the human heart, and then from there we point to and transfer it to the corporeal nature. For that reason, too, the heart for us is as much the seat of religion as it is its nearest world. The universe reproduces itself in the inner life, and only through spiritual nature, the interior, does the corporeal first become understandable. Yet, if it is to generate and nourish religion, the human heart must also operate on us as world and as in a world.

Let me disclose a secret to you lying almost hidden in one of the most ancient sources of poetry and religion.[45] As long the first human being was alone with himself and with nature, the deity certainly ruled over him, spoke to him in different ways; but, since he did not answer, he did not understand the deity. His paradise was beautiful and the stars twinkled down at him from a beautiful heaven, but the sense for the world did not open up to him, nor did he develop out of the interior of his soul. His heart, however, was moved by the yearning for a world, and so he rounded up before him the animal creation, to see perhaps whether a world might be formed out of that. The deity recognized that the world would be nothing as long as the human person was alone and so created a partner for him. And now, for the first time, living and brilliant sounds stirred within him; now, for the first time, the world took shape before his eyes. In the flesh of his flesh and bone of his bone, he discovered humanity—anticipating all directions and forms of love already in this original love—and in humanity he found the world. From this moment onward he became capable of hearing the voice of the deity and answering it, and from now on the most egregious transgression of the divine law no longer excluded him from intercourse with the eternal being.

---

45. A reference to the creation story in Gen 2.

The history of us all is recounted in this holy saga. Everything is in vain for those who place themselves alone. In order to intuit the world and to have religion, a person must first have found humanity, and humanity is only found in love and by means of love. That is why both are so inwardly and inseparably connected: yearning for love, ever fulfilled and ever renewing itself, becomes at the same time religion. Each one of us loves most dearly the one in whom the world mirrors itself most clearly and most purely to us. We love most tenderly the one in whom, we believe, is concentrated everything that we ourselves lack, in order to constitute humanity. Similarly, we hold those pious feelings most holy that express to us humanity's existence in the whole, be it blessedness or necessity.

In order, therefore, to find the prevailing elements of religion, let us enter into that realm where you are also most properly and best at home, where your most inner life opens up to you, where you see in your mind's eye the goal of all your striving and at the same time feel the inner drive of your powers that leads you toward this goal. Humanity itself is to you really the universe, and you count everything else as being a part of this universe only insofar as it comes into relationship with humanity or encompasses it. Beyond this viewpoint I do not want to lead you. It has often deeply pained me that, for all your interest in humanity and all your fervor for it, you are nevertheless always at odds and embroiled with it, and pure love cannot step out from within you. You agonize over improving and educating humanity, each person according to their own way, but in the end you dismiss what will not approach the goal.

If I may say so, this comes from your lack of religion. You want to work on humanity, and you choose individual human beings as your object of contemplation. You highly disapprove of these people. Of all the thousands of possible reasons for this, indisputably the most beautiful one, the one belonging to the better among you, is that you are far too moral, according to your type of morality. You take humans individually, and so you also have an ideal of an individual to which these individuals do not correspond. This is an altogether backward beginning. With respect to religion you will find yourself far better off if you would but try to change the objects of your operations and your contemplation! Work on the individuals, but with your contemplation, lift yourselves higher on the wings of religion to the infinite, undivided humanity. Seek this humanity in each individual person, behold the existence of each person as a revelation of humanity to you, and no trace of anything that now oppresses you can remain.

I, too, at least pride myself on an ethical disposition. I, too, understand how to prize human excellence. And commoners, considered in themselves, can practically overwhelm me with the unpleasant feeling of contempt—except that religion gives me an eminently great and magnificent view of everything. Simply contemplate the genius of humanity as the most perfect and best all-around artist. Genius cannot make anything that would not have a distinctive existence. Moreover, where a genius only appears to dabble with the colors or sharpen the pencil, there living and significant sketches emerge. The genius imagines countless shapes in a certain way and forms them. Millions carry the fashion of the time and are true images of its requirements and its taste; in others, reminiscences of the primitive world or presentiments of a distant future crop up. Some are the most august and most felicitous imprint of what is most beautiful and most divine; others are grotesque products of the most inventive and fleeting whim of a master. It is an irreligious view (the basis for which is not well enough understood) that the artist fashions repositories of honor and of dishonor.[46] You must contemplate nothing individually but must enjoy each one in the place where it stands. Everything that can be perceived at the same time and stands, as it were, on a canvas belongs to one great historic image that displays a moment of the universe. Would you despise that which elevates the main groups and gives life and abundance to the whole? Should the individual celestial forms not be exalted by the fact that thousands of others bow to them and you can see how everyone looks out at them, relating themselves to them?

There is, in fact, something more in this representation than a vapid simile. Eternal humanity is unweariedly occupied in creating itself and in presenting itself in the most manifold ways in the passing appearance of finite life. That is the harmony of the universe, the marvelous and great unity in its eternal work of art. You, however, blaspheme this magnificence with your demand for a despicable

---

46. See Rom 9:21.

separating out. Because you are preoccupied with the first forecourt of morals—and there, too, still preoccupied with the elements—you spurn high religion. Your need is clearly enough indicated, if you might only recognize it and be content! Search among all the occurrences in which this celestial order copies itself and see whether one will not open itself to you as a divine sign. Entertain an old discarded concept, and search among all the holy people in whom humanity reveals itself immediately, for one who could be the mediator between your limited way of thinking and the world's eternal limits. And when you have found such a mediator, then run through the whole of humanity and let all that until now has seemed other to you be illuminated by the reflection of this new light.

What would the monotonous repetition of a highest ideal be, whereby human beings, removed from time and circumstances, are really all the same—the very same formula bound only with other coefficients? What would it be in comparison to this infinite diversity of human manifestations? Take whichever element of humanity you want. You find each in every possible state, almost from its purity (since this is nowhere to be found entirely) on to every mixture with every other thing, almost to the point of the most inward saturation with all the rest (since this, too, is an unattainable extreme). Prepare the mixture in every possible way, every variation and every rare combination. And if you can still imagine combinations that you do not see, then this gap, too, is a negative revelation of the universe, an indication that this mixture is not possible in the stipulated degrees in the present temperature of the world, and your imagination about it is an outlook beyond the present limits of humanity, a true divine inspiration, an involuntary and unconscious prophecy of what will be in the future. And just as whatever the stipulated infinite multiplicity seems to lack is not really too little, so too what seems to you to be the case from your standpoint is not too much.

Religion declares the excess of the commonest forms of humanity, so often deplored and always recurring unvaried in a thousand impressions, to be an empty illusion. The eternal understanding commands, and the finite understanding can also appreciate, that the very same configurations in which the individual is most difficult to distinguish must stand pressed up against another in the closest way. But every person has something distinctive. No one is the same as the other, and in the life of each and every person there is some moment when they—like the silver gleam of base metals, be it through the intimate approach of a higher being or through some electrical shock—are what they can be, as it were, lifted out and placed on the highest pinnacle of that moment. They were created for this instant, when they would attain their purpose, and afterward the depleted life power recedes back again inside them. It is a particular pleasure to restore small souls to this moment, or to contemplate them therein. The entire existence of those who have never undergone this, however, necessarily seems superfluous and contemptible.

The existence of each person is thus related to the whole in a double sense. If in thought I impede the course of that restless process of transmission through which all humanity is interwoven with one another and made dependent on one another, then every individual is, according to their inner essence, a necessary supplement to the perfect intuition of humanity. The one shows me how every little part of humanity that is abstracted shapes itself in delicate and measured forms, as long as the inner formative impulse[47] that animates the whole can quietly continue to be effective in it. The other shows me how, from lack of an invigorating and unifying warmth, the hardness of human matter cannot be overcome; or how, in an atmosphere moved too impetuously, the innermost spirit is destroyed in its acting, and everything becomes nondescript and unrecognizable. The one appears as the coarse and animal part of humanity moved only by the first awkward emotions of humanity; the other as the purest dephlogistic[48] spirit that, separated from all that is base and unworthy, simply hovers over the earth with light foot.

---

47. *Bildungstrieb* was a term specific to the late eighteenth century and to Romanticism. It refers to the notion in biology of epigenesis and the self-organizing, driving force that makes up life. See Johann Friedrich Blumenbach, *Über den Bildungstrieb und das Zeugungsgeschäft* (Göttingen, 1781).

48. A reference to Joseph Priestley's (1733–1804) term for oxygen, which he discovered in 1774. Through a series of experiments, Priestly had come to realize that air is not itself an element but is a composition of gases, one of which is colorless and reactive— "dephlogisticated air," or what Antoine Lavoisier (1743–94) later termed *oxygen*. The OED defines *phlogiston* as "a hypothetical substance formerly supposed to exist in combination in all combustible bodies, and to be released in the process of combustion (by some identified with the element fire, conceived as being fixed in flammable substances). Now *hist.*"

All are there in order to show, through their existence, how these different parts of human nature operate separately and in detail. Is it not enough if, among this countless number, there are always at least some who, as exceptional and higher representatives of humanity, strike one or another of the melodious chords that require no added accompaniment and no subsequent resolution, but through their inner harmony enrapture and content the entire soul in one sound? But as even the most noble of these present humanity only in *one* way, and in one of its moments, so too is every one of those others the same in some one sense, each a particular presentation of humanity. Wherever an individual image is missing in this great painting, we would have to forsake assimilating humanity wholly and completely into our feeling. If every person is so essentially connected with what is the inner core of our life, how could we feel anything but this connection, and with inward love and affection embrace all without distinction of disposition or power of spirit?

If I observe the eternal wheels of humanity in its progress, this unsurveyable interlocking—according to which nothing movable is moved entirely by itself, and nothing moving moves only itself alone—mightily reassures me about your complaint that reason and soul, sensuality and ethics, understanding and blind power appear in masses thus separated. Why do you see everything individually that surely does not operate individually or for itself? The reason of the one and the soul of the other affect each other so closely as could only happen in *one* subject.[49] Ethics, to which that sensuality belongs, is set apart from sensuality. Is its authority thereby more constricted? And do you believe sensuality would be better governed, if ethics were allocated to every individual in small, barely noticeable portions? The blind power allocated to the mobs is not left to its own devices or to a brute, hostile whim in its operations on the whole; on the contrary, often without knowing it, that understanding that you find accumulated at other points in such great measure leads it, and the blind force obeys it just as unknowingly in invisible bonds.

Thus, from my point of view, the contours of personality, which appear to you so definitely, disappear to me. The magical circle of reigning opinions and contagious feelings encircles and swirls around

---

49. Emphasis in original.

everything, like an atmosphere charged with dispersing and magnetic powers. It coalesces and unites everything and, by means of the most living diffusiveness, places what is most remote in active contact; and it energetically spreads around the effluences[50] of those in whom light and truth dwell self-contained, so that they permeate some and, for others, at least light up the surface in a glittery and illusory way.

In this connection of all individuals within the sphere to which each belongs and in which each has significance, everything is good and divine. And those who but let themselves be influenced in this great interconnection feel an abundance of joy and tranquility, but they also feel how contemplation isolates the individual in discrete moments. Consider, in contrast, when we are moved by the customary doings of people who know nothing of this dependence, how they cling and cleave to this and that in order to barricade their "I"[51] and girdle it with various external works, so that they might conduct their isolated existence according to their own free choice. But the eternal current of the world unhinges them slightly. Then Fate necessarily blurs all of this, wounding and afflicting them in a thousand ways. When we see this, what is more natural than the most genial sympathy for all the pain and suffering that arises out of this uneven conflict and for all the blows that awful Nemesis metes out on all sides?

From these peregrinations through the entire realm of humanity, the pious feeling then returns, more honed and better educated, to its own "I" and finds at last within its very self everything that would otherwise stimulate it by flowing together out from the farthest reaches. For certainly, when, at first and still newly consecrated by contact with the world, we attend to how we ourselves feel in this feeling, then we discover how our "I" disappears against the entire scope of humanity—not only into what is small and insignificant, but also into one-sidedness, inadequate and null in itself. At that point, what can be closer to mortality than true, uncontrived humility? And when we gradually become alive and alert in our feeling to that which in the progress of humanity is justly preserved and supported, as opposed to that which must sooner or later be conquered and destroyed if it is not reshaped or transformed: then we look from

---

50. Effluences are of light, electricity, and magnetism—thus he carries through the analogy.

51. *Ich.*

this law to our own acting in the world. What is more natural than sincere regret over everything in us that is hostile toward the genius of humanity, than that humble wish to propitiate the deity, than the ardent desire to turn back and to repair ourselves along with everything that belongs to us to that sacred realm, where alone there is security against death and destruction? And when we further progressively perceive how the whole only becomes clear to us, and we only arrive at the intuition of it and at being one with it in fellowship with others, and by means of the influence of such people who— long ago freed from dependency upon their own perishable existence and from the striving to expand and to isolate it—also enjoy communicating their higher life to others: then how could we resist that feeling of a special affinity with those whose actions have championed our existence and who have safely led it through the dangers that threatened it? Or how could we resist that feeling of gratitude that impels us to pay homage to those who have earlier already united themselves with the whole, and who now are conscious of their life in the whole and also through us?

Only by going through these feelings do you finally find in yourselves the principal features of the most beautiful and most base, of the most noble and most contemptible, which you have perceived in others as unique sides of humanity; and only then do you discover in yourselves at different times all the manifold degrees of human powers. Not only this, but also all the countless mixtures of different compositions that you have intuited in the characters of others appear to you as but moments captured from your own life. There were instances when you thought, felt, acted just like this or that person, when you really were this or that person, despite all distinctions of gender, education, or external environments. You really have passed through all these different configurations in your own order. You are yourself a compendium of humanity, your unique existence encompasses in a certain sense the entire human nature, and this is in all its presentations nothing other than your own "I"—duplicated, more clearly excellent, and eternalized in all its modifications. With the purest, most irreproachable love you can then also love yourself; the feeling of being a center point of the universe can also stand side by side with the humility that never leaves you; and regret of all bitterness can sweeten into joyous self-sufficiency. The person in whom religion has in turn worked itself back into the interior and has also found there the infinite, in whom religion is perfected from all these sides, requires no mediator for any one intuition of humanity—and can be a mediator for many.

It is not only in the present, however, that feeling hovers this way in its expressions between the world and the individual in whom it dwells, drifting nearer toward the one, then toward the other. Rather, as everything that moves us is a becoming, and as we ourselves are not otherwise so moved and do not otherwise comprehend, so too are we as feeling persons always driven back to the past. Indeed one could say, as our piety chiefly nourishes itself more on the side of the spirit, so history is immediately and initially the highest object of religion in the most proper sense—not so as to expedite and govern the progression of humanity in its development, but so as to observe the most universal and greatest action of the universe. In this sense, religion certainly begins and ends with history. Prophecy is in its eyes also history, and the two are indistinguishable. All true history has originally had a religious end and has assumed religious ideas.

Moreover, what is finest and most tender in history can never be comprehended scientifically but only in the feeling of a religious heart. Such a heart recognizes the peregrination of spirits and souls, which already seems but a tender poem, in more than one sense as a wonderful performance of the universe, making it possible to compare the different periods of humanity to a reliable standard. Soon, after a long interval in which nature could produce nothing similar, some excellent individual returns again fully the same. But only the seers[52] recognize this person, and only they are to judge, from the operations that now produce this person, the signs of different times. Soon, a single moment of humanity returns completely, as though a bygone prehistory has left you its image, and, from the different causes through which it has now been generated, you are to recognize the progress of the universe and the formula of its laws. Soon, the genius of some special human predisposition awakens from its slumber. Rising and falling here and there, it had already completed its course and appears in one or another place and under different

---

52. *Die Seher.*

circumstances in a new life. Its faster flourishing, its deeper operating, its more beautiful and more powerful configuration should indicate how the climate of humanity has been improved and how much more suitable the ground for the nourishing of noble plants has become.

Here, peoples and generations of mortals appear to you just as different in remarkableness and worth, but also just as equally necessary for the whole of history, just as the most diverse things in individuals must exist next to one another, simultaneously. Some are dignified and brilliant, powerfully continuing to exert an influence in the infinite without regard to space and time. Others are common and insignificant, destined only to lend particular nuance to an individual form of life or form of union, really only living and noticeable in a moment, only intended to present one thought, to produce one concept, and then hastening toward destruction, so that what generated its most recent growth can be instilled in another. As vegetable nature, through the decline of entire species and out of the decomposition of entire generations of plants, brings forth and nourishes a new generation, so you see here, too, spiritual nature, out of the ruins of a glorious and beautiful human world, generates a new world, which sucks its first life power from the decayed and marvelously reshaped elements of the former.

If here, in the being-seized by a universal connection, your glance is led frequently and immediately from the smallest to the greatest, and from the latter back again to the former, and if it shifts between these two in living oscillation to the dizzying point that it can no longer distinguish great or small, cause or effect, preservation or destruction—then the form of eternal fate, whose pulls entirely bear the imprint of this state, appears to you. It is a marvelous mixture of stark obstinacy and deep wisdom, of coarse, unfeeling violence and intimate love. Soon the one, soon the other alternately seizes you, inviting you now to powerless defiance, now to childlike devotion. If you then compare the secluded striving of the individual, who has arisen out of these opposing views, with the steady and uniform progress of the whole, then you see how the high world-spirit strides smilingly away from all that vociferously resists it. You see how the sublime Nemesis, tirelessly following its steps, crosses the earth, how she metes out chastisement and retributions to the haughty who struggle against the gods, and how with an iron hand she scythes also the bravest and most felicitous who—perhaps with laudable and most admirable mettle—would not bow down before the gentle breath of the great spirit.

If you finally want to grasp the distinctive character of all modifications and all advances of humanity, then your feeling, resting on history, shows you more securely than anything else how the living gods hate nothing as much as death, how nothing ought to be pursued and toppled more than death—the first and last enemy of humanity. The coarse, the barbaric, the unscrupulous ought to be devoured and reshaped in organic formation. Nothing should be dead mass, moved only through dead impact and resisted only through unconscious friction. Everything should be life: distinct, connected, devoured, and raised many times over. Blind instinct, unthinking habituation, dead obedience, everything inert and passive—all these woeful symptoms of the asphyxia of freedom and humanity—should be annihilated. The occupation of the moment and the occupation of the centuries point to the great, always ongoing redemptive work of eternal love.

I have but sketched the basic contours of some of the prominent intuitions of religion in the sphere of nature and of humanity. In doing so, I have at the same time led you to the final limit of your horizon. Here is the end and the pinnacle of religion for all to whom humanity and universe count equally. From here I could only lead you back again into the individual and to what is smaller. Just keep in mind that there is something in your feeling that disdains this limit, in virtue of which it really cannot remain standing here but rightly looks beyond to the other side of this point and into the infinite. I will not speak of presentiments that become more pronounced in thoughts and get subtly established—namely that, if humanity itself is moveable and malleable, if it not only presents itself differently in the individual but also *becomes*[53] different here and there, then it cannot possibly be the sole and highest thing that presents the unity of spirit and matter. In fact, just as the individual person is related to humanity, so humanity can present only one particular form of this unity. Next to it there are necessarily still other such

---

53. Emphasis in original.

207

forms by which it is delimited and thus to which it stands opposed. I only want to allude to this: in our feeling we all find the same. For innate to our life and imprinted in the earth, and therefore also in the highest unity that generated it, is dependence on other worlds. Hence this always active but seldom understood presentiment of something else emergent and finite, but exterior to and above humanity—of a higher, more unified marriage of spirit and matter generating more beautiful configurations. Except certainly here every contour is already too definite. Each reverberation of feeling can only be fleeting and loose, hence exposed to misunderstanding and so commonly taken for foolishness and superstition.

Enough with this intimation about what lies so infinitely far from you! Any further word about it would be an inscrutable speech, and you wouldn't know where it came from or where it was going. If only you had the religion you could have, and if only you were conscious of what you actually already do have! For in fact, if you contemplate only the few religious perceptions and feelings that I have been delineating with minor strokes, then you will find that they are not all alien to you, not at all. I dare say something similar to this has entered your heart before. I do not know, however, which is the greater misfortune—for you to lack them entirely, or for you not to understand them. In the one case they fail to achieve their effect, and in the other you thereby deceive yourselves.

In light of what has been presented, and anything else like that, I might accuse you of two things especially. You pick out one thing and stamp it exclusively as "religion," and the other you want to take away from religion as belonging immediately to ethical acting—both presumably for the same reason. The retribution that strikes everything that tries to go against the spirit of the whole; the active hatred everywhere of all those who are high-spirited and audacious; the continual progression of all human things to an end—a progression so certain that, after many failed attempts, we actually finally see every particular thought and plan that draws the whole nearer to this end succeed. You are conscious of the feeling that is suggestive of this, and you would gladly preserve and spread this feeling, purified of all abuses. But this, you then insist, ought exclusively to be religion. You thus want to drive out everything else that nevertheless arises out of the very same behavior of the heart and fully in the very same way. How is it you have come to these broken fragments? I will tell you. You do not really consider this to be religion but instead a reverberation of ethical acting, and you intend to foist the name *religion* upon what we now commonly consider it to be, in order to serve the last blow to religion itself. For you do not find this yourselves exclusively in the sphere of ethics in the narrow sense in which you take it.

Feeling knows nothing of this kind of narrow-minded partiality. For religion, too, the moral world is not the universe, and what would apply only to this moral world is, for religion, no intuition of the universe. In everything that belongs to human doing—in play as in earnestness, in the smallest as in the greatest—religion knows to discover and to track these actions of the world-spirit. Whatever it should perceive it must be able to perceive everywhere, for only thereby does it become religion's. And thus religion also finds herein a divine Nemesis: the very people who, because only the ethical or the legal dominates in them, make an inconsequential appendage of morals out of religion. Such people only want to take from religion what lets itself be shaped to this, and in doing so they irretrievably corrupt their morals, however much it may also be purified by religion, and scatter the seed into new errors. It sounds very beautiful: if someone perishes by ethical actions, it would be the will of the eternal being, and what does not happen through us will come to be at another time. Yet this grand consolation also does not belong to ethical acting, otherwise ethics would depend on the degree to which each person is receptive in each instant to this consolation. Acting cannot appropriate anything whatsoever from feeling immediately into itself without its original power and purity being at once clouded.

In other ways you chase it with all those feelings of love, humility, joy, and the other feelings I delineated for you whereby the heart hovers between two points, the universe being one and in some way your own "I" being the other. The ancients well knew what was right. They called all these feelings *piety*, and they referred them immediately to religion, taking them to be the noblest part of religion. You, too, are acquainted with them, but when you encounter something like this, you try to persuade yourselves it is an immediate component of ethical acting, and in morals you want to assign their place to moral sentiments. Morals, however, do not covet them, nor do they suffer them. For acting ought not to follow immediately from the stimuli of love and affection, else it would become uncertain and imprudent; nor should it be generated through the instantaneous influence of its external object. Hence morals are acquainted with no awe except that before its own law. It damns as impure and self-seeking what can occur out of sympathy and gratitude. It humiliates—nay, even despises—humility. And when you allude to regret, then it speaks of a lost time that you uselessly aggrandize. Moreover, your innermost feeling must assent to this: that it has not gone after immediately acting with all these sentiments. They come for themselves and end in themselves as functions of your innermost and highest life.

Why do you get all wound up, begging for grace for them there, where they do not belong? If it pleases you to consider that they are religion, then you need to demand nothing for them except religion's own strict right, and you will not deceive yourselves with ungrounded claims you are prone to make in its name. Wherever else you try to assign a spot to these feelings, they will not be able to abide there. Bring them back to religion. To it alone this treasure belongs. As the owner of this treasure, religion is to ethics and to anything else that is an object of human doing not servant but indispensable friend, their fully valid advocate, and intermediary with humanity.[54]

This is the level at which religion stands insofar as it is the embodiment of all higher feelings. I have already intimated that religion alone releases human beings of one-sidedness and narrow-mindedness. Now I can explain this in more detail. In all acting and working, be it ethical or artistic, humans are supposed to strive after mastery. But, for those who are completely inwardly possessed by the object being mastered, all mastery narrows them, making them cold, one-sided, and hard. Mastery initially directs the human heart toward one point, but this one point cannot satisfy it. Can we really expend our entire power proceeding from one narrow opus[55] to the other? Or, in fact, will the greater part of that very power not lie

---

54. This is a highly gender-inflected sentence and could also be translated in this way: "As mistress of this treasure, religion is to ethics and to all else that is an object of human doing not handmaid but indispensable friend, their fully valid advocate, and mediatrix with humanity."

55. *Werk* here and in the following paragraph carries the sense of an "opus," "oeuvre"—a great work of art or achievement of genius; hence, the Latin has been used to capture that.

unused, thus turning against and consuming the self? How many of you fall apart because these powers are themselves too great? There is an overabundance in power and impulse that never once summons forth an opus because none would be suitable for it. It drives them around erratically and is their corruption.

Is it that you want to so quash this evil anew that a person in whom one object is too great should unite all objects of human striving—art, science, and life? Or, if you know of any more objects, those as well? That would certainly be your old desire: to have humanity everywhere cut out of one, ever-recurring piece. Were it only possible! If only those objects did not, as soon as they are envisaged individually, in a very similar way so animate and strive to dominate the heart. Each of them wants to complete great works, each has an ideal to strive toward and a totality to achieve, and this rivalry cannot end otherwise than in one eliminating the other. Yes, within every such sphere, whoever wants to attain to a more eminent mastery must be narrowed all the more to a single thing. But if this completely occupies us, and we live only in this production, then how shall we attain our full portion in the world, and how shall our life become a whole? Hence the one-sidedness and poverty of most *virtuosi*: outside their sphere, they are sunk in a baser kind of existence. And there is no other cure for this evil than that each one, while active in a definite manner in a finite realm, lets their own self at the same time, without definite activity, be affected by the infinite and, in religious feelings of every kind, become aware of all that lies outside of that realm. This is within reach for each of you, since whichever object of your free and artistic activity you have chosen, it takes but little thought to move out from there to find the universe, and in this you then discover the rest as commandment, inspiration, or revelation of the universe.

Thusly comprehending and enjoying them in the whole is the only way that you, with an already chosen direction of the heart, can possess also what lies outside of that—not again, as art, out of free choice, but as religion, out of instinct for the universe. And because they also rival anew in the religious form, religion also therefore seems more often isolated—as a certain distinctive receptivity and taste for art, philosophy, or ethics—than as complete in its entire configuration and as uniting everything. So, alongside the finite that especially and in a narrowing way determines us, we set an infinite. And alongside the tightened striving after something definite and complete, we set a hovering that expands out into the undetermined and the uncreated. Thus do we establish the equilibrium and harmony of our being, which gets lost irretrievably if we, without having religion at the same time, surrender ourselves to one particular direction. For each of us, our specific calling is, as it were, the melody of our life, and our life remains a plain, paltry series of sounds if religion does not accompany those in infinitely rich variety with all sounds that do not wholly resist it. Thus does religion lift up the plain song to a symphonious and splendid harmony.

If what I have indicated (hopefully) coherently enough for all of you really does constitute the essence of religion, then it is not difficult to answer the question, "Where, then, do those dogmas and doctrines really belong? And how are they related to what is essential?" In fact, I have already given you the answer above. For all these propositions are nothing other than the result of that contemplation of feeling, that comparative reflection upon what we have already addressed. And the concepts that underlie these propositions are, just as is true with your concepts of experience, nothing other than the common expression for a determinate feeling—which expression, however, religion does not require for itself, hardly even for communicating about itself, but reflection requires and creates it. Miracles, inspirations, revelations, supernatural sensations—one can have much piety without being in need of any one of these concepts. Yet whoever reflects comparatively on his or her own religion finds it ineluctably, in a very specific way, and cannot possibly evade it. In this sense, all these concepts admittedly belong in the sphere of religion, and indeed do so unconditionally, without anyone being permitted to define the least thing beyond the limits of its application.

The quarreling over which event is really a miracle, over what really constitutes the character of a miracle, over how much revelation there may well be, and the degree to which and the reasons why someone may really believe in it; and the obvious ambition to disavow decency and respect, pushing them to the side as much as possible, according to the silly opinion that philosophy and reason are thereby served—such quarreling is one of the childish operations of the metaphysicians and moralists in religion. They throw all points of view together and bring religion into disrepute to usurp the universal validity of scientific and physical judgments. Pray, do not let yourselves be confused to the detriment of religion by their sophisticated disputations or their sanctimonious concealment of what they would all too gladly like to make public. Religion leaves you your physics and, God willing, also your psychology untouched—however loudly it also demands back all those ill-reputed concepts.

What, then, is a *miracle*? Do you not know that what we call *miracle* in a religious sense is everywhere else referred to as sign, as indication? And that our name, which simply points to the state of mind of the person who is looking, is respectable only insofar as it is what a sign should be, the more so when it is still something else? It must be so natured that it and its characteristic power will be noticed. In this sense, however, every finite thing is a sign of the infinite, and so all those expressions signify nothing except the immediate relationship of a phenomenon to the infinite, to the universe. Does that, however, rule out that there is not just one immediate relation to the finite and to nature? *Miracle* is only the religious name for event. Every event, even the most all-natural and most common, as soon as it lends itself to this—that the religious view of it can be the dominant one—is a miracle. To me, everything is miracle. But in your sense of the term, only what is inexplicable and foreign is a miracle to me; this is no miracle in my sense of the term. The more religious you would be, the more miracles you would see everywhere, and every quarreling here and there over particular events, whether they deserve to be called miracle, only gives me the painful impression of how poor and base the religious sense of those doing the arguing is. The one side proves this by protesting everywhere against miracle; thereby they only prove their refusal to see anything of the immediate relationship to the infinite and to divinity. And the other side proves it by insisting that for them it depends on the particulars and that a phenomenon must be shaped especially fantastically for them to consider it a miracle; whereby they only certify how unobservant they are.

What is called *revelation*? Every original and new communication of the universe to human beings is a revelation, and so would every moment I have already noted above be a revelation, if only you were aware of them. Every intuition and every feeling, whenever they develop originally from such a moment, has emerged out of a revelation. Admittedly, we cannot demonstrate this to be a revelation, since it lies beyond consciousness. We must, however, presuppose it both in general and in the particular. Yes, each person must know best what is repeated and experienced elsewhere, or what is original and new. And if something original and new has not quite yet generated itself in you, then someone else's revelation will become one for you, too. I advise you to entertain it well.

What is called *inspiration*? It is only the general expression for the feeling of true ethics and freedom. Understand me well. I do not mean that fantastical and much-vaunted ethics and freedom that only understands acting as accompanying and adorning extended deliberations. I mean, rather, *inspiration* is the expression for the feeling that activity emerges from the interior of the person, despite all or without regard to all exterior inducement. For, to the degree that it is plucked away from worldly entanglement, it is felt as a divine feeling and is attributed to God.

What is *prophecy*? Every religious pre-shaping of the other half of a religious event, the one half having been given, is prophecy. It was very religious of the ancient Hebrews to gauge the divinity of a prophet not according to how difficult the prophesying was or according to how great the subject matter, but entirely and simply according to the issuance. For, more likely, we cannot know from the individual how completely the feeling has formed itself in everyone until we see whether the prophet has accurately captured the religious view of this definite, motivating relationship.

What is called the *operation of grace*? Clearly, this is nothing else than the common expression for revelation and inspiration, for that play between the world entering people through intuition and feeling, and people stepping into the world through activity and culture, both in its originality and its divine character, so that the entire life of the pious person forms only a single series of operations of grace.

You see, all these concepts, insofar as religion requires concepts or can assimilate them, are the first and most essential. They designate, in the most characteristic way, individuals' consciousness of their own religion, what must necessarily and universally be included in it. Yes, those who do not see unique miracles in the standpoint from which they contemplate the world and in whose interiors distinct revelation does not ascend; whose souls do not ache to suck in the beauty of the world and to be permeated by its spirit; who do not, in the most meaningful moments, feel with the most living conviction that a divine spirit drives them and that they speak and act out of holy inspiration; who are not at least conscious, for this is in fact the minimal degree, of their feelings as immediate operations of the universe and who do not recognize something distinct in them that cannot be reproduced, but that rather authenticates its pure origin out of their innermost being—such people have no religion.

To know oneself, however, to possess this is true *faith*. In contrast, *to believe* as it is commonly used is to accept what someone else has done, to want to think and feel what another has thought and felt. This is a bitter and unworthy service. Instead of being the highest in religion, as is wrongly imagined, it must be cast off straight away by anyone who wants to penetrate into religion's sanctuary. To wish to have and to hold it proves that one is incapable of religion. To demand it from others shows that one does not understand religion. *You* want everywhere to stand on your own feet and go your own way, and this worthy intention should not make you shrink back from religion. Religion is neither slavery nor captivity. Here, too, you should belong to your own selves—yes, this is actually a requisite condition to participating in religion. Everyone, with the exception of a few chosen ones, surely requires a mediator, a guide, who awakens their sense of religion from the first slumber and gives them their first bearings. This, however, should only be a temporary state. Everyone ought then to see with their own eyes and to bank a contribution to religion's treasury, otherwise they do not deserve a place in religion's empire, nor do they obtain one. You are right to despise the wretched parroters, who derive their religion entirely from someone else or who cling to a dead scripture, swearing by it and proving on the basis of it.

Every sacred scripture is in itself a magnificent product, a speaking memorial from the heroic time of the religion. To the servile cult, however, scripture is merely a mausoleum, a memorial that a greater spirit *was* here but no more exists here. For, if this spirit still lived and were effective, would it really look more upon its earlier work with love and with the feeling of identity, which can be only a weak copy of it? Not every person who believes in a sacred scripture has religion. Only those who understand sacred scripture in a living and immediate way have religion—and for that reason only they could most easily do without scripture.

Even your contempt against the pathetic and powerless devotees of religion in whom religion has already died from lack of nourishment before birth—even this contempt demonstrates to me that there is in you an aptitude for religion. And this opinion of mine is confirmed by the respect that you always show to all its true heroes, however much you also rebel against the way that they have been misused and disgraced through idolatry. I have shown you what religion really is. Have you found anything at all there that would be unworthy of you or of the highest human culture? To the contrary, must you not yearn for that universal linking with the world, which is only possible through feeling, the more you are separated and isolated in feeling by means of the most defined culture and individuality? And have you not often felt this holy desire as something unknown? I beseech you to become aware of the call of your innermost nature and follow it. Banish the false shame before an age that should not define you but that should be defined and created by you! Return to that which lies so near to you—especially to you—and the violent separation from which destroys, without fail, the most beautiful part of your existence.

Yet it seems to me as though many among you do not believe that I could want to end my present occupation here or that I could have spoken exhaustively of the essence of religion, since I have said nothing at all of immortality and have talked about God only in passing, although both of these should be the hinge and main article of religion. Except I disagree with you about both of these. That is to say, I do *not* believe that I have said nothing about immortality and so little about God; I believe, rather, that both of these have been in each and every thing that I have established for you as an element of religion, for only what is divine and immortal can have space in religion, wherever religion is spoken of. And, I dare say, just as wrong are those who consider God and immortality, as these are commonly understood, as the most important things in religion—since only what is feeling and immediate perception belongs to that. Your "god" and your "immortality," however, are concepts and thus can have no greater worth in religion than that accorded to concepts, as I have shown you. Still, lest you think that, on the one hand, I am afraid of saying an ordinary word about this subject matter because it would be dangerous to speak about it before a definition of *God* and *existence*,[56] consistent with the law and court, has been set in the light of day and has been sanctioned in the German empire; or lest you believe perhaps that, on the other hand, I am playing a pious deception and want, in order to be everything to everyone, to depreciate with seeming indifference what must be of disparately greater importance for me than I want to admit—I will with pleasure stand my speech up to you and try to make clear to you that it really is as I have just argued it is.

Remember, in the first place, that we took every feeling as a stirring of piety only insofar as, in that same feeling, it is not the individual as such that affects us but the whole, in and with the individual. Therefore, it is not the individual and finite that enters our life, but precisely God, in whom alone the particular is one and all. And so, too, it is not this or that individual function in us that is excited and that steps forward, but our entire being—how we confront the world and are at the same time in it—hence immediately the divine in us. How could anyone therefore say that I have portrayed for you a religion without God, since I have presented nothing other than the immediate and original existence of God in us through feeling? Or is God not the sole and highest unity? Is it not God alone before whom and in whom everything individual dissolves? And when you see the world as a whole and as a totality, could you see this in any different way than in God? Otherwise, tell me something else, if it is not this, through which the highest being, the original and eternal existence, should differentiate itself from what is individual, temporal, and derived! But you cannot have God in feeling in any other way than through these stimuli of the universe, and for that reason God has not been spoken of in any other way. Therefore, if you do not accept this as a knowing about God, as a having of God, then I cannot instruct you further or mean anything to you, but I can only say that whoever denies this will become godless in feeling to me. And I do not want not to condemn how it will also stand concerning their cognizing. For in this area there is certainly also an imme-

---

56. Emphases in original.

diate knowing about God that is the source of all other knowing, except we were speaking not about science but about religion.

The former way, however, having God in consciousness, is neither the idea of God[57] nor the feeling of God. It is for religion something completely subordinate, because it is only a concept. This concept is put together out of features that they call *divine attributes*, but collectively these are nothing other than the grasping and sorting of the different ways in which the unity of the individual and of the whole expresses itself in feeling. For no one will deny that exactly in this manner the individual attributes of God aligned the particular concepts to make them corresponded to other similar feelings. Hence, I cannot apply anything to this concept differently from what I have said in general about concepts in relation to religion—namely, that there can be much piety without them, and that they initially form themselves when piety itself again becomes an object of contemplation. Except this concept of God, as it is so thought, does not stand on the same level as that mentioned above. Because it seeks to be the highest and to stand over all, it actually itself stands under an opposition, and it subordinates existence to thought. Therefore another concept, one conveying the inverse relation, stands in opposition to it and is just as inadequate.

Now how is it fitting that an adherent of the one concept claims so firmly that without it there would be no religion? Everyone can be pious. We hold to this or that concept, but our piety, the divine in our feeling, must be better than our concept. The more we seek the divine in this concept, the less we understand ourselves. Just see how humanly divinity is presented in the one concept, and in turn how dead and rigid it is in the other—in both cases, the more so the concept is taken literally. And admit that both are lacking, that neither of the two can be a demonstration of piety, except insofar as the concept really is self-formed and also necessarily presents one element, at least, of feeling—but if this is not the case, both concepts are worthless. Or is it not manifest that many do believe in and suppose such a God but are nothing less than pious, and also that this concept is never the seed out of which their piety can mature, because the concept has no life in itself but only through feeling? So the

---

57. Schleiermacher clarifies this in the third edition: "...neither the idea of God, which you place at the apex of all knowing, as the undivided unity pouring out of everything...."

speech can also not be about the position that the possession of the one or the other of these two concepts could be the sign of a complete or incomplete religion. In fact, both are changed in the same way, according to the degree to the religious sense is cultivated—and this we can really view as different levels. Listen carefully to this, for I know of nothing further to say about this topic so as to bring us to agreement.

Where a person's feeling is still a dim instinct; where a person's overall relationship to the world has not yet blossomed to clarity; where, too, for that person the world can be nothing more than a oneness in which nothing manifold can be distinguished, nothing but a uniform chaos in confusion, without distinction, order, or law, and out of which nothing individual can be separated out unless it is arbitrarily cut out in time and space—there you will naturally find little difference, whether the concept, to the extent that traces of it even appear, inclines to one side or the other. For certainly you will not wish to place different value on whether the character of the whole is presented as a blind fate that can be identified only by means of magical performance, or whether it is presented as a being that should indeed be living but without determined attributes—an idol, a fetish—regardless of how many there may be because they are distinguishable only through arbitrarily established boundaries of their spheres.

Progressing further, the feeling becomes more conscious. Relationships emerge more clearly in their manifoldness and definiteness. But for that reason, too, in the feeling of the universe there emerges the multiplicity of heterogeneous elements and forces, whose continual and eternal conflict determines its manifestations. Then, too, the result of the contemplation of feeling changes proportionately, and the opposing forms of concept emerge more definitely. Blind fate morphs into a higher necessity in which cause and connectedness rest, albeit inaccessibly and inscrutably. In the same way, the concept of the personal god increases, except at the same time dividing and copying itself. Those forces and elements being especially ensouled, gods are generated in endless number, distinguishable through different objects of their activity, through different inclinations and dispositions. You must grant that this already presents to us in feeling a more powerful and more beautiful life of the universe than that earlier state—the most beautiful where the acquired manifold and the indwelling highest unity are bound in a most interior way in feeling, as you also find in the Hellenes, whom you rightly so revere. In reflection, both forms come to agreement: the one cultivated more for thought, the other more in the arts; the latter presenting more the multiplicity, the former more the unity. Where, however, such an agreement does not exist, will you nevertheless admit that whoever has risen to this level is also more perfect in religion than whoever is still limited to the first level? That, therefore, whoever has bowed at the higher level before the eternal and inaccessible necessity is more perfect than the coarse worshiper of a fetish?

Now let us ascend higher, there where all those quarrelling become one again, where the universe presents itself as totality, as unity in multiplicity, as system, and so for the first time it merits its name. Shouldn't they who so perceive the universe as one and all, and so confront the whole in the most perfect way—shouldn't such people be considered more fortunate for their religion, as well as for how their concept may shape itself from it, than those who have not yet blossomed so far? Therefore, here and elsewhere, decide the value of someone's religion by the manner in which the deity is present to that person in feeling, and not by the manner in which the deity is imaged, always inadequately, in the concept, about which we are now concerned. Therefore, if you name whoever occupies this level but who scorns the concept of a personal god after Spinoza (as you do, although whether rightly so I do not want to decide here), then just grant that this scorning does not rule out the presence of the deity in that person's feeling. Couldn't such a person stand just as far above the worshiper of the twelve great gods as a pious person on this second level, whom you with equal right could name after Lucretius, stands above an idolater?

But this is the old illogic, this is the obfuscating sign of the lack of culture: they furthest discard those who stand with them on one level, simply at a different point on that very level! The level to which we rise authenticates our sense for divinity. This is the real measure of our religiosity. Yet whichever of those concepts we will adopt—to the degree that we still actually need it—depends solely on what we need it for and toward what side our imagination primarily tends.

Does it tend toward existence and nature, or toward consciousness and thinking? I hope you will not take it as sacrilege or contradiction that leaning toward this concept of a personal God or rejecting it should depend on the direction of the imagination. You will know that under "imagination" I mean that which is highest and most original in us, and anything outside of imagination can be only reflection on it and is thus also dependent upon it. You will know that your imagination is the means by which you arrive at the world and at divinity, also per feeling, and then initially arrive at that concept, which creates the world for you, and that you could have no God without world. The concept will not become more ambiguous to anyone thereby. If anything, a person will be better able to break away from the almost irrevocable, encroaching necessity by knowing where this necessity comes from.

Besides, among truly religious persons there were never zealots, enthusiasts, or fanatics for this concept. Whenever the rejection of this concept of God is called *atheism*, they have looked aside with great equanimity. And there has always been something that to them appears irreligious, whatever else it is—namely, when one of those dispense with having divinity immediately present in feeling. Except truly religious people cannot believe that such people are completely without religion, because they otherwise would have to be also completely without feeling and completely sunk with their actual existence into what is brutish, since such people could become nothing inside apart from the God in us and in the world, apart from the divine living and operating of the universe.

Yet originally religion had nothing to do with the personal God, the extramundane God exercising control imperiously from outside. And those who place him over everything, so independently of feeling, are those who also want something that is foreign to religion— namely, that God should, from outside, guarantee their happiness and incite them toward ethics. They like to watch how that goes. A free being cannot want to influence a free being otherwise than by giving itself to the other to recognize, irrespective of whether through pain or desire, because this is determined not by freedom but by necessity. Moreover, a free being cannot incite us to ethics, since it will not contemplate differently from acting, and cannot have acted on our ethics, and no acting on ethics can be thought.

Concerning immortality, however, I cannot salvage the fact that here still far fewer correspond to the way in which all pious people carry an immutable and eternal existence within themselves. And this, I believe, I have plainly presented to you. For when our feeling clings nowhere to the individual, when its content is rather our relation to God, in whom everything individual and fleeting perishes, then there is nothing fleeting in it, only something eternal, and it can rightly be said that the religious life is one in which we have already sacrificed and realized everything mortal, and really enjoy immortality. But the way in which most people take "immortality," and their yearning for it, is entirely irreligious, directly contrary to the spirit of religion. Their wish has no other cause than resentment of what is the aim of religion.

Remember how in religion everything gravitates toward expanding the sharply cut-out contours of our personality, so that they should gradually lose themselves in the infinite and we should, through the intuition of the universe, become one with it as much as possible. They, however, bristle against this. They do not want out of the accustomed narrowness. They want to be nothing but their appearance and are anxiously concerned about their personality. They are, therefore, very far from wanting to seize the unique opportunity that death presents to them, in order to overcome the very same. In fact, they tremble about how they will carry their personality to the other side of this life, and they strive the highest after wider eyes and better limbs. But God speaks to them as it is written: whoever loses his life for my sake will receive it, and whoever would preserve it, will lose it.[58] The life they want to preserve is a wretched one. If for them it has to do with the eternity of their person, why are they not as anxiously concerned about what the person *has been* as they are about what the person *will be*? And what help is it to them going forward if they cannot go backward? Over the search for an immortality, which is no immortality and over which they are not masters, they lose the immortality they could have, and their mortal life besides, with thoughts that distress and afflict them to no avail.

Seek rather to abandon your life to God out of love. Strive to annihilate here already your personality and to live in the one and

---

58. See Matt 10:39, 16:25; Mark 8:35; Luke 9:24.

all. Strive to be more than yourself. Thereby you lose little when you lose yourself. And when you are as merged with the universe, as much as you find of it here and a greater and holier longing has arisen in you, then we will speak further about the hopes that death gives us and about the infinity toward which we swing ourselves aloft unfailingly through death.

This, then, is my attitude about these topics. God, as is commonly conceived as a solitary being outside of the world and behind the world, is not the one and all in religion, but is only an accidental and inadequate way of articulating religion. Whoever believes in such an especial God believes in this God not out of free choice or because they wish to need this God for consolation and help, but because somehow or another they are brought necessarily through their own way to think this. The true essence of religion, however, is in fact the divinity in the world, which is one and at the same time all. And the character of a religious life is immortality, not how you wish yourselves outside of time and behind time, but how we have it immediately, how it is a challenge with which we are constantly engaged. To become one with the infinite in the midst of the finite, and to exist eternally in each moment, that is the immortality of religion.

4

SERMONS

Pentecost Sunday (May 1825):
The Spirit from God and the Human Spirit[1]

These things God has revealed to us through the Spirit;
for the Spirit searches everything, even the depths of God.
For what human being knows what is truly human except
the human spirit that is within? So also no one compre-
hends what is truly God's except the Spirit of God. Now
we have received not the spirit of the world, but the Spirit
that is from God, so that we may understand the gifts
bestowed on us by God.

(1 Cor 2:10–12)[2]

My devout friends, the words we have just heard, having an
immediate bearing as they do on our celebration here today, are profound and (we can certainly not deny it) mysterious. Nonetheless, the
Apostle speaks these words to those to whom, as he himself puts it, he
can as yet communicate nothing except the first and essential elements
of the gospel. He thus is counting on the fact that we should, on the
whole, already understand these words. My dear friends, these words,
probably more than any others, speak so definitively of the distinctive
nature and descent of the Spirit that is poured over the disciples of the
Lord. The Apostle compares the Spirit from God, which we have
received, with a person's own spirit, with the innermost power of our
life, by virtue of which we know our very selves; and, he says, this

---

1. *SW* 2/2:231–48.

2. NRSV. Since Schleiermacher uses Luther's translation of the Greek into German, and
that determines certain meanings, translations of these two sermons often reflect such
particular meanings rather than always relying strictly on the NRSV.

Spirit from God is related to God in the same way that the human spirit is related to a human person. What greater thing than this could be said? And how close it comes to the words of another apostle: we have become participants in the divine nature![3]

Yet, as we all well know, my dear friends, all along Christians have thought and spoken about these topics in such different ways. All of the distinct qualities that Christians ascribe to themselves rest ultimately on the special divine communication to the human race, as much in the person of the Redeemer as through the Spirit, who reigns in Christ's community and is poured out over the members of his body. And yet, concerning the true content and actual connection of this, the most diverse representations and views have persisted next to one another, mutually contradicting and constricting one another. How could it possibly come about (though not, at least, for those who concede that outside of this realm of Christianity the human person attains neither unclouded peace nor the highest vitality and activity) that these people could also have all agreed to appropriate everything that is great, excellent, and always the most glorious of what Scripture pronounces about the Redeemer and about the divine Spirit as well? For my part, I know of no other reason to offer than a certain despondency of the human soul that has not dared to believe in what is greatest and most glorious, especially in relation to the soul itself.

We, however, want to rely on these words of the Apostle. Since we discussed the role and work of the divine Spirit in the souls of believers yesterday, let us now turn our attention to what the Apostle says about the origin and source of this Spirit. Inasmuch as we always beneficially have all the instructions we need for the maintenance and fortification of our faith at hand, let us appropriate what the Apostle says for this purpose. Then, from what he has to say *about the innermost being and about the origin of the Spirit from God*, we shall see that it follows that, on the one side, the effects of the same Spirit are *unique in their kind* and, on the other side, that everything that comes to us from the Spirit is fully *certain and sound* and, finally, is totally *sufficient* for all of our spiritual needs.[4]

---

3. 2 Pet 1:4 (Schleiermacher's note).

4. Emphasis in original.

1. In saying that the Spirit is from God (the Spirit that he had lauded in the preceding passage), in saying that what no human eye has seen nor the human heart conceived[5] has become manifest to us through the Spirit, and in saying that this indeed is the Spirit of God, just as each person's spirit is itself the innermost being of that person— the Apostle leaves us with no doubt that, inasmuch as this Spirit from God was poured out over the Lord's disciples, the divine being itself was communicated to us. Yet this divine being, my dear friends, is *one*—distinct from all else and exalted above all else. And to be poured over and penetrated by this, as has also happened, must generate an effect *unique in its kind*[6] that can never be attained in any other way.

The Apostle even wants to make this point to us in a still more definite way with the words, "Now we have received not the spirit of the world, but the Spirit that is from God." By *world* Scripture does not always mean that which is opposed to the kingdom of God, nor by *the spirit of the world* does it even necessarily mean the evil and pernicious spirit opposed to the Spirit of God. And this is the case here. For this expression, *spirit of the world*, refers to what the Apostle had already treated earlier in this same epistle, from the beginning on, when he says that not many who are wise according to the flesh, nor many who are distinguished and esteemed according to the flesh, will be called; rather, God chose what to the world is lowly and despised.[7] Before God, my good friends, the difference is indeed slight and to be reckoned as nothing. The difference takes place here in this context, and people frequently stress it (yes, we may as well admit it, stress it too much). That is to say, we often stress how one person may surpass others in natural gifts, as well as in the possession of external means that contribute in no small way to the expanding and beautifying of the spiritual life; and, relatedly, how in some individuals a greater proficiency of the spiritual nature develops, whether in general or in particular performances and dealings, than would have happened without such means of support.

The Apostle then leads us to this point: such distinctions completely disappear when we take into account how distant we all are

---

5. See 1 Cor 2:9.

6. Emphasis in original.

7. See 1 Cor 1:26–29.

from the highest being, so that if we contemplate ourselves before God, we cannot possibly appear to ourselves as any wiser than any other, or of greater importance in God's creation, or yet of greater merit than any other. But certainly on the basis of this you do not believe that the Apostle means that therefore—because someone on the lowest level of spiritual development stands no further from God than the wisest, and also, according to the same standard, that whatever human wisdom may be acquired in a hundred years can be nothing more than a day's work before God—the highest being has in point of fact a special preference for those who, among their equals, were esteemed as little and who lag behind in spiritual development. The fact of the matter is, rather, only this: in some people, the consciousness of their needful condition is easy enough to sustain actively, and, because they must confess that they are not in a position to help themselves out, they will then also be more inclined to accept any help offered. The more other people, however, are pleased with themselves and know to enumerate how they have already acquired one splendid thing after another that they wished for, and the more easily they gradually imagine themselves to be free already, through their own efforts, from what was imperfect and defective, or uncomfortable and distasteful, all the more satisfied they are with their condition, gaining ever more confidence in themselves and fortifying themselves in prideful delusion. For them no spiritual need could arise that they would not know how to satisfy in the same manner, and for that reason they find it even harder to believe in or to seek special help from above.

Yet everything that a person can attain in the way I have just described, everything that we can exercise in ourselves with such help from our equals—all of this comes to us from nowhere other than the world. The human spirit is a part of the world, and therefore all works of creation with which it can occupy itself, likewise all of its investigations, are from the spirit of the world. Human society is a part of the world, and all its orderings and conventions are also likewise from the spirit of the world. Thus whatever people have already gained in this way, or could ever gain, belongs to the spirit of the world. It is not as though all of this contains nothing good, nor as though it belongs essentially and wholly and completely to what, considered in and for itself, is wrong—that is, to what resists the divine Spirit. On the contrary, there *is* a satisfaction of spiritual needs in it, but only partially so. It all belongs to the development of human nature, but it is not its perfection, and certainly without exception it has a part in human imperfection and in human corruption. For this very reason, it is completely divorced from the divine Spirit, which has no part in this. And so the Apostle, by designating all that lies within these natural means and can be acquired through them as "the spirit of the world," is quite right to say that we, in having received the Spirit of God, have received nothing from the spirit of the world.

Therefore, when he adds that we have received not the spirit of the world but the Spirit from God, so that we might grasp what God has given us, he thereby also gives us this so that we may recognize what he means: the person who only has the spirit of the world, who is merely equipped with natural resources, even if these resources be of the kind that only the most perfect development of earthly life can offer—this person will still not be in any position to grasp what God has given us. Is it then also only the Spirit of God that opens our eyes so that we might understand God's conduct toward us, so that we understand God's gracious decree concerning us? We would do well to compare this recognition with that of the immediate relations between God and us, for then we would see how true it is that God's working in our souls is entirely singular and cannot be replaced by anything else.

Certainly, this is also our most deeply held conviction: the spirit of the world, as the epitome of all human wisdom, however much it may yet develop, and the cooperative power of human appointments and human orderings, however elaborate they may be, however beneficial they are in their influences, or however they fortify themselves—these cannot replace that which has come to be through the communication of the Spirit to us from God. We can do nothing else but accept that all who believe in the Redeemer, if they themselves would only become clear about their faith, must also share this conviction with us. And it is probably lacking in many only as long as they have not properly gathered the courage to express it in a definite way.

If now the spirit of the world, in this superior sense of the word, reveals itself with ever greater richness; if our knowledge of the earth, this particular piece of God's creation given over to us by God, continually expands itself through increased intercourse with all parts of the world; if through continual observation, through astute attempts to be more and more rid of errors about the powers of nature so that dull superstition loses its foundation; if human dominance is ever more secured over all forces subordinate to it that stir in the world—we may then with the times arrive at the point of saying, with greater right than earlier generations, that the spirit of the world dwelling within us, as the inspirited parts of the world, has searched the depths of the world. And if we were to penetrate even further into the interior of the human spirit, this precious and highest of all earthly powers, and if the mystery of the interconnection of all its inner workings were to be entirely penetrable by us—we would then be able to say that the human spirit has finally searched its own depths, but these depths are not the depths of the Godhead.

Yes, it might possibly have been that in the age of some earlier wisdom the depths of the world and the depths of the human spirit were already discovered, and that at that time everyone had already realized what was only a mystery for a few: the divine being, the highest source of all existence and of all powers, could not be split among many individuals, but could only be *one*. Yet, much would still have been missing had the spirit of the world searched the depths of the Godhead, even if it could grasp the unity and ungrudgingness of the highest being. When justice and order become ever more common among humans, and everything unworthy continues to disappear; when violence and oppression cease, and only wisdom and equity apply; when we hear no more of bloody disputes, and instead peace reigns from one end of the earth to the other over the entire human race—oh, that would be the highest triumph of the human spirit, which is from the spirit of the world! Yet would this concord be the same that exists wherever the Spirit of God in a person calls out, "Dear Father"?

What a difference when we become aware of our common relation to the very same concord and so also of the call to inviolate, allaround cooperation, and when we love one another with brotherly love in God, the common Father! Yes, the world can awaken us to everything else by means of common reason, but to search the depths of the Godhead and call out "Abba, beloved Father"—neither of which can be thought without the other—*that* only the Spirit from God can do, can give, when it has descended upon the human spirit.

Our heart and our conscience teach us very clearly to distinguish these two and to recognize especially whether, in any given moment, we are being moved by the spirit of the world or by the Spirit of God. If the dominant direction of our heart points toward the depths of the Godhead, and if the love for God is the deepest and most primal thing that stirs us, then we must confess that; however much praiseworthy aspiration there may be outside the community in which the Spirit of God presides, nevertheless this life in the depths of the Godhead, this blessedness of filial calling upward to the Father, has been found nowhere else. How could we not be sorry if, this notwithstanding, there are some among us who misconceive this distinction between the spirit of the world and the Spirit from God? Do they not really deprive God of the credit that is due when they ascribe the more imperfect and more common gifts of God to reason, when in fact they possess their share of that only through the higher (though not yet everywhere dispersed) gift, through the Spirit from God? Really, do they not think too little of human beings, whose nature they nonetheless wish to raise up and exalt, if they believe that extraordinary divine interventions for human welfare were only an aid for the earlier childish and imperfect times of humanity—but that humans, when more mature and developed, must retreat again to a greater distance from the highest being and must create everything all the more clearly and more powerfully out of their own inner being, apart from every special divine communication?

If this seems to us to be a questionable detour, grounded even more in the contrariness of the human heart than in its despondency, alarming for those who hammer it in but even more alarming through their influence on the youth when they still wish to rear a generation that shall present a greater perfection out of itself, without the connection to divine revelation in Christ—then what shouldn't we gladly do so as to dissuade anybody from that, rightly redirecting them toward the joy in the divine revelation, a joy that is prepared and granted to us all by God? But believe me, beloved friends, how willingly we long for this jewel of our faith. Seldom will words get it done. The deed will have to speak more powerfully. If we prove to everyone in faith's circle how much we all know to treasure and use those praiseworthy and useful things that the spirit of the world produces in the human person, not at all like those who pass off as lowly and expendable what is too high for them to attain; and if in the process they just as clearly saw that our contentedness is based only on what we search by the other way of the depths of the Godhead, and that this contentedness stands the test as something more imperturbable and more joyous in itself than theirs—then perhaps at that point it will dawn on them how it really stands between the spirit of the world and the Spirit from God.

If we faithfully keep together with them in everything that aims to achieve the welfare of humanity and that relates to the improvement of human affairs (though *not* like those who do not think it worth the effort, because they have no appetite to exert themselves); if they could but see at the same time that not only is irreproachable fidelity completely independent of success, as it is tireless before adversity, but also that we carry a love in our heart that, just as it covers a host of sins, is the ribbon of all perfection—then perhaps they would begin to realize an essential difference between, on the one hand, their awe of the divine wisdom and acquiescence to divine providence and, on the other hand, the childlike relation of those who, in Christ, are children of God according to the inheritance of the promise and also who, with Christ, are faithful like children in the Father's house, for they always cry, "Dear Father." Yes, beloved friends, we would all like to impart the faith to those who live around us, the faith that everything we receive with and through the Spirit from God is unique in this way and cannot be obtained from any other source. So let us everywhere disclose to them as well the fear of the Spirit in such a way that our light really shines as a heavenly light, and such that they must praise our good works as truly having been done in God.

2. *Secondly*, when I have proclaimed in the words of the Apostle about the being and the origin of the Spirit from God, it also stands that everything awakened inwardly in us through this Spirit from God is *incontrovertible and reliable.*[8] This is shown primarily in the words of the Apostle: "No one knows what is in a person except the human spirit that is in that person; neither therefore does anyone

---

8. Emphasis in original.

know what is in God except the Spirit of God." If what only the human spirit knows about what is within a person is unmistakably and incontrovertibly certain, so too will what only the Spirit of God reveals to us of God be just as reliable.

So let us ask, first, what is it about us that only the human spirit within us can know? It is certainly not the external experiences and events of our life, since our own spirit does not know much at all about these but is, rather, acquainted with them only from other people's accounts. Yes, others often even know later incidents just as well as we ourselves do, and they often recall some that have already slipped from our own memory. Nor does the human spirit alone know what we have done and organized in the world. For how much and how often does not the smallest of things come about through us, or at least in their first seeds are stimulated by us, without our being aware of the situation? But it is also true of whatever does not escape our notice that the more it has already attracted something interior in other people, the more these people will know better than ourselves what we have effected in and upon them. And this already leads us to the point that is innermost for each person: a person's most distinct disposition. *This* is the most real consciousness of our own selves that only a person's own spirit itself can have. It is that from which all individual actions arise, and the manner and way in which each of us processes what comes to us from without and what we encounter in ourselves; it is this innermost connection, this deepest ground of the heart, and with it all the various forms of its life in their various moments.

Anyone else can only arrive at an always-uncertain notion that never corresponds perfectly to the truth. In individual cases, we might correctly guess some connection of actions or thoughts of another person, but we remain ever uncertain about the innermost unity out of which everything arises. If several people lead a life in common, they mutually know about this common life, for it is the same in all. Yet only in the most intimate interconnection of those who are one through common lineage or have become one through the holiest love is there a knowledge approaching the truth about the innermost being of the other; otherwise, this is reserved only for the spirit of each person. This proper human knowledge of our selves, however, is then also the most immediate and most authentic truth of our existence, unmistakably always standing the test anew, and at each moment carrying along the entire past and entire future in itself according to nature.

My devout friends, it hardly seems necessary to consider that some people might perhaps object to this. If their judgment of themselves contains the most perfect truth, whence do so many complaints arise about humanity's own ingrained darkness? And why do we not then believe ourselves capable of warning others wholeheartedly and urgently enough, so that they in turn would not deceive themselves about themselves? You already say as much yourself: this is not something new today but has rather always already been so, such that it could not have escaped the Apostle either. And that notwithstanding, he does compare the knowledge that the spirit within a person has of that person with the knowledge that the Spirit from God has concerning the depths of the Godhead. And certainly he did not believe from this that it is deception, and definitely not only more involuntary but also more self-productive, as we believe that humans do not always involuntarily delude themselves about themselves. Just as little will Paul have believed that the Spirit from God will not know the truth about the depths of the Godhead until some future time, as we believe that not until that day will the truth about a person be revealed to that person.

Yet, when we look at it more closely, how does it really stand with these self-deceptions? For truly they are not infrequent, but occur often enough and stir up much deceit. The darkness, however, is a nature so petty that it always adheres to the individual. In particular matters, people do a little good. Just as, in Christ's parables, the conceited Pharisee, in his prayer to the Lord, calculated the particular ways of acting and rules of life, so too do people gladly deceive themselves about the particulars—always inflating the good, covering and palliating the blameworthy, or turning things around until they win for themselves a more pleasing side. And when they do compare themselves with others about the particulars, what is the most profitable game of that same masterly deceitful darkness, according to which it is valid to make oneself appear grand and, in contrast, the other small? All self-deception is bound within these limits. On the contrary, people either do not even begin to look into the innermost part of their own souls because they are afraid of themselves (and that itself is evidence of the fact that they believe in the truth of such a consciousness), or, if they do look into their own soul, they cannot see themselves except as they really are, since they cannot value themselves higher than they are actually worth, and since they know what moves and defines them and what does not.

If we put all particulars aside and ask what, according to the law, the standard of all our actions is; if we do not fully understand a single moment and do not wish to envision a single individual action; but if we, rather, contemplate ourselves in the unity of our entire being—then there is and remains what our own spirit says to us about ourselves, the complete and authentic truth.

It is just the same with God, the Apostle says in our text. No one but the Spirit of God delves into the depths of God's own being. Were this not the same in us, were God rather entirely beyond us, then our cognition[9] of God would be no better than other people's cognition of us in comparison with what each and everyone's own spirit says about itself. Just as we inadequately and uncertainly judge a person on the basis of actions and works and nonetheless always manage to feel that there is no certainty or truth in this, and just as we always manage to waver between opposing opinions, so too our cognition of God would be an uncertain presentiment about the highest being taken from the piecemeal cognition of divine works! Even if these presentiments were a little clearer for some, even if the oscillations were of a lesser degree for some steadier spirits, even if some were to believe that they had grasped the complete truth of the highest being and stood secure in perfect certainty of the cognition of God, these still would certainly be the kind of people who deceive themselves about this one thing and who would not yet have sincerely questioned their own spirit concerning the truth of their own spiritual capacity. And what else is all purely human wisdom about God apart from a variegated image of such uncertain presentiments passing one over another?

For some people, this fog of thinking collects itself into nearly graspable forms until they shudder before wanting to gauge the highest being according to such measurements. For others, it volatilizes itself ever more finely, until they become aware, horrified, that nothing hovers before them anymore. This is why Paul is right

---

9. *Erkenntniß.* See above, 153, about this term.

to say that, without God's Spirit, no one knows what is in God. What those who have God's Spirit know is true and authentic, like the most secret, innermost knowledge people can have of themselves. They know that this Spirit of truth is in them. And this knowledge is the great act of divine communication by which the innermost truth of the divine being is also planted in our soul. Only in this way did it become clear to us in our inner selves and in the most exact interconnection with our most interior consciousness of ourselves, so intelligible and audible does it now appear to everyone since this divine communication. In no other way could it have penetrated our spiritual ear or spiritual eye, so as to be heard and grasped.

That is why I scarcely believe that any of you questions what this is in our cognition of God, which cohabitates in us, because it has come to us through the Spirit of God with an unshakable certainty. I don't believe that anyone asking about this abundance could expect any other answer but this: "God is love."[10] Nowhere has the Spirit said, "God is justice," or "God is omnipotence," or "God is wisdom." The Spirit does, however, say "God is love" through the mouth of the Apostle, whose discourses are the most trusted reverberation from the discourses of the Redeemer. Christ still says this through us all by exclaiming in us "Abba, Father," since where there is a father, there is also love.

Now this conviction does not exist where the Spirit from God does not speak. The God of Israel, who wanted to afflict the iniquities of the fathers onto their progeny until the third and fourth generations, was not recognized as father. And among the heathen, what room would there have been for a fatherly love of the highest being in the multifarious splitting up of the same, since there cannot be several fathers harmonious in one household, much less with these so-called deities who always stood opposed to one another? The wisest among them thought it folly to split up the deity, but even they could only reach the point of saying that the highest being was ungrudging and knew no envy.[11] How far, however, this still is from trust in fatherly love.

And certainly this trust is what is most solid and truly unshakable in our cognition of God. For how could we remain in the free-

---

10. 1 John 4:16.
11. See Plato, *Timaeus* 29c.

dom of the children of God if, out of fear, we would have to be ser-vants again, as in ancient times? If we became wavering in the con-viction that God is love, then right away the fear before an omnipotence about whose disposition there would be no certitude would immediately take up the place in the heart that had become empty. Then, in place of the worship of God in the Spirit and in truth, just as the blessed-making truth grows dim, a legal servitude to the letter creeps in again, which is always a child of fear. Is there, however, anything more wavering or more uncertain than the servi-tude of the letter and of the law? Here a rule and there a rule, here a prohibition and there a prohibition; here they want to outdo human addenda and there destroy contending interpretations, the same whether it is a letter of the precept or a letter of doctrine. And as from that point on the world was always full of the most diverse forms, and human weakness always ever leans in that direction, so also would Christianity, the kingdom of grace and freedom, be transformed back again into those same old forms—if it did not rest upon this unshakable certainty!

These two are inseparable from one another. No one calls God "Father" except through the Holy Spirit, for no one knows the Father except the Son and those to whom the Son wishes to reveal it.[12] In turn, where the Spirit of God is, there also God is called "Father." Whatever else in the womb of Christianity might change in our cog-nition of God, as it befits human observation and human reflection about revelation and the operations of the Spirit to be nothing other than mutable, this conviction that God is love remains exempt from all change. It does not originate with humans, though indeed it would not escape them; it is, rather, the original and essential word of the Spirit in our soul. And as the knowledge of the Spirit of God that is conferred to us concerning what is in God (so eternal and unchangeable like the Spirit of God itself), so too this conviction is always the innermost and soundest truth of our existence and, as a matter of fact, is that in which we live, move, and have our being.[13]

3. Yet just as equally certain for us is what the Spirit of God communicates to us from its knowledge of what is in God—and this,

---

12. See Matt 11:27.
13. See Acts 17:28.

too, must be perfectly *sufficient* for us.[14] Must it not seem sacrilegious, and simultaneously confused and contradictory, to want to think only of something else when we are filled with the weighty words of the Apostle? If what the Spirit of God gives us to hear were not sufficient, then we would have to wait for yet another revelation or we would be the most hapless people! But then where shall it come from, if only lesser things can come from humans themselves? I nevertheless believe that many (if they want to be honest) will own up to the fact that, if what until now has been set apart shall be all that is communicable to us of what God's Spirit searches of depths of the Godhead, then this is not enough for them. Needs would arise deep from the heart, wishes would absorb them in the prime of life— none of which would find satisfaction in that certainty. This is why it is necessary to ask whether this inadequacy is really well founded, whether it does not indicate that whatever a person yearns for, but is not given, would also not have been adequate for their salvation.

And so let us next look to see whether it does not happen in just the same way in relation to what is human. The Apostle also seems to consider this to be the highest knowledge of a human being: what only the human spirit within a person knows about that person. This, however, just does not satisfy many. To become acquainted with our innermost disposition, to know what stirs us within and powerfully moves us, to have searched the fundamental law and measure of our spiritual life—that is beautiful. It is also salutary for us. For the more this is present to us, the less we will neglect to take care wherever danger threatens us. But however deserving of thanks this may be, only a very few will be satisfied with it.

They would well like to penetrate the unsearchable connection between the bodily and the spiritual of our nature. They would like to search the first unconscious beginning of our earthly existence, this meaningful piece of our life, which for each person is wrapped in irretrievable forgetfulness and about which we get to know only the most extrinsic part, and that through others. They would like to trace how the spiritual life gradually took form from these faint beginnings. They would like, where possible, to peer beyond the limits of earthly life in order to experience how it was with the human

---

14. Emphasis in original.

spirit within them before this earthly efficacy of the same spirit began, and likewise, having passed through this state, how and in what relationship the beautiful and comforting promises of the divine word apply and then grow to fulfillment. But the human spirit within says nothing to that person concerning any of that. And that is why so many people complain about the deficiency of the knowledge we have of our own accord. But why is it deficient? Would we better solve any part of the challenge of our lives? Would anything we have to struggle against become unpowerful or easier to overcome? Would we behold the flux of earthly life any differently because of it? Who, knowing anything of the human soul, would dare answer yes to even one of these questions?

So it is also with what the Spirit of God, which is also in us, reveals to us from the depths of the Godhead. The Apostle says we have received the Spirit so that we could know what God has given us, or rather, as it should really read, what God has done for us out of love and pleasure. Now this is nothing other than what we have addressed earlier, though instead of more, it seems to be even less and is, if anything, a restricting expression. For God is love. Hence, God's creative omnipotence is nothing other than the extent of God's love. Hence, too, everything that belongs to the work of creation and to the proceeding of providence must exist principally to declare this love. Indeed, we also have a definite feeling of this when the Spirit in us calls out "Father." The Spirit, however, does not show us the particulars of this insight; rather, all that we can know is what God has done for us out of love. Everything that the Spirit communicates to us from the depths of the Godhead is therefore limited to the admittedly great mystery of God's revelation in the flesh.[15] The eternal decree of divine love for the salvation and glorification of humanity through the sending of him through whose righteousness the justified life for all humanity might come about,[16] because God was in him, in order to reconcile the world to God; the existence of a kingdom of God that not even the gates of hell could overpower; the descent of the Father with the Son in order to dwell in the hearts of human beings; the intuition of the Father in the Son, who is the exact

---

15. See 1 Tim 3:16.

16. Rom 5:18 (Schleiermacher's note).

likeness of God's being and the reflection of God's glory—see here, this and what depends upon it is the development, suitable to our powers and our being, of the one great fact: that God is love. And these are the depths of the Godhead, which the Spirit from God discloses to us, that we may know what God has done for us out of love.

There are, however, other depths of the Godhead that God's Spirit does not reveal to us. We yearn for these just as much as we do for what the human spirit in us likewise does not reveal to us about ourselves. Mysteries of creation—into which God's Spirit does not instruct us to penetrate, but leaves rather to human study; yet how little will our understanding approach the infinite goal, even in a number of centuries. Mysteries of the inaccessible light—in which light human reason cannot bathe itself even once; our understanding cannot even dip into its buckets and pour out into its forms.[17] For who would want to adjudicate about the highest being from human speech, or how close it comes to the actual truth of its existence? Mysteries of the indwelling—we do not always know where the Spirit comes from or where it is going; and this applies not just to those who hear the blowing and booming of the divine Spirit externally, but also in many ways to those who know and possess in themselves the Spirit's doings and dispensing. About all of this the Spirit has only an unspoken sigh for us.

And just as we must allow ourselves to be satisfied concerning the depths of our own being, so too must we be content to look into the depths and abundance of divine grace without desiring that our incapacity to fathom the depths of the divine being be taken from us. Without the Spirit's revelations extending further, we can be the most blessed instruments of the divine Spirit. Thus equipped, we are able to attest to it, in the power of the Spirit according to the word of the Redeemer, to punish the world for its sin and to represent this to the world as the epitome of sin: that it does not believe in him. We are able to announce to the world that now all justice is fulfilled and that whatever is lacking is restored[18] by the Spirit living in the community of believers, since the Redeemer has now returned to the Father. We are able to proclaim to the world in an encouraging way

---

17. The imagery here is more artisanal than philosophical insofar as it has to do with pouring a liquid or pliable material into a set mold in order to give it definite form.

18. See 1 Thess 3:10.

that now the kingdom of God is secured and entrance to it is open to all, but the prince of this world is judged.[19]

To preach this Word, to spread this belief is the daily task shared by all together in the vineyard of the Lord. We lack nothing in performing it, since we can know what God has done for us out of love. Let us not, however, look to the work that we have to perform; let us look instead to the peace that is promised to us. Oh! Then, through what God's Spirit reveals to us about the depths of the Godhead, we might enjoy this peace to the fullest. We lack nothing of the most blessed fellowship in which we stand with God when the Spirit from God reveals to us God's love as the innermost depths of God's being. We lack nothing when the loving decree, which has moved God's fatherly heart toward the human race from the beginning on, becomes clear to us. We lack nothing when all infirmity of our nature can be healed through the fullness of the Godhead that lives in Christ, who shares in our very nature. We lack nothing when through him the Spirit from God spreads itself over all who believe in Christ as a vivifying and fortifying power, transfiguring the Redeemer to them and making the Father present to them in Christ.

How shall such a state not be the most perfect satisfaction of the heart, so that there remains no essential lack in our spiritual life, since all the glorious fruit of the Spirit must come forth from this fellowship with God, in which fruit the likeness to God declares itself? Since we already carry the eternal with us, how shall we, being conscious of this fellowship, not also confidently cut ourselves off from this earthly life at the determined hour and throw ourselves with complete confidence into the arms of the eternal fatherly love, which we recognize as living—or rather, which has accepted us and has given us the Spirit as the pledge for all that we may yet anticipate?

Accordingly, we are not to ask for anything more. God's decree is fulfilled. What the eternal love could give humanity has become ours through the Redeemer and through the Spirit of truth and of consolation who is poured out over his own. Certainly, we cannot set for ourselves a greater task, but for that reason it is a task we cannot complete during our entire earthly life: to hold fast to the conviction that just as the Spirit weds with the human spirit within us in the most intimate

---

19. See John 16:11.

way, so too the Spirit unveils the depths of our own being more thoroughly and consolingly than our own spirit does, since the Spirit opens up for us the depths of the Godhead, which our own spirit would have been too weak to seek out; and to let this Spirit from God cultivate all our powers into the Spirit's instruments, so that we ourselves see everything in the Spirit's light and illuminate everything around us with this same light, and so that the love for God and Christ, which the Spirit pours out into our hearts, proves also to be a spiritually helpful and blessed-making love for our brothers and sisters. In this way, the Spirit records in our souls the kingdom of God, whose image, as one of a kingdom of truth and love, the Spirit continually revitalizes and renews. And in this way the kingdom of God is brought to life in us and is continually further advanced.

Therein do we have the peace and the blessedness that the Lord has promised to his own. Therein ceases all being-labored and being-burdened, which is indisputably the correct expression for the earlier condition of the human person, and which we can now see as the condition under the law or under sin. Thereby all that is lost is found and brought back into living fellowship with God, whose very self has been revealed to us in the Son. And to God, with this Spirit from God that has been given to us, be praise and honor and glory forever. Amen.

Second Sunday of Advent (December 1832): Christ Is Like Us in All Things but Sin[20]

For we do not have a high priest who is unable to sympathize with our weaknesses, but we have one who in every respect has been tested as we are, yet without sin.

(Heb 4:15)[21]

These first Sundays of our church year, specially intended as they are for preparing us for the worthy celebration of our Redeemer's appearance in this earthly world, are for this reason also especially and wholly suited for us to consider together general views about the

---

20. *SW* 2/3:427–35.

21. NRSV.

relation between him and us, and to keep this vividly before our eyes in its broad contours. That relation consists preeminently and essentially in this: on the one hand, he must have been one of us as the originator and perfector of our faith, as the one who made us worthy to be called his brothers; on the other hand, he must have been separate from all humankind and elevated above all others as the one in whom the glory of the only begotten Son of the Father appeared and without whom we could not come to the Father.

If we contemplate our Christian change in faith in him and the way in which our living fellowship with him increasingly develops and strengthens, then certainly we all find and know that our faith is nourished from both of these roots. If, however, we contemplate the history of the Christian Church, then we glimpse a lively debate, ever regenerating itself under various forms, over these two attributes of the Redeemer. We find this debate from the beginning as well as from one age to another, renewing itself under different guises. It takes place among those confessing the same Lord, those who are not merely Christian by name—for how else did they come to the same faith, to the same hopes, to the same power of love through which faith is active?

And that is simple enough to explain. For if we pull ourselves back from life into contemplation and bring to mind one of the two apart from the other, and reflect on that, then it will seem to almost anyone as though, by directing our thought to the other, we necessarily lose track of the first. This is why so many Christians now cling exclusively to the pure humanity of the Redeemer while others cling exclusively to his divine worth, and that is why both parties are ready, if necessary, to abandon the other side entirely for the sake of their own. No words or sayings from the holy books of our New Testament take any part in this debate, nor are they the cause of it. They all hold closer to the very immediacy of life in Christ, to which they bear the purest, plainest, and most valid witness. So it is in our text. If we read both—he could "sympathize with our weaknesses" and he "has been tested as we are, yet without sin"—then we must turn as much toward the one as to the other, back and forth between both, and we must recognize him as our equal and at the same time as one elevated infinitely above us.

Therefore let us then turn our contemplation to these words, so that we convince ourselves how, in both, *the speech is about both: the identity of our Redeemer with us and the glory of the only begotten Son of the Father are inseparably bound with one another—yes, they are one in the same.*[22]

1. Let us first envisage what our text expresses with the words, *He has been tempted* everywhere the same as us, *but without sin.*[23]

Temptation and sin. We all constantly experience how the two are related. Generally, temptation comes before sin. A sin that is not preceded by a temptation, viewed from one side, would certainly point to a much greater sway of the evil and corruption in the person, but viewed from the other side, such a deed would appear to us not as a peculiar, new moment or as a fresh expression of life, but rather only as a consequence of something already long enduring. Every time, however, temptation has preceded sin, we also know that all too often sin really does follow from the temptation. So where does sin begin?

As Scripture says, when desire has conceived and appetite is excited, the might of conscience pushes it back before it can grasp its object.[24] When the soul is influenced from outside in such a way that the passion is excited and fermented in it, but there is a strength of the will that can arrest these surges of the heart and say, "Here and no further!" and thus it becomes subdued before it has even come out in form, in motions, or in words—oh, that is a beautiful victory! But it is not without sin. Those motions themselves were already sin, and a dark spot is left behind on the innermost ground of the soul that cannot be so easily washed away again. Yes, if sin has been in us already somehow before the temptation, then we also know that each one exerts a certain consequence such that, if similar circumstances recur even after such a hard won victory, they still receive a greater power from the earlier sway of the desire and passion. Yes, if we go back even further, we will have to say that unfortunately there exists in the human heart preparations for sin, which themselves do not seem to be sin at all but are already effective before a temptation can arise in us, in this or that sphere of our life. If habits have already

---

22. Emphasis in original.
23. Emphasis in original.
24. See Jas 1:15.

been established in us, or if we have distanced ourselves from much—however the moment now enters—then this or that has mastery in the soul, making us then fall prey almost irresistibly to sin.

What then does it mean for the Redeemer to have been tempted in all things, but without sin? It must be that nowhere in the innermost of his heart is there any kind of movement that the spirit, resurgent in that moment, would have needed to dampen or deprecate. From earliest childhood on, therefore, there was in his life no such habit that later provoked or lured him to sin, no such weaning or estrangement from what was burdensome to him or captured his indolence. Thus he must have been able to be tempted in all, but without sin.

But then what, my devout friends, remains in his life and in the movements of his soul that we can call still call *temptation*? His human soul shows in the totality of his appearance, as it manifests itself to us in all the individual features of his life. It is also already expressed when it is said of him, "He has shared in flesh and blood like all human beings,"[25] and, "He has become like us in all things except sin." His human soul, I say, had the same variability in every detail as our souls have. As in our souls, the opposition of desire and aversion, of joy and pain was also in his soul. And in such oppositions his power must stand the test—that is to say, must turn back temptation.

Everything, therefore, that moves us internally such that afterward a sin emerges out of us also moved him, but without sin emerging in him. He was able to say, "My soul is sorrowful unto death,"[26] but in this affliction there was no trace of a will, or even a wish, to be allowed to step back from the course enjoined upon him. He was able to say, "I thank you, Father, because you have hidden it from the wise and have revealed it to those not of age."[27] In this passage we find expression of pure joy over the fact that through him the gospel was announced to the poor. Yet in this joy there is no trace of antipathy, reluctance, or enmity toward those who were puffed up in their wisdom; no antipathy to answering their questions; no wish that it might also remain so and that they might always be excluded from

25. See Heb 2:14.

26. See Matt 26:38; Mark 14:34.

27. See Matt 11:25.

the pleasure of his goodness. He knew that he had come to light a fire and certainly wished that it might burn soon,[28] but the wish did not turn into impatience over the slow course that the Father had determined for his cause.

And so externally he was also exposed to all changes of life that affect us and thus also tempt us. Accordingly, insofar as these changes bring to earthly life the kind of disparity that lures the rest of us from the right path, they tempted him as well. But no sin arose from it. He endured rumors both good and bad: admired as a prophet, marveled as a miracle worker, disparaged as one who did not know Scripture, suspected of leading the people astray. Nevertheless, the former did not excite him to vanity or hubris, nor was the latter able to intimidate him. In a given moment, because he was avoided and rejected, he did not know where he would lay his head down. Never once, however, was such a situation able to injure his courage or disturb his joyfulness. Often he found himself cared for in his earthly life and carried by the hand of tender love and reverence; yet, without the smallest trace of effeminacy[29] in his heart, he was always where he was, not because it suited him but rather because his calling entailed it to be so. Here and there he knew want and plenty, and he felt this disparity of earthly life as we do, but this disparity had no influence over the constant expression of his spiritual power, over the way he always looked at the works that his Father in heaven showed to him. In no moment was he chagrined or ill-tempered. His joyfulness, his obedience, and his love all remained ever the same.

That, my friends, is what it means for the Redeemer to be tempted without sin. If we wish to comprehend it, we can only do so by contemplating the human being simultaneously as the Word become flesh, in which the glory of the only begotten Son of the Father appeared; as he who could say of himself that he is one with the Father; as he who was allowed to speak the great word about himself that he does nothing from himself. For whatever human beings do from themselves alone carries with it not only the traces of

---

28. See Luke 12:49.

29. *Verweichlichung*. A form of weakness that is gender inflected, standing in contrast to "manly" courage and bodily strength. This stands in tension, e.g., with the *Christmas Dialogue*, where Schleiermacher underscores the affinities between Christ and women. See above, 102, 124–25.

human weakness but also that of human fragility. But everything that Christ did, he did out of pure obedience to the commandment revealed to him and living in him, out of pure obedience to the will of his Father, which he always fulfilled.

2. And this now leads us right to the second part of our contemplation: namely, how the author of our epistle says in the words of our text, "We could not have a high priest who could not have *sympathized with our weakness.*"[30]

This was the true effect of his having been tempted in all things, except without sin: he could now sympathize with our weakness. But when our text expresses it in this way, "We could *not* have such a high priest, who could *not* have sympathized with our weakness,"[31] then we can plainly see that he had in mind another high priest about whom this very thing could indeed be said.[32] And so it was even with the high priest of the Jewish people, who was taken from among humans, with whom the author compares the Redeemer in these words and in many places of the epistle. Through his birth, this high priest was already destined to the great call to be the mediator between God and the people, and for this reason from childhood on he was viewed and guided differently from how others were. All requests, all sacrifices and gifts of the people were offered up to the Highest through him. The other priests and those who took charge of the service in the lesser affairs of the temple were only his instruments and obeyed his direction. On that one great day of the year, however, he personally was called to offer the common sacrifice of reconciliation for all those trespasses of the people that were still unrecognized and still unatoned. At the same time, he was also so entirely set apart and separated from the rest of human life that he had no immediate intuition of those conditions of the people that make it most necessary to offer before God prayer and intercession for forgiveness.

It counted for just this reason: because it was so alien and stood

---

30. Emphasis in original.

31. Emphasis in original.

32. Schleiermacher is right to point out that the double negative is meant to highlight Christ's sympathy, but in what follows he exaggerates what the texts says about the separation of the high priest from the people (Heb 5:1–3). For more on this, see Alan C. Mitchell, *Hebrews*, Sacra Pagina 13 (Collegeville, MN: Liturgical Press, 2007), 106–7.

so far from him, as did what Scripture itself says of the people through the mouth of the prophets, "This people honors me with their lips, but their hearts are far from me."[33] Certainly, he had first to offer sacrifice to God for himself and his own sins, but this served to nourish in him the consciousness that he, too, was a sinful person, even though he was virtually never caught up in the situations, nor was he touched by all the movements of the heart that arise from the hardship of the soil or by all the sinful emotions that arise out of relationships of competition and conflict among human beings. For he was raised far above all of that, and he stood at a height to which no other could reach. This is why, then, even his prayers were merely words, and the sacrifices he offered only gifts, which according to the author of our epistle are capable of obtaining nothing other than "a reminder of sin."[34] We neither should nor could have had this sort of high priest, otherwise we would have prospered no further and the human race would always have remained in that same spot, able to bring nothing before God but the (over and over again) renewed reminder of sins (over and over again) committed, and sin would always have exercised the same sway over human hearts.

So that he could have such a complete compassion[35] for our weakness, far distinct from that former high priest of his people, the Redeemer took on the form of a servant.[36] Endowed with these gifts and powers, externally he could have walked among people like God, so to speak. But this is why he instead had to take on the form of servant—in order to be thrown into the midst of the full mêlée of humanity, so to speak, and to see with his own eyes the several ways in which they go astray, all the ways that batter the lost sheep of his people. He would himself have surely been aware of the power that always elevated him upward toward his Father and to beholding the Father's operations and will—and thereby even raised him above sin. At the same time, however, he carried in himself that same variability of the human heart. All this is why he could have a clear understanding of what we lack as well as a living compassion for our

---

33. Mark 7:6, NRSV; see Isa 29:13.
34. Heb 10:3 (Schleiermacher's note).
35. *Mitgefühl.*
36. See Phil 2:6–7.

247

weakness. Weakness is lack. And as he turned out to be, inwardly in his entire existence, the kingdom and the fullness of divine potency, so he could recognize in the aberrations of humans—in how each and every smallest temptation became sin to them—what they lacked and what he alone was in a position to give them.

Such was the compassion he was able to have with our weakness. He could feel it from the identity of his human soul with ours, from the identity of the movements that were in him as they are in us. In us, however, the movements break out differently from how they did in him. For in him dwelt the fullness of the Godhead, which we lack, as all human beings have drifted away from God and are lacking in the splendor that they should have before God. On that account, just as the former high priest of the Jewish people could not have had this kind of compassion for the weakness of his brethren, and thus his prayers were only words and remained only words, so in contrast the Redeemer's sympathy[37] was the intercession with which he substituted for us as our high priest, and that was not words and sentiment but deed. Therefore, as the sacrifice offered by the former high priest could establish nothing more than a reminder of sin, so was the sacrifice of him who could sympathize with our weakness and who simultaneously withstood the test of human life as one tempted in everything but without sin—that is to say, so was the sacrifice of our high priest his whole life. He offered his whole life for our sins, not to establish a reminder of our sins but rather so that his power would pass over into us through the Spirit, which he sent to his own; so that we, in fellowship with him, would have been permeated by his life and in his life would have been made holy before God; and so that we, as one with him, might also have free access to the Father just like him.

Dear friends, we had to have just such a high priest! But as he is our high priest—the only one who deserves the name, the only intermediary between God and human beings, and he whose high priestly accomplishment is eternally effective—we are thus also called to be a priestly people. He was tempted in everything like us, but without sin. We are tempted, and we fall. But when we cleave to him, then we always get up again. And the more his life passes into us, the more the power he communicates to us grows as well. This power could only

---

37. *Mitleiden.*

have come to us from him: it makes it easier for us to get up again, fall less frequently over time, and in this way attain greater sway over everything that tempts us and normally leads us to sin. And thus in his power we build ourselves as a community into the kind of city built on the hill,[38] the true heavenly Zion, which cannot hide itself. There the good works of all human weakness and infirmity should produce holy deeds that entice the hearts of people to praise the Father in heaven for having given them the very might that abides in his Son.

We ourselves are subject to the weakness with which he could only sympathize! But when we cleave to him, then there is soon something that lies behind us that we are allowed to forget, if only we never cease reaching for that which lies before us. If we become strong in faith in him, then his power shows itself mightily in the weak, and his Spirit in us is ever more victorious over the dominance of the flesh. Then in us the consciousness of human weakness and the consciousness of our own suffering that results from that weakness morph ever more into the priestly compassion with those who are still bound by strong earthly ties. In his service, we likewise extend our hand to the weak, as he has extended his to the entire human race. And as his servants in the spiritual temple of God, we invite people with the voice of his love, that they, the weary and burdened, might come to him in order to find rest and rejuvenation for their souls. Only then does it become patently clear to us how right the Apostle is in saying, "For all things are yours!"[39] And also, that power by which he rises above all things will be ours ever more; also, the blessed fellowship with God our heavenly Father grows ever more finely in us; then also, we feel in ourselves only his life and we speak truly, "The life we live, we live in his Spirit and no more in the flesh."[40] And then is his sacrifice, and then is his high priestly prayer, also fulfilled in us, and the Word answers our prayer that we are one with him, as he is one with the Father. Amen.

Hymn 101, 6–8

---

38. See Matt 5:14.
39. See 1 Cor 3:21.
40. See Rom 8:4, 9; Gal 5:16.

5

CORRESPONDENCE

Schleiermacher to his Father, J. G. A. Schleyermacher. Barby, January 21, 1787[1]

Tenderly beloved Father!

I send my New Year greeting. Although late, it is not on that account any less earnest or fervent. The older we get, best Father, and the more we watch the course of things in the world, the more we become convinced that, out of fear of wishing something evil, we ought to wish nothing of what we really want for ourselves or, generally speaking, for others. Under certain circumstances, everything is fortune, under other circumstances misfortune. But what I wish for you is that you experience calm and equanimity of the heart in all circumstances and (what more than this can be wished for a father?) to experience joy in your children. As your son, the more I wish you this from a full, filial heart, the more dearly it costs me and the more it gnaws at the innermost part of my soul to have to now inform you of something that must cause your hope in the fulfillment of this wish to waver. In my last letter, I confessed to you my unhappiness about my constricted situation. I told you how easily it can feed religious doubt—doubts that emerge so easily for young people in our times—and I sought thereby to prepare you for the news that this has been the case for me. Yet I was not successful in that. You believed that you had appeased me with

---

1. Letter 53, *KGA* 5/1:49–52.

your answer, and for six entire months I held my tongue, not having the heart to wrench you from this misapprehension. Faith is a divine prerogative, you wrote to me. Oh, best Father! If you believe that without this faith there is no blessedness—at least not blessedness in the next life, nor rest in this life, except for those with faith—and, yes, you do believe that—oh, then pray to God that he bestows it on me, since right now it is lost for me.

I cannot believe that he who called himself only the Son of Man was the true, eternal God. I cannot believe that his death was a vicarious atonement, because he himself never expressly said it, and because I cannot believe that atonement had been necessary, since God, who clearly created human beings not for perfection but only for the pursuit of perfection, could not possibly want to punish humans eternally because they have not become perfect. Oh, best Father, the deep, penetrating grief that I am feeling in writing this letter hinders me from explaining to you in detail the history of my soul regarding my opinions and all my strong grounds for them. But I entreat you, do not deem my thoughts as temporary or as not deeply rooted. For almost a year now, they have stuck with me—a long, intense reflection determined that it be so for me. I entreat you, do not withhold from me your strongest reasons for refuting my own, but in all honesty I do not believe that they will convince me *now*,[2] for I stand firmly by them.

So the news is out—this news that must horrify you so much. Try to understand my soul completely, with my—I can give testimony with a clear conscience, and I know that you are yourself convinced about it—with my very great tender filial love to a father as good as you, whom I have to thank for everything, and who loves me so affectionately. Perhaps you can imagine to some extent what these lines have cost me. They are being written with trembling hand and with tears, but I would still not send them off now had my superiors not prompted me to do so and had they not, in a manner of speaking, charged me with writing it to you. Take heart, dearest Father! I know that

---

2. Emphasis in original.

you had, for a long time, been in the same situation I am in. Doubt once assailed you in the same way as it now assails me, and yet you have become what you are now. Think, hope, believe that it could go the same way with me, and be assured, as long as I am not of one faith with you, that I will always endeavor to become an upright and useful person, and that is the main thing.

I have candidly stated my thoughts to my local superiors, and nevertheless I have on the whole been treated in an abundantly kind manner. They have told me that they still want to wait and see whether the hour of a providential change might not soon strike. It has, however, also been said to me, often and clearly, what is self-evident: that I could not count on even the least position in the Congregation[3] until I retune my convictions. I know, best Father, how much heartache I am now causing you, too—even so, you will not deprive me of your fatherly love and provision. You yourself will see that, in the event that this change does not happen soon (regrettably, I am firmly convinced that it will not), it is necessary to take measures so that I may educate myself to be a practical man apart from the Congregation, since for the foreseeable future I cannot be a part of it.

If your circumstances at all allow it, let me move to Halle, if only for two years. My getting by in this life, you see, depends on that. I hardly believe that you will acquiesce with my continuing to study theology there, for you will probably not want to give our fatherland one more heterodox teacher. If, however, you could do it with a clear conscience, since I would probably commit myself only to a scholarly discipline, that is what would be most preferable to me, because I would be best prepared for that and am inclined toward that. I would also sooner be able to change my thinking there than by studying in the Congregation. I would have more opportunity to test everything and would perhaps see that, on the one hand, some reasons are not as strong as I thought, and, on the other hand, some stronger than I thought. What I should study, however, is up to you alone. The downside about studying law is that a jurist

---

3. A reference to the *Herrnhuter Brüdergemeine*, the Moravian Church.

from the burgher class seldom finds a position, and the downside about studying medicine is that I would need more than two years, due to the dearth of necessary preliminary knowledge, and in any case medical schools are much more expensive. Perhaps my uncle[4] can provide free room or free board in his home; perhaps there is a possibility of receiving free meals[5] elsewhere or even a small stipend. Six young brethren are already now studying law at Halle, and they—along with Wenzel, my old friend from Breslau, and Mr. S.—would be sufficient company for me, such that from this side you would not have to be afraid of the corruption of the universities for my sake. I would need all my time for studying and would live secluded under the supervision of my uncle.

If you now communicate with my siblings in Herrnhut about this and present the matter to them, then perhaps you will bring it about that I go to Halle with their approval, so that if my attitudes do change, the option of returning to the Congregation would be open to me. My sister and brother will well realize that this diversion of my thinking to wholly other subjects is the best means to accomplish this by and by. Should I, however, also be wholly separated from the Congregation for a time, then it is indeed better, if I do not change my mind, than leading an unhappy and inactive life in the Congregation; or, if I do change my mind in Halle, then it is not impossible that I would also then return to the Congregation again.

You will see in this letter, most loved Father, how corrosive it has become for me. May God give you the strength to receive this news without damage to your health, without too great affliction, and without it rupturing your fatherly love for me. God only knows what it costs me to give you this news. Only this single plea: decide as soon as possible. All courses at Halle begin at Easter, and what help is it, if I am still here for another

---

4. The reference is to his mother's brother, Samuel Ernst Timotheus Stubenrauch (1738–1807).

5. *Freitisch* refers to a tradition in Germany of providing meals for poor students, whether by inviting them into private homes or by giving extra money for the purpose.

six months, if I eat up yet more money here, and if afterward it must still come to the same point? With mournful longing[6] I kiss your hands, best Father, and ask you to view everything from the best side and to consider it all carefully, and still in the future to give me, as much as it is possible for you, the gift of your fatherly love so priceless to me, as

Your afflicted son, who worships you dearly,
Fr. Schleyermacher

Schleiermacher to Henriette Herz.
Monday, January 1, 1798[7]

Here you have your fragment, dear friend. The convictions it contains stand on their own, but your enduring goodness may make the prospects come true for me.

When a calm and beautiful soul moves between the sweet banks of benevolence and love, its entire life turns out similarly. It resembles a silent brook, which not only mirrors the blueness of the sky in complete clarity, but also out of this mirror itself reflects the grey, dreary clouds back in more mild form, because the beautiful images of the flowers of many different colors that cover those banks all over intermingle directly with its bleaker tints. If the tender expressions of such a heart reveal themselves only to confidants—as only he who reposes on the breast of the friend hears his friend's heart beat—then in return it amplifies his entire, beautiful existence. For whoever may intuit a beautifully formed life, delighting in and with it, assuredly his own life flows calmly alongside that; and to whom it is granted to linger, gazing into the calm of a well-ordered heart, this person's life cannot thus remain without traces of beauty,

---

6. *Wehmuth.*
7. Letter 435, *KGA* 5/2:244.

because such a sight disarms and displaces with beneficial enchantment everything that is antagonistic to the graces [...]

Schleiermacher to G. A. Reimer. Gnadenfrei, April 30, 1802[8]

Yesterday, when I had to decide to remain here a few days longer than I had originally intended, the first thing that occurred to me was that then, plainly, I would not see you for some time, and under these circumstances I cannot deny myself the pleasure of writing a couple words to you, at the very least. I will probably not meet Schlegel and his wife[9] again, either, but I view this from the standpoint that it spares me having to bid farewell. I am quite well here with a tenderly loved sister, in a splendid region amidst the marvelous impressions of an earlier time of life. No other place has fostered the lively reminiscence of the entire course of my spirit as this place has—from the first awakening of the better things up to the point where I now stand. Here arose in me, for the first time, the consciousness of the relation of the human person to a higher world—admittedly in an inferior form. It is said that spirits often appear as children or dwarfs, but they are nonetheless spirits, and for anything essential it is all the same. Here, for the first time, emerged the mystical predisposition that is so essential to me and that has sustained me through all storms of skepticism and rescued me. Back then it was only budding, now it is formed, and I can say that I have become a Moravian again after all, only of a higher order. You can imagine how alive and how deep in my very self I exist here. Here, I have a sister nearby whom I sincerely love and with whom I stand continually in a very candid and deeply engaging correspondence. It is thus a splendid treat to behold at once and to enjoy immediately what for the past six years has been read and experienced through letters on a page.

---

8. Letter 1220, *KGA* 5/5:392–93.
9. Dorothea Mendelssohn Veit Schlegel.

So it is with me, dear friend. What, meanwhile, have you been doing? Has Heinrich's presence been for you quite pleasant and useful?

Had I known that I would not see you for so long, I would have forthwith begged you to write to me at once—by now, it is too late to do that, and in Leipzig, I well know, there is no time. If you return from Leipzig as soon as it gets done, then it must remain at my departure from Berlin on the 31st of May, and then we can enjoy reprimanding each other. —I will find the *Ofterdingen*[10] well done, right?

Give Minchen and Ludchen my greetings. I arrive on Sunday the ninth, and you shall see how soon I will seek you at home. Adieu, dear friend. It is high time that I seal the letter, which ought to be posted.

Schleiermacher

Schleiermacher to Eleanore Grunow. Stolp, December 10, 1802[11]

You will be faring, dear friend, inversely as shall I. You will receive my birthday greetings a day before your birthday. Your birthday will join the series of melancholic[12] days that you have spent so far; it will stand out from all its predecessors by being the last time, a fact that will also force itself on you. I will be thinking much about this, and it will grieve me that I cannot share your grief and your melancholy right now. It is a holy year of your life that you are completing and that you are starting.

---

10. A reference to Novalis's unfinished novel, *Heinrich von Ofterdingen*, published posthumously in 1802.

11. Letters 1402, 1403, *KGA* 5/6:234–36.

12. In this paragraph he frequently uses the terms *wehmüthig* and *Wehmuth*, which are translated as "melancholic" and "melancholy," but also could be translated as "nostalgic" and "nostalgia," or "mournful" and "mournful longing." For the Romantics, the term conveyed an aestheticized, poetic idea of melancholy as mournfulness linked to an idea of acute pain and longing.

You are completing a year during which you have lost the presence of a dear friend,[13] who feels it with melancholic joy that he was ever something to you and that his existence has brought forth much that is beautiful in you. You are starting a year that will rob you of your dear and tenderly loved mother. I shall say nothing more to you about how I love you for your filial love and for all the sorrows it has already caused you. Thinking of the remarkable content of your new year, let us also think with melancholic joy about how the passing time really does not take anything away, however much it also seems to do so. You will lose your mother no more, for even now your beautiful love for her and the image you carry of her in your heart is the only way that you possess her—and in exactly this sense, almost retaining the same words, you have also not lost me. And I hope you will remain true to our beautiful covenant to hold firmly to eternal youth and also, through this, to rejuvenate temporal life. And I hope your soul will, as it befits every phoenix, arise out of the fire of holy grief more beautifully rejuvenated. This is how I hope to see you in the new year of your life, and to show you that, amidst all the deprivations and not a few sorrows, the joyous feeling of my beautiful fate has faithfully kept the covenant of this day. May everything beautiful that my grateful heart wishes for you only grow during this year.

I had come up with the idea of a present for you that would have given you certain joy. I hoped in Königsberg to be able to collect the rare, earlier literary attempts of Hippel, except I was not at all successful, and so I present to you now nothing but a couple of little things by him and about him, which Jette[14] will deliver to you. I take slight comfort in the fact that it is not more than this. What is best about presents that a friendly heart sets out to give is precisely the presence—the love that expresses itself as much in accepting as in giving. It is this love that must primarily constitute the greatness of the gift. Indeed, I had

---

13. A reference to himself and to their recent attempt to end their relationship. The final separation would not occur until 1805.

14. A reference to Henriette Herz.

nearly forgotten that you, at least it is my view, will also welcome the *Heinrich von Ofterdingen*.[15] Accept it right now, as though from my hands. A book such as this—a memorial of a heart so pure and high, which draws every similar heart to itself and also willingly submits itself to every worthy attunement of such a heart—is a beautiful possession at any time.

You have not, I believe, been misunderstood by me, but allow me my legitimate little war with the dead letter. Am I not now gladly suffering as much by means of it as the Apostle did by means of Alexander the Smith?[16] For only consider, I should now really be writing the *Critique of Morals*.[17] So many dead letters about the holiest, most living subject! And so beyond what I have already said of the dead letter, I at least do not want to waste any further words. I am not wrong about this. I have never before complained about the dead letter to which a woman gave life; rather, I feel, and certainly very inwardly, what is beautiful to me—truly, not just a little—has been given in this way.

[Later that same day]

It must have been a beautiful morning that you have celebrated there with the others, well worthy of all sorrows and tears—and how deeply piercing into your pious, so complexly sensitive heart! Assuredly there is no more beautiful act than to part with beloved souls in a calm and collected manner and to bring the real close of life—after this, physical death can come, whenever it wants. And, I might say, if Christ had only instituted the Last Supper, I would have loved him to the point of adoration.

---

15. See n. 10, above.

16. A reference to 2 Tim 4:14. In 1805 at Halle, Schleiermacher developed his lectures on hermeneutics based in large part on his translation and ordering of Plato's dialogues (*Platons Werke*). He applied his interpretive theory to 1 Tim and concluded (correctly) that the letter was not authentically Pauline; he later judged (incorrectly) that 2 Tim was authentically Pauline.

17. A reference to his *Grundlinien einer Kritik der bisherigen Sittenlehre* (*Basic Principles of a Critique of Previous Ethical Theory*, 1803).

Schleiermacher to Henriette Herz.
Stolp, Thursday, January 20, 1803[18]

Yesterday I was terribly distressed in spirits, and I mused about how I should arrange my sick room. Today I am perfectly well and do not comprehend any of this. My work is going tolerably well but still not quite quickly enough. I promised Reimer that I would send the first book[19] at the end of this month. At the start of tomorrow a fair copy of the first third will have been made, and the second third will almost be ready in draft (as you know, it is still incomplete); the last third is yet to be entirely written. For that I now have only one week left, and I need to see what I can accomplish in this time. I have not even dared myself to touch the splendid things in the second part of the Novalis book (which part I have only now obtained), even though it would very necessarily inspire me sometimes to sound a higher note than the dry *Critique of Morals* does. Ach, writing is a great distress, but a book of this kind—not again in my life. I don't believe I have had more than six clever thoughts this entire time, nothing but critical shavings. The only fun is when I imagine to myself how Fichte will be agitated and will despise me even more deeply; how A. W. Schlegel will wrinkle his nose that it is nothing more than that and also that no Schellingianism can be found in it at all; and how the old men will wonder how I became so jejune and exhaustive a critic, and will wait to see whether I outlive such transformation. Soon enough, though, they shall see that I am still the same old mystic.

Long letters to Friedrich and Dorothea lie begun before me; God knows when they will be finished. To Eichmann and to Willich I would also happily write; I see no time. The waters sweep over my head, King David would say.[20] Are you familiar with the sensation of not being able to hold breath under water? It is quite accurate. On top of all that, tomorrow and the day after, I shall have to go

---

18. Letter 1424, *KGA* 5/6:276–77.

19. *Basic Principles of a Critique of Previous Ethical Theory.*

20. See Ps 69.

into society. Since Tuesday I have been entirely quiet at
home—more alone than you, oh, much more alone!
Be good and calm and strong and write to me as much as
you can.

Schleiermacher to F. H. Jacobi.
Berlin, March 30, 1818[21]

Most admired man! It has been a long time since I have been
as seriously angry with a dear friend as I am now with Göschen,
who has only just now relayed to me your friendly request or
informed me of your letter to Reinhold.[22] Nevertheless, so that I
do him no injustice, and so that you will not well believe what he
told me a long time ago: I do think very highly of you, and right
from the heart. What he had told me did leave me with the sting
of a desire to declare myself against you. Yet I must have rebelled
against this because I did not believe myself entitled to indulging
this desire. Now that I have obtained this, he also desires your
letter back immediately, and therefore I cannot write a letter to
you as I would like—which would be a book instead or, better
still where possible, a dialogue. I must rather content myself with
a few winged words. That is otherwise not my way; to me, it is
too juvenile. But even so, already aging somewhat myself, I must
perhaps become young again by approaching you, not to declare
to you my admiration but to register what *is* and what has
always accompanied me, ever since the most beautiful times of
my youth, even though it entered relatively late for me.

From your writings and from the reports of good people, an

---

21. See *ASL* 2:349–53. To date the *KGA* has completed only through volume 9 (1807) of
Schleiermacher's correspondence. This translation is based on two recent editions:
Martin Cordes, "Der Brief Schleiermachers an Jacobi: Ein Beitrag zu seiner Entstehung
und Überlieferung," *Zeitschrift für Theologie und Kirche* 68, no. 2 (1971): 195–212; and
Walter Jaeschke, ed., *Religionsphilosophie und spekulative Theologie 3.1: Der Streit um
die Göttlichen Dinge (1799–1812), Quellenband* (Hamburg: Felix Meiner, 1994), 394–98.

22. He is referring to a letter Jacobi wrote to the philosopher Karl Leonhard Reinhold
(1757–1823), October 8, 1817 (in Jaeschke, *Religionsphilosophie und spekulative
Theologie,* 391–94).

image has taken shape for me. You yourself must be aware of it, how very much it can captivate the heart. And if you have believed that I had to steel myself, on account of dissenting views, against the effects of this image, then that can only sadden me, but I cannot accuse you for that reason. Why is it you had excepted me from the great crowd of those coldly dismissive, scornful, philosophical youth, into which I had nevertheless been incorporated and to whom I might have, from a distance, appeared similar? I will say nothing further about this. I will instead respond only to your call to seek an agreement about the different views. Yet I can only really do it on the boldest presupposition that one word will lead to another, and, as bold this also is, I would come across as immodest if I wanted to attempt more than this.

You yourself direct me to your letter to Reinhold. In this letter, I find, presented in a couple of simple formulas, the complaint that runs throughout all your writings. I quite gladly keep to these two in order to submit to you, on the basis of them and simply for the time being, how I differ from you on the matter. *You are a heathen with respect to the intellect, a Christian with respect to feeling.* Against this, my dialectics retorts: heathen and Christian are, as such, opposed to one another in the same sphere—namely, in the sphere of religion. Do understanding and feeling have such equal claims in this sphere that they could divide into the opposing forms? Religiosity is the affair of feeling. In contrast to that, what we call *religion*, but what is always more or less dogmatics, is only the understanding's interpretation of the feeling, an interpretation that has emerged only by means of reflection. If your feeling is Christian, can your understanding then interpret in a heathen manner? On this point, I cannot find myself in agreement. My counterproposition, therefore, is this: with respect to understanding, I am a philosopher, for that is the independent and original activity of the understanding, and with respect to feeling I am wholly a pious person—in particular, a Christian. I have removed heathenism entirely or, better put, never had it in me. You, however, as we all know, are also a philosopher with respect to the understanding, and are—against all who believe it necessary to become Catholic—firmly resolved always to continue philosophizing.[23] On this point, we are already in complete agreement, for I, too, would never let myself be deprived of continued philosophizing.

When you therefore say that you are at the same time a heathen with respect to the understanding, then this invariably can only mean that your philosophizing understanding cannot accept, at the same time with its philosophy, whatever it must interpret from your Christian feeling. But certainly, if you had a heathen religious feeling, then your understanding would still not be able to accept what it must have interpreted from this feeling. You simply call this negation *heathen* because it is grounded in the fact that your understanding does not want to extend beyond nature. Neither, however, does mine—except, since I, too, want there to be absolutely no contradiction, I have established the foothold for myself that I will allow no one to prove to me where nature ends. If then my Christian feeling is conscious of a divine spirit within me, which is something other than my reason, I never want to give up seeking this in the deepest depths of the nature of the soul. And if my Christian feeling becomes conscious of a Son of God, who is distinguished from the best of us in a different way from being a "better still," then I never want to stop seeking the generation of the Son of God in the deepest depths of nature and telling myself that I will comprehend the other Adam probably just as soon as the first Adam, or the first Adams, whom I must also accept without comprehending.

This is my way of equilibrium in the two waters.[24] Admittedly, it is nothing other than an alternating between being buoyed up by the one and being plunged by the other. But why is it we

---

23. He is using the language from Jacobi's letter, where Jacobi talks about the "sphere of Catholicism," contrasting it with "always continuing philosophizing."

24. He is referring to an image Jacobi uses in his letter to Reinhold: "You see, dear Reinhold, that I am ever the same, completely a heathen with respect to the understanding, a Christian with respect to the whole heart. I swim between two waters that will not unite in me and that, in concert with each other, deceive me: just as one continuously lifts me, so simultaneously the other plunges me" (in Jaeschke, *Religionsphilosophie und spekulative Theologie*, 393).

would rather *not* put up with that? Oscillation is the universal form of all finite existence. There is, in fact, an immediate consciousness that this undulating proceeds from the two foci of my own ellipse, and in this undulating I have the entire abundance of my earthly life. My philosophy and my dogmatics, therefore, are firmly determined not to contradict each other, but also for that very reason can they never wish to be finished. As far back as I can think, they have always been reciprocally tuning themselves and also always drawing nearer to each other.

I believe that, after this statement, I scarcely need to make a confession to you about the return to the letter currently in Christianity. One age bears the debt of another, but it seldom knows how to clear that without incurring new debt. All historical connection was abolished by the total annihilation of the letter; and it is the very same madness to abolish that connection in the religious sphere and to abolish it in the political. *That,* therefore, had to be established. If, however, one now wants to screw the piece back, to use Tieck's excellent expression, then the historical connection is thereby abolished, but in a reverse manner. The Bible is the original interpretation of the Christian feeling, and for just this reason is so established that it might always be better understood and developed. I, as a Protestant theologian, will not let anyone deprive me of this right of development. Mind you, however, I am thereby of the opinion that dogmatic language, as it has formed itself since Augustine, is so deep and rich that, if one handles it judiciously, it will grow toward that possible convergence of philosophy and dogmatics. Indeed, this and only this will I allow. What concerns the difference of our philosophy turns me back to your other proposition.

There is no third alternative to the deification of nature and to anthropomorphism. I have also been told that you were of the opinion that I, for just this reason, could not think much of you, since the foundation of your philosophy is the idea of a personal God, and I abolish this. You have also enunciated this basic principle in that proposition in your letter to Reinhold. At least, to me, both seem to be the same. Because you see no third alternative and because you do not want to deify nature, you deify consciousness. But, dear man! In my eyes, the one deification is certainly just as good as the other. And precisely this insight—that each one is only a deification—is for me the third. We *cannot* extricate ourselves from the antithesis between the ideal and the real, or however else you want to designate it, as it is all the same to me. Are you any better able to view God as person than as *natura naturans*?[25] If you want to form for yourself a vivid concept of a person, must that person not necessarily become something finite to you? Are an infinite understanding and an infinite will something other than empty words, given that understanding and will are, while different, also necessarily delimited? And, in your wanting to give up differentiating understanding and will, does not the concept of the person collapse back on itself?

I find the same thing on the other side as well. Anthropomorphism—or, if you allow me, I prefer to say ideo*morphism*—is unavoidable in the sphere of the interpretation of religious feeling; whether hylo*morphism*[26] (and I do not mean that atomistically speaking, but as it conveys the most living physics) is not just as indispensable on the side of natural history, I do not want to decide, since I understand too little about it. The former, however, I use in the religious sphere, whereas in the sphere of philosophy I affirm that it is just as good an expression and just as incomplete as the other. I do so with complete right precisely because of that insight that we *cannot* frame a real concept of the highest being, but that all proper philosophy consists only in the insight that this inexpressible truth of the highest being underlies all our thinking and sensing. The development of this insight is precisely what, I am convinced, Plato meant by *dialectics*. Any further than this, I believe, we cannot venture.

---

25. "Naturing nature." A reference to the philosophy of Spinoza and to the Pantheist Controversy in the 1780s.

26. Emphases in the original.

That is my one word on the matter. Allow me the hope that it will lead to one from you, and that it also be only this, admired man: that in your heart you absolve me of whatever caused you to disbelieve my reverence for you. In order to illustrate our difference, it also occurs to me that, on the basis of your image, the two masses will not unite for you. Nor will they for me. But whereas you wish for this union and sorely miss it, I put up with the separation. For me, understanding and feeling remain next to one another, but they touch and form a Galvanic pile.[27] For me, the innermost life of the spirit exists only in this Galvanic operation, in the feeling of understanding and in the understanding of feeling, whereby nevertheless both poles always remain averted from the other.

I became acquainted with your friend Reinhold in the autumn of 1816—although it was only a fleeting quarter hour. He received me in a quite friendly and cordial manner. Unfortunately, I could draw little benefit from it, since I was unendingly afflicted and exhausted. But, with you, I regret he is not to be brought back from the dry precipice. This is the curse that (according to my experience and according to my feeling) always occurs when someone only philosophizes, without a real engagement with history or natural science, which fertilizes speculation, or without an artistic striving bound up with it, which alleviates the stiffening effect of purely formal substance. Reinhold seems to me so mindful and amiable that, with you, I am convinced the aridity is not in him. May I be so fortunate as to see you and to be uplifted by the affectionate old man who also carries the weakness of old age with loving surrender—you, who, more than any one person I can think of, represents and connects two eras? Who knows! It has already happened to me even more than I could have hoped. May the New Year give you new power—then the prospect of seeing you might remain open

---

27. A reference to the precursor of the electrical battery: the discovery by Luigi Galvani (1737–98) of an electrochemical cell that consisted of two half cells separated by a porous membrane.

to me for a long time! And pardon me, if I have encroached upon your request. The intention was shorter than the execution.

From the heart, Your grateful and devoted
Schleiermacher

BIBLIOGRAPHY

Schleiermacher's Works Cited
(See Also Abbreviations)

German Texts (Listed Chronologically)

Friedrich Daniel Ernst Schleiermacher Kritische Gesamtausgabe. Edited by Hans-Joachim Birkner, Gerhard Ebeling, Hermann Fischer, Günter Meckenstock, Kurt-Victor Selge, et al. Berlin and New York: Walter de Gruyter, 1983–.

Schleiermacher, Friedrich D. E. "Spinozismus," and "Kurze Darstellung des Spinozistischen Systems." In *KGA* 1/1, *Jugendschriften 1787–1796*, edited by Günter Meckenstock, 511–58 and 559–82. Berlin and New York: Walter de Gruyter, 1984.

————. *Über die Religion. Reden an die Gebildeten unter ihren Verächtern* (1st edition, 1799). In *KGA* 1/2, *Schriften aus der Berliner Zeit 1796–1799*, edited by Günter Meckenstock, 185–325. Berlin and New York: Walter de Gruyter, 1984.

————. *Monologen: Eine Neujahrsgabe* (1800). In *KGA* 1/3, *Schriften aus der Berliner Zeit 1800–1802*, edited by Günter Meckenstock, 1–61. Berlin and New York: Walter de Gruyter, 1988.

————. *Platons Werke von F. Schleiermacher* (1804–28). Berlin: Reimer, 1/1, 1804; 1/2 and 2/1, 1805; 2/2, 1807; 2/3, 1809; 3/1, 1828; 2nd ed., 1817.

————. *Die Weihnachtsfeier: Ein Gespräch* (1806). In *KGA* 1/5, *Schriften aus der Hallenser Zeit 1804–1807*, edited by Hermann Patsch, 43–98. Berlin and New York: Walter de Gruyter, 1995.

————. *Über die Religion. Reden an die Gebildeten unter ihren Verächtern* (2nd edition, 1806). In *KGA* 1/12, *Über die Religion*

(2.–) 4. Auflage, Monologen (2.–) 4. Auflage, edited by Günter Meckenstock, 1–321. Berlin: Walter de Gruyter, 1995.

———. *Über die Religion. Reden an die Gebildeten unter ihren Verächtern 1799/1806/1821*. Edited by Niklaus Peter, Frank Bestebreurtje, and Anna Büsching. Zürich: Theologischer Verlag, 2012.

———. *Der christliche Glaube nach den Grundsätzen der evangelischen Kirche im Zusammenhange dargestellt* (2nd edition, 1830/31). 2 vols. In *KGA* 1:13/1–2. Edited by Rolf Schäfer. Berlin and New York: Walter de Gruyter, 2003.

English Translations of Schleiermacher's Texts Cited

Dinsmore, Patrick D., ed. *A Facing-Page Translation from German into English of Friedrich Schleiermacher's 'Kurze Darstellung des Spinozistischen Systems' and 'Spinozismus.'* Lewiston, NY: Edwin Mellen, 2013.

Rowan, Frederica, ed. *The Life of Schleiermacher as Unfolded in His Autobiography and Letters*. 2 volumes. London: Smith, Elder and Co.: 1860.

Schleiermacher, Friedrich D. E. *Christmas Eve: A Dialogue on the Celebration of Christmas*. Translated by W. Hastie. Edinburgh: T & T Clark, 1890.

———. *Christmas Eve: Dialogue on the Incarnation*. Translated by Terrence N. Tice. Richmond, VA: John Knox Press, 1967. Revised version: *Christmas Eve Celebration: A Dialogue*. Eugene, OR: Cascade Books, 2010.

———. *The Life of Jesus*. Edited by Jack C. Verheyden. Translated by S. MacLean Gilmour. Philadelphia: Fortress Press, 1975.

———. *Occasional Thoughts on Universities in the German Sense* (1808). Translated by Terrence N. Tice and Edwina Lawler. Lewiston, NY: Edwin Mellen, 1991.

———. *On the Glaubenslehre: Two Letters to Dr. Lücke*. Translated by James Duke and Francis Schüssler Fiorenza. American Academy of Religion: Texts and Translations 3. Chico, CA: Scholars Press, 1981.

BIBLIOGRAPHY

————. *On the Highest Good* (1789). Schleiermacher: Studies and Translations 10. Translated by H. Victor Froese. Lewiston, NY: Edwin Mellen, 1992.

————. *On Religion: Speeches to Its Cultured Despisers* (1799). Translated by Richard Crouter. Cambridge: Cambridge University Press, 1988.

————. *On Religion: Speeches to Its Cultured Despisers* (1821). Translated by John Oman. New York: Harper, 1958.

————. *Soliloquies: A New Year's Gift.* Translated by Horace Leland Friess. Chicago: Open Court Pub. Co., 1957.

General Bibliography

Albrecht, Ruth. "'We Kiss Our Dearest Redeemer through Inward Prayer': Mystical Traditions in Pietism." In *The Wiley-Blackwell Companion to Christian Mysticism*, edited by Julia A. Lamm, 473–88. Oxford: Blackwell, 2013.

Altmann, Alexander. "The New Style of Preaching in Nineteenth-Century German Jewry." In *Studies in Nineteenth-Century Jewish Intellectual History*, 65–116. Cambridge, MA: Harvard University Press, 1964.

————. "Zur Frühgeschichte der jüdischen Predigt in Deutschland: Leopold Zunz als Prediger." In *Von der mittelalterlichen zur modernen Aufklärung: Studien zur jüdischen Geistesgeschichte*, 249–99. Tübingen: J.C.B. Mohr/Paul Siebeck, 1987.

Arndt, Andreas, ed. *Wissenschaft und Geselligkeit: Friedrich Schleiermacher in Berlin 1796–1802.* Berlin: Walter de Gruyter, 2009.

Beiser, Frederick C. *The Romantic Imperative: The Concept of Early German Romanticism.* Cambridge, MA: Harvard University Press, 2003.

Blackwell, Albert L. "The Antagonistic Correspondence of 1801 between Chaplain Sack and His Protégé Schleiermacher." *Harvard Theological Review* 74, no. 1 (1981): 101–21.

————. *Schleiermacher's Early Philosophy of Life: Determinism, Freedom, and Phantasy.* Harvard Theological Studies 33. Chico, CA: Scholars Press, 1982.

————. "Schleiermacher's Sermon at Nathanael's Grave." *The Journal of Religion* 57, no. 1 (1977): 64–75.

Calvin, John. *Institutes of the Christian Religion.* Translated by Ford Lewis Battles. Edited by John T. McNeill. 2 volumes. Louisville: Westminster John Knox Press, 1960.

Capetz, Paul E. "Friedrich Schleiermacher on the Old Testament." *Harvard Theological Review* 102, no. 3 (2009): 297–326.

———. "The Old Testament as a Witness to Jesus Christ: Historical Criticism and Theological Exegesis of the Bible according to Karl Barth." *The Journal of Religion* 90, no. 4 (2010): 475–506.

Cordes, Martin. "Der Brief Schleiermachers an Jacobi: Ein Beitrage zu seiner Entstehung und Überlieferung." *Zeitschrift für Theologie und Kirche* 68, no. 2 (1971): 195–212.

Crouter, Richard. *Friedrich Schleiermacher: Between Enlightenment and Romanticism.* New York: Cambridge University Press, 2005.

———. "Shaping an Academic Discipline: The *Brief Outline on the Study of Theology.*" In *The Cambridge Companion to Friedrich Schleiermacher*, edited by Jacqueline Mariña, 111–28. New York: Cambridge University Press, 2005.

Crouter, Richard, and Julie Klassen, eds. *A Debate on Jewish Emancipation and Christian Theology in Old Berlin.* Indianapolis: Hackett, 2004.

Dahlhaus, Carl. *The Idea of Absolute Music.* Translated by Roger Lustig. Chicago: University of Chicago Press, 1989.

DeVries, Dawn. *Jesus Christ in the Preaching of Calvin and Schleiermacher.* Louisville: Westminster John Knox Press, 1996.

———, ed. *Servant of the Word: Selected Sermons of Friedrich Schleiermacher.* Philadelphia: Fortress Press, 1987.

DeVries, Dawn, and B. A. Gerrish. "Providence and Grace: Schleiermacher on Justification and Election." In *The Cambridge Companion to Friedrich Schleiermacher*, edited by Jacqueline Mariña, 189–207. New York: Cambridge University Press, 2005.

Fiorenza, Francis Schüssler. "Schleiermacher's Understanding of God as Triune." In *The Cambridge Companion to Friedrich Schleiermacher.* Edited by Jacqueline Mariña, 171–88. New York: Cambridge University Press, 2005.

Frohlich, Mary, RSCJ. "Mystics of the Twentieth Century." In *The Wiley-Blackwell Companion to Christian Mysticism*, edited by Julia A. Lamm, 515–30. Oxford: Blackwell, 2013.

Gerber, Simon. "Seelsorge ganz unten—Schleiermacher, Der Charité-Prediger." In *Wissenschaft und Geselligkeit: Friedrich Schleiermacher in Berlin 1796–1802*, edited by Andreas Arndt, 15–42. Berlin: Walter de Gruyter, 2009.

Gerrish, B. A. *Continuing the Reformation: Essays on Modern Religious Thought.* Chicago: University of Chicago Press, 1993.

———. *The Old Protestantism and the New: Essays on the Reformation Heritage.* Chicago: University of Chicago Press, 1982.

———. *A Prince of the Church: Schleiermacher and the Beginnings of Modern Theology.* Philadelphia: Fortress Press, 1984.

———. *Tradition and the Modern World: Reformed Theology in the Nineteenth Century.* Chicago: University of Chicago Press, 1978.

Hadot, Pierre. *Exercices spirituels et philosophie antique.* Paris: Études Augustiniennes, 1981.

———. *The Inner Citadel: The Meditations of Marcus Aurelius.* Translated by Michael Chase. Cambridge, MA: Harvard University Press, 1998.

———. *Philosophy as a Way of Life: Spiritual Exercises from Socrates to Foucault.* Edited by Arnold I. Davidson. Translated by Michael Chase. Cambridge, MA: Blackwell, 1995.

Hartlieb, Elisabeth. *Geschlechterdifferenz im Denken Friederich Schleiermachers.* New York: Walter de Gruyter, 2006.

Helmer, Christine. "Mysticism and Metaphysics: Schleiermacher and a Historical-Theological Trajectory." *The Journal of Religion* 83, no. 4 (2003): 517–38.

———. "Schleiermacher's Exegetical Theology and the New Testament." In *The Cambridge Companion to Friedrich Schleiermacher*, edited by Jacqueline Mariña, 229–47. Cambridge: Cambridge University Press, 2005.

Holder, Arthur, ed. *The Blackwell Companion to Christian Spirituality.* Oxford: Blackwell Publishing, 2005.

Jaeschke, Walter, ed. *Religionsphilosophie und spekulative Theologie 3.1: Der Streit um die Göttlichen Dinge (1799–1812): Quellenband.* Hamburg: Felix Meiner, 1994.

Klein, Ursula. "Der Chemiekult der Frühromantik." In *Wissenschaft und Geselligkeit: Friedrich Schleiermacher in Berlin 1796–1802,* edited by Andreas Arndt, 67–92. Berlin: Walter de Gruyter, 2009.

Kolb, Robert, and Timothy J. Wengert, eds. *The Book of Concord: The Confessions of the Evangelical Lutheran Church*. Minneapolis: Fortress Press, 2000.

Lamm, Julia A. "The Early Philosophical Roots of Schleiermacher's Notion of Gefühl, 1788–1794." *Harvard Theological Review* 87, no. 1 (1994): 67–105.

————. *The Living God: Schleiermacher's Theological Appropriation of Spinoza*. University Park, PA: Pennsylvania State University Press, 1996.

————. "Pantheism and Romanticism." In *The Nineteenth-Century Theologians*, edited by David Ferguson, 165–86. Oxford: Blackwell, 2010.

————. "Reading Plato's Dialectics: Schleiermacher's Insistence on Dialectics as Dialogical." *Zeitschrift für neuere Theologiegeschichte / Journal for the History of Modern Theology* 10, no. 1 (2003): 1–25.

————. "Schleiermacher as Plato Scholar." *The Journal of Religion* 80, no. 2 (2000): 206–39.

————. "Schleiermacher's *Christmas Dialogue* as Platonic Dialogue." *The Journal of Religion* 92, no. 3 (2012): 392–420.

————. "Schleiermacher's Post-Kantian Spinozism: The Early Essays on Spinoza, 1793–94." *The Journal of Religion* 74, no. 4 (1994): 476–505.

————. "Schleiermacher's Treatise on Grace." *Harvard Theological Review* 101, no. 2 (2008): 133–68.

————, ed. *The Wiley-Blackwell Companion to Christian Mysticism*. Oxford: Blackwell, 2013.

La Vopa, Anthony J. "The Politics of Enlightenment: Friedrich Gedike and German Professional Ideology." *The Journal of Modern History* 62, no. 1 (1990): 34–56.

Mariña, Jacqueline, ed. *The Cambridge Companion to Friedrich Schleiermacher*. Cambridge: Cambridge University Press, 2005.

McGinn, Bernard. *The Foundations of Mysticism*. Volume 1 of *The Presence of God: A History of Western Christian Mysticism*. New York: Crossroad, 1991.

————. *The Presence of God: A History of Western Christian Mysticism.* 7 volumes. New York: The Crossroad Publishing Co., 1991–.

————. "The Letter and the Spirit: Spirituality as an Academic Discipline." In *Minding the Spirit: The Study of Christian Spirituality,* edited by Elizabeth Dreyer and Mark Burrows, 25–41. Baltimore: Johns Hopkins University Press, 2005.

Mitchell, Alan C. *Hebrews.* Sacra Pagina 13. Collegeville, MN: Liturgical Press, 2007.

Morgenroth, Matthias. *Weihnachts-Christentum: Moderner Religiosität auf der Spur.* Gütersloh: Chr. Kaiser/Guetersloher Verlagshaus, 2002.

Nicol, Iain G., ed. *Friedrich Schleiermacher on Creeds, Confessions and Church Union: That They May Be One.* Lewiston, NY: Edwin Mellen, 2004.

Niebuhr, Richard R. *Schleiermacher on Christ and Religion: A New Introduction.* New York: Scribner, 1964. Reprint edition, Eugene, OR: Wipf & Stock, 2009.

Nowak, Kurt. "Schleiermacher als Prediger am Charité-Krankenhaus in Berlin (1796–1802)." *Theologische Zeitschrift* 41 (1985): 391–411.

————. *Schleiermacher: Leben, Werk, und Wirkung.* Göttingen: Vandenhoeck & Ruprecht, 2002.

Patsch, Hermann. "Der 'Erdgeist' als philosophischer Topos bei Friedrich Schlegel, Schleiermacher, Schelling und Hegel." In *Schleiermacher's Philosophy and the Philosophical Tradition,* edited by Sergio Sorrentino, 75–90. Lewiston, NY: Edwin Mellen, 1992.

————. "Die esoterische Kommunikationsstruktur der 'Weihnachtsfeier.' Über Anspielungen und Zitate." In *Schleiermacher in Context: Papers from the 1988 International Symposium on Schleiermacher at Hernnhut,* edited by Ruth Drucilla Richardson, 132–56. Lewiston: Edwin Mellen, 1991.

————. "Metamorphosen des Erdgeistes. Zu einer mythologischen Metapher in der Philosophie der Goethe-Zeit." *New Athenaeum/Neues Athenaeum* 1 (1989): 246–79.

————. "Die zeitgenössische Rezeption der 'Weihnachtsfeier.'" In *Internationaler Schleiermacher-Kongreß Berlin 1984*, edited by Kurt-Victor Selge, 1215–28. Berlin: Walter de Gruyter, 1985.

Pearson, Lori. "Schleiermacher and the Christologies behind Chalcedon." *Harvard Theological Review* 96, no. 3 (July, 2003): 349–67.

Proudfoot, Wayne. *Religious Experience.* Berkeley: University of California Press, 1985.

Rahner, Karl, SJ. *The Practice of Faith: A Handbook of Contemporary Spirituality.* Edited and translated by Karl Lehmann and Alfred Raffelt. New York: Crossroad, 1983.

Redeker, Martin. *Schleiermacher: Life and Thought.* Translated by John Wallhausser. Philadelphia: Fortress Press, 1973.

Richardson, Ruth Drucilla. "Friedrich Schleiermacher's *Weihnachtsfeier* as 'Universal Poetry': The Impact of Friedrich Schlegel on the Intellectual Development of the Young Schleiermacher." PhD Dissertation, Drew University, 1985.

————. *The Role of Women in the Life and Thought of the Early Schleiermacher (1768–1806): An Historical Overview.* Lewiston, NY: Edwin Mellen, 1991.

Riesebrodt, Martin. *The Promise of Salvation: A Theory of Religion.* Chicago: University of Chicago Press, 2010.

Schlegel, Friedrich. *Philosophical Fragments.* Translated by Peter Firchow. Minneapolis, MN: University of Minnesota Press, 1991.

Schmidt, Leigh Eric. "The Making of 'Mysticism' in the Anglo-American World: From Henry Coventry to William James." In *The Wiley-Blackwell Companion to Christian Mysticism*, edited by Julia A. Lamm, 452–72. Oxford: Blackwell Publishing, 2013.

Schneiders, Sandra M. "Approaches to the Study of Christian Spirituality." In *The Blackwell Companion to Christian Spirituality*, edited by Arthur Holder, 15–33. Oxford: Blackwell, 2005.

Sheldrake, Philip F. "A Critical Theological Perspective." In *The Wiley-Blackwell Companion to Christian Mysticism*, edited by Julia A. Lamm, 533–49. Oxford: Wiley-Blackwell, 2013.

————. *Explorations in Spirituality: History, Theology and Social Practice.* Mahwah, NJ: Paulist Press, 2010.

Sockness, Brent W. "The Forgotten Moralist: Friedrich Schleiermacher and the Science of Spirit." *Harvard Theological Review* 96, no. 3 (2003): 317–48.

———. "Schleiermacher and the Ethics of Authenticity: The *Monologen* of 1800." *The Journal of Religious Ethics* 32, no. 3 (2004): 477–517.

———. "Was Schleiermacher a Virtue Ethicist? *Tugend* and *Bildung* in the Early Ethical Writings." *Zeitschrift für neuere Theologiegeschichte* 8, no. 1 (2001): 1–33.

Steiner, Peter M., ed. *Friedrich Daniel Ernst Schleiermacher, Über die Philosophie Platons*. Hamburg: Felix Meiner, 1996.

Terrence N. Tice. "Schleiermacher's Interpretation of Christmas: 'Christmas Eve,' 'The Christian Faith,' and the Christmas Sermons." *The Journal of Religion* 47, no. 2 (1967): 100–26.

Thiel, John E. *Imagination & Authority: Theological Authorship in the Modern Tradition*. Minneapolis: Fortress Press, 1991.

———. *Nonfoundationalism*. Minneapolis: Fortress Press, 1994.

Vallée, Gérard, ed. *The Spinoza Conversations between Lessing & Jacobi: Text with Excerpts from the Ensuing Controversy*. Translated by G. Vallée, J. B. Lawson, and C. G. Chapple. Lanham, NY: University Press of America, 1988.

Vial, Theodore M. "Friedrich Schleiermacher on the Central Place of Worship in Theology." *Harvard Theological Review* 91, no. 1 (1998): 59–73.

Williams, Raymond. *Key Words: A Vocabulary of Culture and Society*. London: Fontana Press, 1988.

Williams, Rowan. *The Wound of Knowledge: Christian Spirituality from the New Testament to St. John of the Cross*. Revised edition. London: Darton Longman and Todd, 1990.

Wyman, Walter E., Jr. "Rethinking the Christian Doctrine of Sin: Friedrich Schleiermacher and Hick's 'Irenaean Type.'" *The Journal of Religion* 74, no. 2 (1994): 199–217.

———. "The Role of the Protestant Confessions in Schleiermacher's *The Christian Faith*." *The Journal of Religion* 87, no. 3 (2007): 355–85.

———. "Sin and Redemption." In *The Cambridge Companion to Friedrich Schleiermacher*, edited by Jacqueline Mariña, 129–49. Cambridge: Cambridge University Press, 2005.

INDEX

Abba, 229–30, 235
Absolute dependence. *See under*
  Dependence
Act of writing, 37–38, 259–60
Acting: art and, 154–55; ethics
  and, 163–64, 187–88,
  208–9; existence and, 171;
  feeling versus, 63, 184–86;
  of God, 64; life and,
  154–55; in *On Religion:
  Speeches to Its Cultured
  Despisers*, 154–55, 160,
  163–64, 171, 175, 184–88,
  208; piety and, 19, 155,
  186; power and, 209;
  religion and, 17, 19, 41–42,
  62, 154–55, 163–64,
  183–86; secondhand, 187;
  suffering and, 180. *See also*
  Doing
Action: knowledge and, 165;
  modes of, 33–34, 43–44;
  religion and, 185
Activity: of Christ, 35; divine,
  20–21, 33; solitary, 37
Adam (first man), 60, 262
Albertini, Johann Baptist von, 7
Anthropomorphism, 72, 263
Anti-eudemonism, 11
Apologetics, 18–19, 33

"Apology" (Friedrich
  Schleiermacher), 16
Apophatic language, 62–63, 71
Arrogance, 19, 178
Art: acting and, 154–55; doing
  and, 41–42; imagination
  and, 155; judging, 194; life
  and, 13–14, 116; in *On
  Religion: Speeches to Its
  Cultured Despisers*, 156,
  167–68; religion and, 116,
  156; science and, 13; unity
  with science and religion,
  167–68, 211–12. *See also*
  Music
Artist, 155–56, 163, 168–69
Atheism, 21, 221
Atonement, 47, 51, 139
Awe, 193

Baptism, 130–32
Barby (seminary), 8–9, 47
Barth, Karl, 74
*Basic Principles of Critique of
  Previous Ethical Theories*
  (Friedrich
  Schleiermacher), 25
Being: divine, 226, 229, 235,
  239; in existence, 11, 16,
  35, 50, 148, 160–62, 169,

277